P9-DZY-977

BEYOND
TOLERANCE
RELIGION AND GLOBAL COMMUNITY

DEDICATION

This book is dedicated to my daughter and son, Erin and John, and their generation's efforts at making a better world.

BEYOND TOLERANCE

TOLERANCE

RELIGION AND GLOBAL COMMUNITY

ALLEN M^cKIEL Ph.D

INTERFAITH RESOURCES

BEYOND TOLERANCE
Religion and Global Community

©2007 Dr. Allen McKiel Ph.D.

All rights reserved.

Published by:
Interfaith Resources
www.InterfaithResources.com
1-800-326-1197
511 Diamond Rd.
Heltonville IN 47436

Cover and Text Design
Justice St Rain

ISBN 978-1-88547-19-1
First Printing 2007

CONTENTS

PREFACE

The positions presented in this book derive from my reading of scripture. They have evolved through daily prayer and meditation and from facilitating and participating in weekly religious discussion groups over the past twenty-five years with individuals from a variety of faith traditions. I believe that guidance and inspiration are available to all who sincerely seek the will of God. My expectation is that readers will undertake the continued development of their own understandings through reasoned investigation of scripture. The arguments presented here have a bias. They are intended to promote the development of an understanding of the world's religions as guidance from the one God who created and sustains us all. I believe the world's scriptures can assist us in the pursuit of harmonious global community. This discussion will reference the world's scriptures for inspiration, direction, and validation.

The work is organized in two parts. The first part explores passages of the world's scriptures through ten themed chapters. The second part contains ten chapters that present teachings of the Baha'i Faith concerning global community. This is a personal presentation of those teachings, not an authoritative one. I have adopted an informal, sometimes narrative style that occasionally uses the first person. I do not believe that I have anything other than a personal view to offer. Constant references to the fact that this is just my opinion would become tedious in the writing. Where the writing style appears to be stating facts or sounds preachy or authoritative, I apologize in advance.

Acknowledgements

I was raised as a Christian and am most familiar with the Bible, so my references from the New Testament are dominant throughout the first part of the book. This is not meant to indicate that they are better than the scriptures of other faith traditions. I identify myself as a member of the Baha'i Faith. The concepts presented throughout this work derive particularly from my understanding of Baha'i scripture.

This work has been built upon the efforts of the editors of and contributors to *World Scripture: A Comparative Anthology of Sacred Texts*. The book was originally published in 1991 by Paragon House of St. Paul Minnesota as a Project of the International Religious Foundation. Their work provides invaluable subject access to a significant offering of the world's scriptures.

I would like to acknowledge the debt owed to the editor, Tamea Rector. She not only cleaned up my shaky grammar, but helped me to clarify passages, correct the myriad mistakes, and point out style, meaning, and attitude problems.

To my publisher, Justice St. Rain, I owe thanks for helping me to navigate the processes of publication. I am also grateful for the depth of conversation and friendship that has accompanied the process.

Tom McFaul, author of *The Future of Peace and Justice in the Global Village: Role of the World Religions in the 21st Century*, and Michel Laurent, a friend for over twenty-five years who arranged and participated in the meeting, I would like to thank for a wonderful day of conversation over the two manuscripts.

Roy Duval provided art work for multiple iterations of the cover sustaining his efforts through the twists, turns, and reversals of the decision-making process.

Last, but certainly not least, my wife, Carol, is part author of this work through section by section discussions of the book and as the final editor.

INTRODUCTION

Human beings are unfolding capacity in a manner that echoes all of nature. Nothing stands still. Everything progresses through stages of development. We are at a significant juncture in the development of social order—its globalization. I believe this is good and that spiritual guidance can enable us to avoid the more destructive hazards and reap the benefits latent in this stage of human social evolution.

An experience traveling by train from Xian from Beijing provides a small, personalized example of the difficulties of globalization. The young man sitting next to me expressed his concern over my presence on the train. The objection was not personal. It was cultural. My presence represented the American influence infringing on the cultural integrity of China. I told him of my regrets and honest empathy with respect to the spread of the more pernicious aspects of America's version of modern materialism—drugs, violence, moral laxity, and the dissolution of the family among the most obvious. However, with respect to the preservation of our respective ancestral heritages, I told him that I believed the time had passed for the maintenance of boundaries against the influences of modern global community. The two of us sitting on that train in our blue jeans, sipping Cokes with hands banded in digital watches, listening to hybrid Western/Asian music over the speaker system, were culturally closer to each other than either of us was to our ancestors of two hundred years ago.

Our shared global culture included more than the superficial accoutrements of marketing and the distribution of goods and services. Our common cosmology included concepts of an expanding universe that initiated from a 'Big Bang', the relative nature of time as well as morality, the existence of black holes, evolution, DNA, space flight, Marxism, capital-ism, existentialism, atomic fusion, and global village to name a few. I was not arguing against the presence of a significant cultural influence in each of our lives distinct to our individual heritages; I was suggesting that the influence of global culture was more pervasive and significant. Moreover, I believe that the evolving global culture is good.

Modern human society, relying on empirical investigation and technical progress, sustains life for more human beings over longer average life spans with at least materially improved quality. I prefer the quality of my modern, middle class life to the material benefits associated with the life of Solomon who was at the apex of his social order. I have better food, intellectual stimulation, medicines, mobility, scriptural guidance, artistic experience, and creature comforts. This is not yet the norm for the majority of our planet's populations. Working toward these benefits as sustainable norms for global culture is a noble human endeavor.

Information and Society

Many of today's institutions originated from the minds of men who understood the earth as the center of the firmament that had been created by the hand of God who reigned with his angels just above the clouds. The minds of many, who are today reshaping the institutions for the future, carry images of the earth as a globe that moves around one of more than a hundred billion suns in a galaxy that is one of more than fifty billion in the currently measured universe. The mind of man has constructed images of the heavens and the earth with an increasing zeal to uncover the details of an ever more fascinating creation. From sub-atomic particles to black holes, descriptions of the phenomenon of human reality fill millions of books, periodicals, audio/video images, and web pages.

The magnitude of the paradigm shift associated with the emergence of global civilization can be glimpsed by examining the change of information production and transmission. Scientific investigation into all aspects of reality is the central defining characteristic of the emerging global society. It has been responsible for the creation of a vast depth and breadth of information. Viewed in relation to the production of information in the past, the last one hundred and fifty years could be characterized as an explosion. Our information infrastructure informs our collective understanding of the world we live in and thereby affects the nature of the institutions we create. An examination of the changing information infrastructure of society provides a glimpse of the varying stages of its evolution. So, before proceeding with a thematic presentation of some of the world's scriptures and how they apply to global community, we will view a sketch of the progression of society from tribal to global by viewing the relationship between the information handling mechanisms of a culture and its institutions.

The primary mechanism for the conveyance and storage of information for human beings living in tribes was the spoken word, stored in the memory of individuals and passed from generation to generation. Most of us have heard about the game that demonstrates just how unreliable the spoken word is for maintaining information accuracy. If you pass a story through ten individuals, each privately telling the story to the next person, you can end up with an entirely different story at the end of the process. Details often do not withstand the process of hearing, interpreting, reacting, reformatting, and delivering that must happen as the story is heard and retold. The institutions of the tribe are integral to this level of information accuracy as is the size of the population over which the institutions can effectively administer. The tribe is a group of individuals who know each other. The institutions deal with information in real time among members who personally share the daily experiences of the group.

A city-state differs from a tribe in the size and nature of its institutions, the nature and organization of work, the buildings, the number of people, and the way they relate to each other. The information shared by the group is preserved in written documents. Contrast the image you have of Rome two thousand years ago with its sewer systems, public baths, temples, and senators to the image of a small group of people living in temporary dwellings at the side of a river. Cooperative farming and other technologies may be part of the system that produced the necessary amounts of food to sustain the more sophisticated activities of a city-state. But the information systems necessary to control and consolidate technology, wealth, and power were an essential, integral part of the picture. A level of accuracy could be preserved that allowed for the development of more complex religious, political, social, and technical institutions. Ancient Greece, Rome, Egypt, and Imperial China were all expressions of societies that used the written word.

The structures or institutions that created, managed, preserved, and passed on the information of the city-state were limited by the rate at which the information could be proliferated. The rate relied on the number of individuals who participated in the creation and dissemination of the information. In the typical city-state, only a small percentage of the population was literate and privy to the recorded information. That information was often viewed as sacred, and it was expensive. If it took a scribe a year to copy the information and create an additional copy of the text, it was worth a year of his upkeep. The scribe occupied a position of prominence in his day. Viewed in current terms, he was a reasonably well-paid scholar or professional. One copy of a book or scroll was worth roughly $50 to $100 thousand if viewed in the context of today's pay scale. You did not order the copy of a book unless you really felt you needed it. You did not write something down unless it was very important. You did not change it without the sanction of the highest authorities of the day.

The printing press brought the written word into the realm of the profane. It provided for easy and cheap proliferation of information. It was a prerequisite technology to the beginning of global civilization. The printing press drove the price of a book or manuscript from the $50 thousand range down to the $29.95 range. As the market cost of information plummeted, the volume and the quality of the information soared. The content engaged the mental capacities of an ever increasing number of individuals in the creation of still more information. The observations of one individual could be scrutinized from a larger variety of perspectives. Over the course of several centuries the product of all of those contributions to human learning took us through the Renaissance, the Enlightenment, the Scientific Revolution, the Protestant Reformation, the Industrial Revolution, and a series of political revolutions.

There is now available in the libraries of the world, a relatively large volume of information on the effects of these revolutions on the institutions of the modern world. The family, religion, workplace, city, state, indeed, all the institutions of society have gone through more change over the past five hundred years than they had in the previous ten thousand years since the beginnings of agricultural societies.

Computers, along with communication technologies, are opening the contents of the world's knowledge to an expanding number of participants with ever more powerful tools to find, analyze, synthesize, and communicate information. The acceleration of the production of information and the corresponding engagement of human mental capacity is progressing at an exponential rate when compared with former times. The Internet has been characterized as the global societal brain being constructed and used by a global community of participants. The new understandings and consequent actions and reactions of the peoples of the world through the accelerated means of communication are causing the fabric of the social, political, and economic order of the modern world to be undone and rewoven at every level of human experience. Global society is evolving within this expanded information context.

The following three concepts, gleaned from Baha'i scripture, summarize my view of the process of globalization. First, the current stage in our development on this planet is like the transition of the individual from adolescence to adulthood. Global community requires the engagement of reason in the search for meaning and will proceed through choice and consequence. The absolutes of childhood understanding are giving way to the realization of the relative, contingent nature of human understanding. Science and reason as an integral aspect of global society are being harmonized with spiritual experience and understanding. This integration is an essential ingredient for the creation of a hopeful, meaningful, and peaceful global community.

Second, the world's religions all issue from the same source, the same reality of God, and their primary teachings are in complete agreement. The differences in the teachings with respect to the particulars of religious practice and social justice derive from the exigencies of their respective cultures. Their differences are like personalities that reflect individual experiences in reality.

Third, the realm of perfection proceeds from God as He makes Himself known to each of us. The Messengers, i.e. Abraham, Moses, Krishna, Zoroaster, Buddha, Jesus, Muhammad, the Bab, and Baha'u'llah, are the remembrance of God, the voice of God, the word of God. We can experience the one God through Them, but none of us can speak authoritatively for God or His Messengers. What we are to do about our varying conceptions of reality will most productively proceed from consultative, consensus building processes rather than force. Submission to the will of God, respect for each other's capacity to uniquely approach God, and realization that we are not to supplant God's role as the judge of who is best succeeding in following His will, are the foundation of all of the religions of God. They are also the foundation required for global community.

PART ONE

THE SCRIPTURES

– 1 –

THE COMMON LANGUAGE
OF RELIGION

Spirit of God

Hinduism.

Meet together, speak together, let your minds be of one accord, as the Gods of old, being of one mind, accepted their share of the sacrifice. May your counsel be common, your assembly common, common the mind, and the thoughts of these united. A common purpose do I lay before you, and worship with your common oblation. Let your aims be common, and your hearts of one accord, and all of you be of one mind, so you may live well together. (Rig Veda 10.191.204)

May we unite in our minds, unite in our purposes, and not fight against the divine spirit within us. (Atharva Veda 7.52.1-2)

Native American Religions.

My children, war fear, and disunity have brought you from your villages to this sacred council fire. Facing a common danger, and fearing for the lives of your families, you have yet drifted apart, each tribe thinking and acting only for itself. Remember how I took you from one small band and nursed you into many nations. You must reunite now and act as one. No tribe alone can withstand our savage enemies, who care nothing about the eternal law, who sweep upon us like the storms of winter, spreading death and destruction everywhere.

My children, listen well. Remember that you are broth-
ers, that the downfall of one means the downfall of all.
You must have one fire, one pipe, one war club. (Hiawatha,
Onondaga Tradition)

Christianity

Now there are varieties of gifts, but the same Spirit;
and there are varieties of service, but the same Lord; and
there are varieties of working, but it is the same God who
inspires them all in every one. To each is given the manifestation of the Spirit for the common good. (1 Corinthians
12:4-7)

Part I of this text is organized around themes common to
all of the world's religions. Passages of scripture are used to
discuss the themes. The selection of themes and passages is
aimed at the improvement of mutual respect and understanding. This work presents a view of the world's religions
that encourages their acceptance as multiple traditions flow-
ing from the same spirit of God. The common language of
religion is the spirit of God that pervades and gives life to
the world's scriptures. The various religions are like lamps
through which the light of guidance radiates. It is the same
light regardless of the lamp.

The premise in this work concerning scriptural interpretation is that we as individuals do not have the authority to
dictate to anyone else the intent or meaning of any scripture.
We should all be given room to express our understandings
and perspectives. Each of us knows the will of God as it
pertains to us through our communion with Him. And each
of us must ultimately answer to God for how well we listen.
The judgment of God as it pertains to anyone else belongs
to God.

In the context of human interaction, we must admit our
own fallibility and seek consensus about what we jointly
choose to do about our common concerns. In a society with
multiple religious belief systems, we must at least permit
peaceful and mutually beneficial social interaction through
civility. Tolerance for religious differences is a common space

for meeting, speaking, and acting together. It is held in place by a suspension of disbelief in much the same manner that we suspend disbelief in order to enjoy a story, play, or movie plot that we do not believe could happen. We set aside our disagreement with the storyteller. In as much as none of us is the author of reality, and our view of it is an image compared to reality itself, to each of us the other's view may appear as a fantasy. Religious tolerance can be viewed as a rational ordering of priorities in the human world so that we may peacefully work and live together without having to agree on the particulars of our differing conceptions concerning trust in God.

This book, however, seeks unity beyond religious tolerance. It promotes reasoned and sincere experience of the common ground provided by the world's scriptures.

> Meet together, speak together, let your minds be of one accord, as the Gods of old, being of one mind, accepted their share of the sacrifice. May your counsel be common, your assembly common, common the mind, and the thoughts of these united. A common purpose do I lay before you, and worship with your common oblation. Let your aims be common, and your hearts of one accord, and all of you be of one mind, so you may live well together. (Hinduism. Rig Veda 10.191.204)

This passage is an admonition and an invocation for unity, which rests upon the sanction and example of the "Gods of old." The Gods of our ancestors are of one mind. The Messengers of the past "accepted their share of the sacrifice" to unify the peoples of the past. It is our time to contribute to the unity of the people. The passage admonishes us to be unified as the Messengers are. The images and theologies that man has constructed of God are infinitely varied. Every culture and every individual carries a unique understanding of God. Our cultural and personal concepts of God also change over time. As we mature, our concepts of God incorporate a deeper set of experiences with life. The reality of

God is not shaped by our images of Him. Only our concepts change. When God makes Himself known to us, it is the same God that communicates with everyone albeit our circumstances and understandings are infinitely varied.

As a global community of nations, we are facing very serious problems that arise from our different faith traditions and the concepts we hold of God. Assumptions about our capacity to make judgments about other's relationships with God based on their religion can cause serious barriers to community. It can also lead to violence. The voices of fanaticism are shrill and destructive. Wisdom from the Onondaga Tradition is both an example of the use of religion to bind people together in a defensive war effort, and applicable to our need to unite against the voices of religious fanaticism.

> My children, war fear, and disunity have brought you from your villages to this sacred council fire. Facing a common danger, and fearing for the lives of your families, you have yet drifted apart, each tribe thinking and acting only for itself. Remember how I took you from one small band and nursed you into many nations. You must reunite now and act as one. No tribe alone can withstand our savage enemies, who care nothing about the eternal law, who sweep upon us like the storms of winter, spreading death and destruction everywhere....My children, listen well. Remember that you are brothers, that the downfall of one means the downfall of all. You must have one fire, one pipe, one war club. (Native American Religions. Hiawatha, Onondaga Tradition)

In the past, religion has aided in efforts to galvanize people in a defensive struggle against the assaults of their enemies. Warriors risked their lives in the defense of their communities. The world community of nations disseminated from one human evolution. It is now converging into a single economically, politically, and socially interdependent community. The technology of war has become a threat to the existence of human community. Human beings now possess the destructive force capable of annihilating human life altogether. The preservation of human life requires that we develop consultative and legislative processes to resolve difficulties and provide for the security and welfare of all nations. "May we unite in our minds, unite in our purposes, and not fight against the divine spirit within us" (Hinduism. Atharva Veda 7.52.1-2).

Citizens of all nations now face a common enemy in religious fanaticism and intolerance. The beginning of a common space within which we can unite requires that we all admit that none of us speaks for God when we are interpreting scripture. The "one war club" that we must collectively embrace is commitment to the unity and well being of humankind under the banner of unity in diversity. None of us can take God's place in determining who is closest to Him.

Unity in the context of diverse understandings of God is sanctioned by all of the scriptures of the world's religions. Diversity is integral to the nature of reality. "Now there are varieties of gifts, but the same Spirit; and there are varieties of service, but the same Lord; and there are varieties of working, but it is the same God who inspires them all in every one. To each is given the manifestation of the Spirit for the common good" (Christianity. 1 Corinthians 12:4-7). No two grains of sand or snowflakes are identical in all of creation. Diversity is also an essential characteristic of human society.

– 2 –

THE ONENESS OF GOD

Oneness

Judaism

Hear O Israel: the Lord our God, the Lord is One. (Deuteronomy 6:4)

I am the Lord, and there is no other, besides me there is no God. (Isaiah 45.5)

Islam

Say, He is God, the One!
God, the eternally Besought of all!
He neither begets nor was begotten,
And there is none comparable unto Him. (Qur'an 112)

Hinduism

He is the one God, hidden in all beings, all-pervading, the Self within all beings, watching over all works, dwelling in all beings, the witness, the perceiver, the only one, free from qualities. (Svetasvatara Upanishad 6.11)

As men approach me, so I receive them. All paths, Arjuna, lead to me. (Bhagavad Gita 4.11)

Sikhism

He is the Sole Supreme Being: of eternal manifestation; Creator, Immanent Reality; without Fear, without Rancor; Timeless Form; Unincarnated; Self-existent; Realized by the grace of the Holy Preceptor. (Adi Granth, Japuji, p. 1)

Taoism

The way that can be spoken of is not the eternal Way. The name that can be named is not the eternal name. (Tao Te Ching 1)

The sage clasps the Primal Unity,
Testing by it everything under heaven. (Tao Te Ching 22)

Buddhism

The Suchness of these dharmas and the Suchness of all dharmas and the Suchness of the Tathagata are simply this one single Suchness. There is no division within Suchness. Just simply one single is this Suchness, not two, nor three. (Perfection of Wisdom in Eight Thoursand Lines 31.1)

Baha'i Faith

There is none other God but Thee, the Inaccessible, the Omnipotent, the Omniscient, the Holy of Holies. (Gleanings, 5)

"As men approach me, so I receive them. All paths, Arjuna, lead to me" (Hinduism. Bhagavad Gita 4.11). This passage is from a conversation between Arjuna and Krishna. The statement can be read as a condition as well as an indication that the paths may be different. "As men approach me" can be understood as "when men approach me." It can also be understood as "no matter how they approach me." The how is less important than the reality of the effort.

The theme of the oneness of God is common to the scriptures of the world's religions: for the Jews and Christians, "the Lord is One"; for the Muslims, "He is God, the One"; for the Hindu, "He is the One God"; for the Buddhist, "this one single Suchness"; for the Taoist God is the "Primal Unity." With each Messenger of God comes the restatement of the oneness of God. The statement can be understood as a realization of the reality rather than a theological position. There is only one God no matter what different people call Him or how they view or understand Him. It is the same God who makes Himself known to all of

us though we have multiple religious traditions and an infinite variety of conceptualizations of Him. All of the Messengers remind us that all of the conceptions of God are not
God. The Messenger brings the realization or recognition of
His oneness beyond human conception.

Individuals understand their experience of God in the
context of the scriptures, practices, and theologies of their
individualized faith traditions. The realization of the oneness
of God provided by Zoroaster, Krishna, Moses, Buddha, Jesus,
and Muhammad become literalized into concepts. As followers of the various religions, we tend to view our concept of
God as God and view with skepticism the concepts others
present of God. The scriptures of all of the religions repeatedly remind us that there is only one God who is not subject
to conceptualization.

The assumption of the absolute rightness of our own
thoughts is a normal human predisposition. My thinking
processes require an assumption of credibility. The assumption is, nevertheless, inaccurate if accepted as absolute. We
do not have the ability to perfectly conceptualize anything.
My thoughts are a partial, incomplete reflection of reality.
To the degree that any of us holds or presents our thoughts
as absolutes, we set a course for conflict with the perceptions
and pronouncements of others.

The tendency to understand our conceptualizations as objective reality is particularly true of our conceptions of God.
This derives from the nature of the experiences we have of
communion with God. When God presents Himself to us,
He is absolutely perfect. However, the instant we turn our
gaze from God to our thoughts of Him we are no longer
gazing toward the realm of perfection. Our thoughts of God
are not God. The scriptures bear evidence to and the Messengers remind us of this repeatedly by providing us with
admonitions against mistaking our images of God for the
remembrance God provides of Himself. We have infinitely
diverse images, perspectives, and understandings of God, but
they are not God. Only God has the capacity to manifest His
own Self.

The realization of the oneness of God with which Jesus inspired the apostle Paul, for example, permitted him to introduce the spirit of God to the Greeks by identifying with a statue of the unknown God. Paul was in Athens. He addressed a gathering of Athenians "in the midst of Mar's hill" concerning their preoccupation with their graven images of God to the point of their having an altar dedicated "to the unknown God" (Christianity. Acts, 17:23). Paul was not confused by images of God. He experienced the realty of God through Jesus and wanted to share the good news. His words and actions demonstrated that he knew the difference between his understanding of God and the reality of God. Paul was not, therefore, threatened by the Greek image of the unknown God nor was he afraid to use it to connect people with the experience of the oneness of God that Jesus brought.

Six hundred years earlier Lao Tze articulated the same principle. "The way that can be spoken of is not the eternal Way. The name that can be named is not the eternal name" (Taoism. Tao Te Ching 1). "The sage clasps the Primal Unity, testing by it everything under heaven" (Tao Te Ching 22). The recognition of the reality of "everything under heaven" is dependent on holding fast, not to a concept or image but to the Primal Unity. God speaks for Himself through His Messengers to the human heart that "clasps" or earnestly seeks understanding through His presence. The spirit of God informs understanding and is primary. Theology is secondary and cannot encompass God.

All Nations Serve the One God

Judaism

For from the rising of the sun to its setting my name is great among the nations, and in every place incense is offered to my name, and a pure offering; for my name is great among the nations, says the Lord of hosts. (Malachi 1:11)

Islam

Unto each nation have We given sacred rites which they are to perform; so let them not dispute with you of the matter, but you summon unto your Lord. (Qur'an 22.67)

Verily We have raised in every nation a messenger, proclaiming, "Serve God and shun false gods." (Qur'an 16.36)

Hinduism

As men approach me, so I receive them. All paths, Arjuna, lead to me. (Bhagavad Gita 4.11)

Sikhism

Some call on the Lord, "Rama," some cry, "Khuda," Some bow to Him as Gosain, some as Allah; He is called the Ground of Grounds and also the Bountiful, the Compassionate One and Gracious. Hindus bathe in holy waters for His sake; Muslims make the pilgrimage to Mecca. The Hindus perform puja; others bow their heads in namaz. There are those who read the Vedas and others—Christians, Jews, Muslims—who read the Semitic scriptures. Some wear blue, some white robes, some call themselves Muslims, others Hindus. Some aspire to bahishat (Muslim heaven), some to swarga (Hindu heaven). Says Nanak, Whoever realizes the will of the Lord, He will find out the Lord's secrets! (Adi Granth, Ramkali, M.5, p. 885)

Baha'i Faith

There can be no doubt that whatever the peoples of the world, of whatever race or religion, they derive their inspiration from one heavenly Source, and are the subjects of one God. The difference between the ordinances under which they abide should be attributed to the varying requirements and exigencies of the age in which they were revealed. All of them, except for a few which are the outcome of human perversity, were ordained of God, and are a reflection of His Will and Purpose. (Gleanings from the Writings of Baha'u'llah 111)

Christianity

And Peter opened his mouth and said, "Truly I perceive that God shows no partiality, but in every nation any one who fears him and does what is right is acceptable to him." *(Acts 10:34-35)*

And I [Jesus] have other sheep, that are not of this fold; I must bring them also, and they will heed my voice. So there shall be one flock, one shepherd. (John 10:16)

Although the concept of "nation" has changed considerably over the centuries in which the various scriptures have used the term, the broader meaning of the word as different peoples or cultures includes the diverse meanings. The following passage from Malachi instructs us that God has a relationship with all nations. "For from the rising of the sun to its setting my name is great among the nations, and in every place incense is offered to my name, and a pure offering; for my name is great among the nations, says the Lord of hosts" (Judaism. Malachi 1:11). The beauty of God is the same beauty no matter who sees it or where they reside. As Peter is quoted, "Truly I perceive that God shows no partiality, but in every nation any one who fears him and does what is right is acceptable to him" (Christianity. Acts 10:34-35).

Every nation has its own traditions and rituals for praising God. The Qur'an explicitly states that it is best not to argue about the manner in which each nation relates to God. "Unto each nation have We given sacred rites which they are to perform; so let them not dispute with you of the matter, but you summon unto your Lord" (Islam. Qur'an 22.67). The application of the open market system for the pursuit of converts ("you summon unto your Lord") was applied in the Americas a thousand years later when the Christians agreed to disagree. Each denomination was allowed to seek converts. The impulse to protect the individual's choice concerning religious belief systems and practices in the new land derived largely from the persecutions and wars concerning religion in Europe. The compromise avoided war. They re-

linquished the impulse to enforce a particular religious orthodoxy in order to survive in a field of competitors that
could not be dominated. Christianity in the context of the
United States thereby articulated an institutional realization
of religious unity and theological relativism within the context of the Christian dispensation.

During the sixteenth century in Northern India, Nanak
explicitly addressed the underlying religious unity of Hinduism, Judaism, Christianity, and Islam, and imparted the scriptural texts of Sikhism.

> Some call on the Lord, "Rama," some cry, "Khuda,"
> Some bow to Him as Gosain, some as Allah; He is called
> the Ground of Grounds and also the Bountiful, the Com-
> passionate One and Gracious. Hindus bathe in holy wa-
> ters for His sake; Muslims make the pilgrimage to Mecca.
> The Hindus perform puja; others bow their heads in namaz.
> There are those who read the Vedas and others—Chris-
> tians, Jews, Muslims—who read the Semitic scriptures. Some
> wear blue, some white robes, some call themselves Mus-
> lims, others Hindus. Some aspire to bahishat (Muslim
> heaven), some to swarga (Hindu heaven). Says Nanak, Who-
> ever realizes the will of the Lord, He will find out the
> Lord's secrets! (Sikhism. Adi Granth, Ramkali, M.5, p.
> 885)

The proof concerning the unity of God among the nations can be discerned by being willing to listen to and
realize the will of God rather than our own will. If we want
to view the will of God, we must submit to Him. Both
Peter ("any one who fears him and does what is right") and
Nanak ("whoever realizes the will of the Lord") in the above
passages remind us that the approach to God is conditioned
on doing His will not on the strength of our particular
theology. The unity of religion can be realized through seeking God's will and purpose rather than insisting on our own
theologies. Religions issue from the will of God. At this
juncture in human history, we cannot use force to establish
the unity of religion. Nor do we have to abandon religion to

create a unified world culture. The unity of religion will be established on the planet and assist in the development of global culture to the degree that we realize that it has always been unified. There has always been one flock and one shepherd—the people of God and His Messengers. All of the Messengers speak as one voice—the voice of God. "And I [Jesus] have other sheep, that are not of this fold; I must bring them also, and they will heed my voice. So there shall be one flock, one shepherd" (Christianity. John 10:16). "Verily We have raised in every nation a messenger, proclaiming, 'Serve God and shun false gods'" (Islam. Qur'an 16.36). The false gods are those of our own making. They are fashioned most intensely through our refusal to accept that God speaks for Himself through His Messengers to whomever He pleases.

— 3 —

THE UNKNOWABLE GOD

The Most Hidden

Hinduism

He truly knows Brahman who knows him as beyond knowledge; he who thinks that he knows, knows not. The ignorant think that Brahman is known, but the wise know him to be beyond knowledge. (Kena Upanishad 2.3)

Judaism

Truly thou art a God who hidest thyself. (Isaiah 45.15)

For my thoughts are not your thoughts, neither are your ways my ways, says the Lord. For as the heavens are higher than the earth, so are my ways higher than your ways and my thoughts than your thoughts. (Isaiah 55.8-9)

Buddhism

Who sees Me by form, who seeks Me in sound, perverted are his footsteps upon the Way; for he cannot perceive the Tathagata. (Diamond Sutra 26)

Jainism

There exists no simile to comprehend him. He is formless existence. He is what baffles all terminology. There is no word to comprehend him. He is neither sound nor form nor odor nor taste nor touch. (Acarangasutra 5.140)

Taoism

The way that can be spoken of is not the eternal Way. The name that can be named is not the eternal name. (Tao Te Ching 1)

Islam

No vision can grasp Him, but His grasp is over all vision. He is above all comprehension, yet is acquainted with all things. (Qur'an 6.103)

Invent not similitudes for God; for God knows, and you know not. (Qur'an 16.74)

Have you seen him who makes his desire his god, and God sends him astray purposely, and seals up his hearing and his heart, and sets on his sight a covering? Who, then, will lead him after God [has condemned him]? Will you not then heed? (Qur'an 45.23)

Baha'i Faith

To every discerning and illuminated heart it is evident that God, the unknowable Essence, the Divine Being, is immensely exalted beyond every human attribute, such as corporeal existence, ascent and descent, egress and regress. Far be it from His glory that human tongue should ad equately recount His fathomless mystery. He is, and hath ever been, veiled in the ancient eternity of His Essence, and will remain in His Reality everlastingly hidden from the sight of men. (Gleanings 46-47)

This people, all of them, have pictured a god in the realm of the mind, and worship that image which they have made for themselves.... Consider then, how all the peoples of the world are bowing the knee to a fancy of their own contriving, how they have created a creator within their own minds, and they call it the Fashioner of all that is—whereas in truth it is but an illusion. Thus are the people worshipping only an error of perception. (Selections from the Writings of Abdul'Baha 53-54)

In the movie version of Carl Sagan's book, *Contact*, the theologian and the scientist address the existence of God. The scientist refers to Occam's Razor—a supposition that all things being equal, the simplest explanation tends to be closest to the truth. The scientist asks if it is more likely that God created human beings and the universe and then hid any trace of Himself or that God simply does not exist and human beings created the concept of God to feel more secure and comfortable in an otherwise mostly enigmatic reality. In the book, God plants an explicit message about His existence in the ranges of the calculation of *pi* that can only be reached by extremely powerful computers. The mechanism is a clever resolution of the conflict between science and religion in the story. As scientific explanations outstrip the utility of religious cosmological explanations concerning the workings of physical reality, the plot of the story allows God to provide unquestionable scientific evidence of His existence. Given the unlikely resolution of the question of God's existence in this manner, modern humans must seek the answer as it has been sought in the past, through His Messengers—His presence.

All of the world's religions present God as beyond human understanding. God is essentially unknowable. Human beings can no more understand the workings of the author of reality than an ant can understand human society. Fewer than half a billion years of evolution separate humans and ants. The distance between humans and the primal cause is infinite. God is the most hidden of the hidden—the primary mystery of the universe. The search to know and understand God is therefore unlimited. There can never be an end to the search. God will always be unattainable. No one can observe God independently of the way in which He makes Himself known.

The scriptures of the world's religions refer to the unknowable and therefore indescribable essence of God and to the tendency of humans, nevertheless, to create descriptions of God that are mistaken for His reality. The Qur'an instructs us to "Invent not similitudes for God; for God knows, and you know not" (Islam. Qur'an 16.74). The first part of the statement is similar to the statement from the Ten Commandments—"You shall have no other gods before Me" (Judaism. Exodus 20:1-2). It is also similar to texts from Jainism and Buddhism. "There exists no simile to comprehend him. He is formless existence. He is what baffles all terminology. There is no word to comprehend him. He is neither sound nor form nor odor nor taste nor touch" (Jainism. Acarangasutra 5.140). "Who sees Me by form, who seeks Me in sound, perverted are his footsteps upon the Way; for he cannot perceive the Tathagata" (Buddhism. Diamond Sutra 26). An image or likeness of God, whether physical or intellectual, is not to be confused with God.

The confusion is nevertheless the norm for most of us most of the time. Our approach to God through this life is intimately related to how we conceive of God. For most of us our religious education involves how we are to think about God. We are taught theology. I remember being told in grade school religion class that the pagans ignorantly bowed down before statues that they had carved and worshiped as God. The statues, I was instructed, were just stone. They were not God and could not fulfill the prayers of their suppliants. I was then instructed in the concept of the Trinity, which, I was assured, was the correct concept of God.

A representative statement from Hinduism teaches, "He truly knows Brahman who knows him as beyond knowledge; he who thinks that he knows, knows not. The ignorant think that Brahman is known, but the wise know him to be beyond knowledge" (Hinduism. Kena Upanishad 2. 1-3). The passage admonishes us not to confuse the concept or image of God with the reality of God. This is not to say that having an understanding of God is not acceptable. Apart from His presence and His revelation of Himself to us, all we have are our images and concepts. Discussing God, particularly in pursuit of a closer relationship with Him, is reasonable for us. The above passage of scripture refers to the difference between two human conditions with respect to the images we hold. Some think of the image as God. Some understand that it is not. The scriptures admonish us to understand the difference. The last chapter referred to the opening line of the Tao concerning the unknowable nature of God. Its reiteration is appropriate as one of the most elegant expressions of the concept. "The way that can be spoken of is not the eternal Way. The name that can be named is not the eternal name" (Taoism. Tao Te Ching 1).

Or, as I have heard it expressed, "if you understand the Tao, it is not the Tao."

The following two passages from the scriptures of the Baha'i Faith, speak directly to the unknowable nature of God and to our tendency to, nevertheless, worship the concepts we hold of God.

> To every discerning and illuminated heart it is evident that God, the unknowable Essence, the Divine Being, is immensely exalted beyond every human attribute, such as corporeal existence, ascent and descent, egress and regress. Far be it from His glory that human tongue should adequately recount His fathomless mystery. He is, and hath ever been, veiled in the ancient eternity of His Essence, and will remain in His Reality everlastingly hidden from the sight of men. (Baha'i Faith. Gleanings from the Writings of Baha'u'llah, 46-47)

> This people, all of them, have pictured a god in the realm of the mind, and worship that image which they have made for themselves.... Consider then, how all the peoples of the world are bowing the knee to a fancy of their own contriving, how they have created a creator within their own minds, and they call it the Fashioner of all that is—whereas in truth it is but an illusion. Thus are the people worshipping only an error of perception. (Baha'i Faith. Selections from the Writings of Abdul'Baha, 53-54)

Knowing the Unknowable

The dichotomy presented by having to know an unknowable God is an essential aspect of the relationship between man and God. The scriptures tell us of God and that the purpose of our existence is to know God. The theme is reiterated throughout the scriptures. The following is an example from the Baha'i scriptures. "The purpose of God in creating man hath been, and will ever be, to enable him to know his Creator and to attain His Presence" (Baha'i Faith. Gleanings from the Writings of Baha'u'llah, 71).

Yet the scriptures also tell us that God is beyond human comprehension. A resolution to the paradox can be glimpsed through examining the verse in Isaiah that refers to God as One "who hidest thyself" (Judaism. Isaiah 45.15). God hides Himself to protect us from His overwhelming presence. None can stand or exist in the presence of God. "For my thoughts are not your thoughts, neither are your ways my ways, says the Lord. For as the heavens are higher than the earth, so are my ways higher than your ways and my thoughts than your thoughts" (Judaism. Isaiah 55.8-9). Free will, or the choice to turn to God, is the measured capacity He gives us to stand in His presence. There is no way to overview God. He cannot be "seen" or "heard" except as He makes Himself known. Implicit in the human situation is the requirement of submission of our view to His view if we are to know Him as other than our image of Him. Finding God is conditioned on both His will and our will.

The capacity of human beings to recognize the excellence of their Creator pivots on their freedom to reject or accept the view. Our freedom of choice is an essential aspect of our capacity to know God. The author of reality makes Himself known to human beings through the mechanism of free will, the independent approach to His presence. God reveals His own Self as the most obvious of the obvious to those who are willing to forgo the primacy of their own view and let God speak for Himself. In order to attain the presence of God, we must willingly accept the primacy of God's view over our own.

False Gods—Idolatry

Judaism

The law against idolatry outweighs all other commandments. (Mekilta Exodus 12:6)

There shall be in you no strange god and you shall not worship a foreign god. (Psalm 81.10)

What is the "foreign god" within a man's body? It is the evil impulse. (Shabbat 105b)

Christianity

For many... live as enemies of the cross of Christ. Their end is destruction, their god is the belly, and they glory in their shame, with minds set on earthly things. (Philippians 3:18-19)

Covetousness, which is idolatry. (Colossians 3:5)

Hinduism

Fools misjudge me when I take a human form, because they do not know my supreme state as Lord of Beings. Unconscious, they fall prey to beguiling nature such as belongs to ogres and demons, for their hopes [ascribing to God human motives] are vain, and so are their rituals and their search for wisdom. (Bhagavad Gita 9.11-12)

Islam

Verily We have raised in every nation a messenger, proclaiming, "Serve God and shun false gods." (Qur'an 16.36)

Have you seen him who makes his desire his god, and God sends him astray purposely, and seals up his hearing and his heart, and sets on his sight a covering? Who, then, will lead him after God [has condemned him]? Will you not then heed? (Islam. Qur'an 45.23)

Buddhism

Who sees Me by form, who seeks Me in sound, perverted are his footsteps upon the Way; for he cannot perceive the Tathagata. (Diamond Sutra 26)

All acquisitions [i.e., grasping] as well as play of concepts [i.e., symbolic representations] are basically in the nature of cessation and quiescence. Any factor of experience with regards to anyone at any place was never taught by the Buddha. (Nagarjuna, Mulamadhyamaka Karika 25)

Intrinsically our transcendental nature is void and not a single thing can be attained. It is the same with the Essence of Mind, which is a state of Absolute Void. (Sutra of Hui Neng 2)

Through the abandonment of desire the Deathless is realized. (Samyutta Nikaya xlvii.37)

The world's scriptures are replete with warnings against the worship of false gods. "Verily We have raised in every nation a messenger, proclaiming, 'Serve God and shun false gods'" (Islam. Qur'an 16.36). "There shall be in you no strange god and you shall not worship a foreign god" (Judaism. Psalm 81.10). Idolatry is the worship of something other than God. "The law against idolatry outweighs all other commandments" (Judaism. Mekilta Exodus 12:6).

The most readily available idols are the objects of our desires. "What is the 'foreign god' within a man's body? It is the evil impulse" (Judaism. Shabbat 105b). When our desires conflict with the way of God, we often choose our way—"the evil impulse." Idolatry is submission to our will when we suspect that it conflicts with the will of God. It is the preference for the ways of the world over the ways of heaven. "For many... live as enemies of the cross of Christ. Their end is destruction, their god is the belly, and they glory in their shame, with minds set on earthly things" (Christianity. Philippians 3:18-19). Another term for submission to our selfish instincts is covetousness—"Covetousness, which is idolatry" (Christianity. Colossians 3:5).

The injunction not to worship a false god pertains primarily to our selfishness and our preference for our will as opposed to the will of God. The warning in the scriptures is directed at our malevolent inclinations. It is not a warning against entrapment by inaccurate theology. Idolatry is submission to our limited desires for our own ends, the worship of things subject to corruption. Some concepts of God might be more sophisticated and inclusive than others; however, the injunction to follow the one true God concerns a choice between our will and God's will. It is not a directive to fight over which concept of God is the "right" one. "Have you seen him who makes his desire his god, and God sends him astray purposely, and seals up his hearing and his heart, and sets on his sight a covering? Who, then, will lead him after God [has condemned him]? Will you not then heed?" (Islam. Qur'an 45.23). God knows our disposition with respect to Him and has the final word about our relationship

with Him. The relative accuracy of our theology is no substi-
tute for His presence, which cannot be attained without
submission to His will over our desires. "Through the abandonment of desire the Deathless is realized" (Buddhism.
Samyutta Nikaya xlvii.37).

– 4 –

THE MESSENGER

Baha'i Faith

Since there can be no tie of direct intercourse to bind
the one true God with His creation, and no resemblance
whatever can exist between the transient and the Eternal,
the contingent and the Absolute, He hath ordained that
in every age and dispensation a pure and stainless Soul be
made manifest in the kingdoms of earth and heaven. Unto
this subtle, this mysterious and ethereal Being He hath
assigned a twofold nature; the physical, pertaining to the
world of matter, and the spiritual, which is born of the
substance of God Himself. He hath, moreover, conferred
upon Him a double station. The first station, which is
related to His innermost reality, representeth Him as One
Whose voice is the voice of God Himself, To this testifieth
the tradition: 'Manifold and mysterious is My relationship
with God. I am He, Himself, and He is I, Myself, except
that I am that I am, and He is that He is.' And in like
manner, the words: 'Arise, O Muhammad, for lo, the Lover
and the Beloved are joined together and made one in Thee.'
He similarly saith: 'There is no distinction whatsoever between Thee and Them, except that They are Thy Servants.'
The second station is the human station, exemplified by
the following verses: 'I am but a man like you.' 'Say, praise
be to my Lord! Am I more than a man, an apostle?' These
Essences of Detachment, these resplendent Realities are
the channels of God's all-pervasive grace. Led by the light
of unfailing guidance, and invested with supreme sovereignty, They are commissioned to use the inspiration of
Their words, the effusions of Their infallible grace and the
sanctifying breeze of Their Revelation for the cleansing of

every longing heart and receptive spirit from the dross and dust of earthly cares and limitations. (Gleanings from the Writings of Baha'u'llah, 66-67)

Judaism

The Eternal thought, "Shall I hide from Abraham what I am going to do, seeing that Abraham is to become a large and powerful nation, and that all nations of the world are to seek bliss like his? I have chosen him that he may charge his sons and his household after him to follow the directions of the Eternal by doing what is good and right." (Genesis 18:17-19)

The Lord your God will raise up for you a prophet like me [Moses] from among you, from your brethren—him you shall heed. (Deuteronomy 18:15)

Buddhism

Homage to Him, the Exalted One, the Arahant, the All-enlightened One. To the Buddha I go for refuge. To the Norm I go for refuge. To the Order I go for refuge. (Khuddaka Patha)

Islam

Say, "Obey God, and obey the Messenger; then, if you turn away, only upon him rests what is laid on him, and upon you rests what is laid on you. If you obey him, you will be guided. It is only for the Messenger to deliver the manifest Message." (Qur'an 24.54)

Muhammad is...the Messenger of God and the Seal of the Prophets. (Qur'an 33.40)

Verily We have sent messengers before you, among them some of those of whom We have told you, and some of whom We have not told you. (Qur'an 40.78)

Christianity

In the beginning was the Word, and the Word was with God, and the Word was God. He was in the beginning with God; all things were made through him, and without him was not anything made that was made. In him was life, and the life was the light of men.... And the Word became flesh and dwelt among us, full of grace and truth; we have beheld his glory, glory as of the only Son of the Father. (John 1:1-4, 14)

Do you not know me, Philip? He who has seen me has seen the Father; how can you say, "Show us the Father?" Do you not believe that I am in the Father and the Father in me? (John 14: 9-10)

Jesus said to them, "Truly, truly, I say to you, before Abraham was, I am." (John 8: 58)

Jesus said to him, "I am the way, the truth, and the life; no one comes to the Father, but by me. (John 14:6)

Sikhism

The whole world seeks to attain the transcendent state. Without the true Preceptor's aid it is not attained. Exhausted with learning, pundits and astrologers fall into sects and are lost in delusion. The transcendent state is attained only on meeting the Preceptor, should He of his will show grace. Brother! Except through the Preceptor the transcendent state may not arise. (Adi Granth, Sri Raga, M.3, p. 68)

Says Nanak, "The Master is the Lord's image; The Lord in the Master pervasive—Brother! Between these lies no difference." (Adi Granth, Asa Chhant, M. 4, p. 442)

The Messenger

The Eternal thought, "Shall I hide from Abraham what I am going to do, seeing that Abraham is to become a large and powerful nation, and that all nations of the world are to seek bliss like his? I have chosen him that he may charge his sons and his household after him to follow the directions of the Eternal by doing what is good and right" (Judaism. Genesis 18:17-19).

The question is rhetorical. God does not intend to hide His will from Abraham or from anyone. He makes Himself known to every human being personally and to society at large through His Messengers and the scriptures provided through them.

The inability of human consciousness to overview the reality of God does not mean that God does not make Himself known. God makes Himself known through all of creation; every atom of existence bears testimony to the existence of a creator. The human mind is stirred as it touches reality itself. The soul "leaps" when it touches the reality of its own being and is fulfilled in its awareness of God. The experience of God, His remembrance, is the Messenger—the word of God. The Messenger is the presence of God to any human being in any context. God speaks to the human soul and to the human mind through His Messengers. Baha'u'llah, the Messenger of the Baha'i Faith, referring to the two natures of the Messenger—physical and spiritual— explains the spiritual nature as "born of the substance of God Himself".

Since there can be no tie of direct intercourse to bind the one true God with His creation, and no resemblance whatever can exist between the transient and the Eternal, the contingent and the Absolute, He hath ordained that in every age and dispensation a pure and stainless Soul be made manifest in the kingdoms of earth and heaven. Unto this subtle, this mysterious and ethereal Being He hath assigned a twofold nature; the physical, pertaining to the world of matter, and the spiritual, which is born of the substance of God Himself. He hath, moreover, conferred upon Him a double station. The first station, which is related to His innermost reality, representeth Him as One Whose voice is the voice of God Himself, To this testifieth the tradition: 'Manifold and mysterious is My relationship with God. I am He, Himself, and He is I, Myself, except that I am that I am, and He is that He is.' And in like manner, the words: 'Arise, O Muhammad, for lo, the Lover and the Beloved are joined together and made one in Thee.' He similarly saith: 'There is no distinction whatsoever between Thee and Them, except that They are Thy Servants.' The second station is the human station, exemplified by the following verses: 'I am but a man like you.' 'Say, praise be to my Lord! Am I more than a man, an apostle?' These

Essences of Detachment, these resplendent Realities are
the channels of God's all-pervasive grace. Led by the light
of unfailing guidance, and invested with supreme sovereignty, They are commissioned to use the inspiration of
Their words, the effusions of Their infallible grace and the
sanctifying breeze of Their Revelation for the cleansing of
every longing heart and receptive spirit from the dross and
dust of earthly cares and limitations." (Baha'i Faith.
Baha'u'llah, Gleanings, 66-67)

The reality of God is articulated into the personal and
cultural fabric of humanity through the Messengers of God—
Abraham, Zoroaster, Moses, Buddha, Krishna, Christ,
Muhammad, the Bab, and Baha'u'llah. As initiators of independent world religions, they are the tether between this
world and God for the individual and for society. The vast
majority of the individuals currently on the earth who profess a personal belief in God do so in the context of religious
experiences associated with one of the world's major faith
traditions.

The Messengers corroborate the Divine and temporal aspects of Their missions through scriptural statements concerning their identity. For example, Jesus comments: "No
one has ever seen God; the only Son, who is in the bosom
of the Father, he has made him known." (Christianity. John
1:18) The reference to Himself as the only Son addresses
His divine nature. Similarly, the Gospel of John begins with
a description of Jesus as the Word of God. "In the beginning was the Word, and the Word was with God, and the
Word was God. He was in the beginning with God; all
things were made through him, and without him was not
anything made that was made. In him was life, and the life
was the light of men" (Christianity. John 1:1-4). The Messenger is the eternal word of God; He who makes God
known.

This passage goes on to address the physical nature of the
Messenger. "And the Word became flesh and dwelt among
us, full of grace and truth; we have beheld his glory, glory as

of the only Son of the Father" (Christianity. John 1:14).
Jesus, as a Messenger of God, is both a human being and the
Word of God. Beholding or recognizing the glory of God is
an experience of the fundamental unity of God. The title
"Son of the Father" is a reference to the divine nature of
Jesus. The physical, historical Jesus that initiated the Christian religious dispensation was the vehicle or lamp associated
with the óne light of God. Experiencing the light of God
through a relationship with Jesus, does not negate the same
experience through a relationship with Moses, Buddha,
Zoroaster, Krishna, Abraham, Muhammad, the Bab, or
Baha'u'llah. There is only one light of God, not knowable
or describable save through His own Self, though there are
many lamps. Recognition of the divine nature of Jesus or the
other Messengers is realization of the Self of God.
Conceptualization of the historical, cultural aspects of the
missions of the Messengers pertains to the temporal nature
of Their dispensations.

The Image of the Messenger

Judaism

You shall have no other gods before Me. (Exodus 20:1-2)

Islam

Invent not similitudes for God; for God knows, and
you know not. (Qur'an 16.74)

Christianity

I am the way, the truth, and the life: no man cometh
unto the Father, but by me. (John 14:6)

That was the true Light, which lighteth every man that
cometh into the world. (John 1:9)

Buddhism

I am the Tathagata, the Most Honored among men; I
appear in the world like unto this great cloud, to pour
enrichment on all parched living beings, to free them from
their misery to attain the joy of peace, joy of the present
world, and joy of Nirvana. (Lotus Sutra 5)

Hinduism

Fools misjudge me when I take a human form, because they do not know my supreme state as Lord of Beings. Unconscious, they fall prey to beguiling nature such as belongs to ogres and demons, for their hopes [ascribing to God human motives] are vain, and so are their rituals and their search for wisdom. (Bhagavad Gita 9.11-12)

I [Krishna] am the goal of the wise man, and I am the way. I am his prosperity. I am his heaven. There is nothing dearer to him than I. (Srimad Bhagavatam 11.12)

Truth is victorious, never untruth. Truth is the way; truth is the goal of life, reached by sages who are free from self-will. (Mundaka Upanishad 3.1.6)

Confusing an image or concept of the Messenger with God's voice or presence is the age old human mistake described in all of the world's scriptures. "Invent not similitudes for God; for God knows, and you know not" (Islam. Qur'an 16.74). "You shall have no other gods before Me" (Judaism. Exodus 20:1-2). Jesus said, "I am the way, the truth, and the life: no man cometh unto the Father, but by me" (Christianity. John 14:6). He did not say that the images you have created in your mind of Me or the interpretations of scripture you have constructed in your thoughts are "the way, the truth, and the life." Placing the image of the Messenger, His life story, rituals, practices, theology, or even our thoughts of His grace before His presence sublimates the Messenger to our will and way.

Fools misjudge me when I take a human form, because they do not know my supreme state as Lord of Beings. Unconscious, they fall prey to beguiling nature such as belongs to ogres and demons, for their hopes [ascribing to God human motives] are vain, and so are their rituals and their search for wisdom. (Hinduism. Bhagavad Gita 9.11-12)

The presence of Jesus, Buddha, Zoroaster, Krishna, Muhammad, Moses, the Bab, and Baha'u'llah is the presence of God. In the beginning of John's Gospel, the Messenger is referred to as the eternal, creative "Word" of God that was in the beginning with God and through which all creation is fashioned. The "Word" that is the "light of men", "that was the true Light, which lighteth every man that cometh into the world" (Christianity. John 1:9). None can adequately describe the remembrance of God that He gives us through His Messengers; not even to ourselves.

The following statement of Krishna echoes the identity statement made by Jesus as "the way, the truth, and the life." "I [Krishna] am the goal of the wise man, and I am the way. I am his prosperity. I am his heaven. There is nothing dearer to him than I" (Hiduism. Srimad Bhagavatam 11.12). In another passage from Hindu scripture, the truth is identified as the way. "Truth is victorious, never untruth. Truth is the way; truth is the goal of life, reached by sages who are free from self-will" (Hinduism. Mundaka Upanishad 3.1.6). The Messenger, God as He makes Himself known, is eternal life, the desire of the heart, and the fulfillment of being. In Buddhism the Messenger is called the Tathagata.

> I am the Tathagata, the Most Honored among men; I appear in the world like unto this great cloud, to pour enrichment on all parched living beings, to free them from their misery to attain the joy of peace, joy of the present world, and joy of Nirvana. (Buddhism. Lotus Sutra 5)

When we enter the presence of God in prayer or meditation or through the activities of our lives and we see with our own eyes the beauty of God and hear with our own ears the accents of His voice, that experience is "the way, the truth, and the life."

A Kingdom Divided

Christianity

> And Jesus knew their thoughts, and said unto them. Every kingdom divided against itself is brought to desolation; and every city or house divided against itself shall not

stand: And if Satan cast out Satan, he is divided against himself; how shall then his kingdom stand?....But if I cast out devils but by the Spirit of God, then the kingdom of God is come unto you. (Christianity. Matthew 12:25-26)

For the Bread of God is he which cometh down from heaven, and giveth life unto the world. (John 6:33)

Follow me and let the dead bury their dead. (Matthew 8:22)

The physical lives of the Messengers, including the histories and reported sayings or the writings of the prophets of God, can be understood as metaphors and mantras directing our attention toward the spirit of God. Jesus directs us toward God when He refers to Himself as the bread of heaven and instructs us that there is no way to heaven except through eating His body and drinking His blood. This can be understood as a metaphor describing the spiritual food that is derived from partaking of the presence of God through Jesus. It was not an instruction to a select few individuals to attain heaven through cannibalism. The incident was a wonderfully eloquent way of admonishing us not to confuse our image of Jesus with the bounty of His presence—not to confuse spiritual bounty with concepts or literal understandings. It is an admonition not to confuse the lamp with the light. Asking which Messenger is the true one is like asking which lamp is the true lamp. Lamps that provide light are true lamps; Messengers who provide the presence of God are true Messengers.

One of the implications of replacing God with concepts of Him can be seen in the context of the current world situation. To the degree that the adherents of the different religions of the world are bringing individuals and their behavior in closer proximity to God, they are all working toward the same end. The result is unity. To the degree that they are using religion to pursue an end other than the spirit of God, the house of global humankind suffers disunity. Jesus said, after being accused of being Satan, that a house divided against itself could not stand.

> And Jesus knew their thoughts, and said unto them.
> Every kingdom divided against itself is brought to desola-
> tion; and every city or house divided against itself shall not
> stand: And if Satan cast out Satan, he is divided against
> himself; how shall then his kingdom stand?....But if I cast
> out devils but by the Spirit of God, then the kingdom of
> God is come unto you. (Christianity. Matthew 12:25-26)

There is only one voice of God manifested through the
various Messengers that have appeared throughout the evolution of people on this planet. Self-righteousness in this
context appears as the rigid human act of joining partners
with God by proclaiming an understanding of God to be
God and a particular religion to be the only true religion.
Righteousness is the infinitely flexible human position that
proceeds from the experience of humility before the Messengers of God. In the context of the current world, humility before the presence of God bears the fruit of religious
unity and the peace that its fellowship affords. Insistence on
the pre-eminence of any understanding of God betrays a lack
of humility before His presence and results in the pursuit of
narrow agendas, alienation, mistrust, intolerance, conflict, and
even war.

The Gospel, along with the scriptures derived from the
all of the Messengers of God, is the word of God, the truth
that is not limited by human conception. Jesus with respect
to the eternal name of God is Moses, Zoroaster, Buddha,
Krishna. The reference to His name is not to followers of a
literal name, but to followers of His reality—the word or
presence of God.

Jesus cautioned His followers not to be literal but to look
toward the spiritual meanings of His teachings. When He
referred to Himself as the "Bread of God," He was not
saying that He was a loaf of bread. "For the Bread of God is
he which cometh down from heaven, and giveth life unto
the world" (Christianity. John 6:33). Jesus also said, "Follow me and let the dead bury their dead" (Christianity.
Matthew 8:22). It is a statement indicating that there were

two kinds of dead. One death is that of the physical body; the other is the death of the spirit. Spiritual life is the word of God that reaches the human heart with the "Good News" of eternal life in the presence of God.

Against Me or For Me

Christianity

But Jesus said, Forbid him not: for there is no man which shall do a miracle in my name, that can lightly speak evil of me. For he that is not against us is on our part. (Mark 9:39-40)

Wherefore I say unto you, All manner of sin and blasphemy shall be forgiven unto men: but the blasphemy against the Holy Ghost shall not be forgiven unto men. And whosoever speaketh a word against the Son of man, it shall be forgiven him: but whosoever speaketh against the Holy Ghost, it shall not be forgiven him, neither in this world, neither in the world to come....For the tree is known by his fruit. (Matthew 28:31-33)

Ye worship ye know not what: we know what we worship: for salvation is of the Jews. But the hour cometh, and now is, when the true worshippers shall worship the Father in spirit and in truth: for the Father seeketh such to worship him. God is a Spirit: and they that worship him must worship him in spirit and in truth. (John. 4:22-24)

Zoroastrianism

Then do I proclaim what the Most Beneficent spoke to me, the Words to be heeded, which are best for mortals: those who shall give hearing and reverence shall attain unto Perfection and Immortality by the deeds of good spirit of the Lord of Wisdom! (Avesta, Yasna 45.5)

An event described in the New Testament can be understood in the context of the underlying unity of the world's prophets. The apostle John approached Jesus and informed Him that there was someone casting out devils in His name but that this person was not one of their followers, so they stopped him. "But Jesus said, Forbid him not: for there is no man which shall do a miracle in my name, that can lightly speak evil of me. For he that is not against us is on our part" (Mark 9 39-40). The primary purpose of the Messenger of God is to bring individuals to the presence of God. The followers of the various religions have their own purpose fulfilled by receiving the gift from the Messenger and by sharing it. Jesus instructed John that the teacher that was casting out devils was not working against him.

In another passage, Jesus explains that the primary responsibility of individuals in this life is to receive the Spirit of God no matter from which Messenger.

> Wherefore I say unto you, All manner of sin and blasphemy shall be forgiven unto men: but the blasphemy against the Holy Ghost shall not be forgiven unto men. And whosoever speaketh a word against the Son of man, it shall be forgiven him: but whosoever speaketh against the Holy Ghost, it shall not be forgiven him, neither in this world, neither in the world to come....For the tree is known by his fruit. (Christianity. Matthew 28:31-33)

Receiving the Holy Ghost, the spirit of God, is the fruit of God's forgiveness. All sins shall be forgiven except sins against the spirit of God even failure to recognize the person of the Messenger, the Son of man. By using the term "Son of man," Jesus was referring to the physical aspect of His station as the Messenger of God. Even if a person did not recognize Jesus as the Messenger of God, forgiveness was still available through recognition of the spirit of God. Individuals who accept the presence of God are by God's presence forgiven of their separation, even those that do not recognize the latest Messenger. There is no cure for refusing to accept the gift of the presence of God.

A similar admonition is provided in Zoroastrian scripture. "Then do I proclaim what the Most Beneficent spoke to me, the Words to be heeded, which are best for mortals: those who shall give hearing and reverence shall attain unto

Perfection and Immortality by the deeds of good spirit of the Lord of Wisdom!" (Zoroastrianism. Avesta, Yasna 45.5). The primary fruit of the Messenger is the realization of eternal life in the presence of God—"Perfection and Immortality by the deeds of good spirit of the Lord of Wisdom."

Speaking to the Samaritan woman at the well Jesus said, "Ye worship ye know not what: we know what we worship: for salvation is of the Jews. But the hour cometh, and now is, when the true worshippers shall worship the Father in spirit and in truth: for the Father seeketh such to worship him. God is a Spirit: and they that worship him must worship him in spirit and in truth" (Christianity. John 4:22-24). The Jews taught the spiritual recognition of God—"we know what we worship: for salvation is of the Jews." Jesus brought the recognition of God to all that were willing to "worship him in spirit and in truth."

The Messenger Enables the Choice

Baha'i Faith

Thus doth the Nightingale utter His call unto you from this prison. He hath but to deliver this clear message. Whosoever desireth, let him turn aside from this counsel and whosoever desireth let him choose the path to his Lord. (Baha'i Prayers, 307-11)

I swear by God, the Peerless, the Incomparable, the True One: for no other reason hath He—the supreme Testimony of God—invested Me with clear signs and tokens than that all men may be enabled to submit to His Cause. (Selections from the Writings of the Bab, 12).

By the righteousness of Him Who is the Absolute Truth, were the veil to be lifted, thou wouldst witness on this earthly plane all men sorely afflicted with the fire of the wrath of God, a fire fiercer and greater than the fire of hell, with the exception of those who have sought shelter beneath the shade of the tree of My love. (Selections from the Writings of the Bab, 12).

All the keys of heaven God hath Chosen to place on My right hand, and all the keys of hell on My left... (Selections from the Writings of the Bab, 12)

I am the Primal Point from which have been generated all created things. I am the Countenance of God Whose splendor can never be obscured, the Light of God Whose radiance can never fade. Whoso recognizeth Me, assurance and all good are in store for him, and whoso faileth to recognize Me, infernal fire and all evil await him... (Selections from the Writings of the Bab, 12)

I testify unto that whereunto have testified all created things, and the Concourse on high, and the inmates of the all-highest paradise, and beyond them the Tongue of Grandeur itself from the all-glorious Horizon, that Thou art God, that there is no God but Thee, and that He Who hath been manifested is the Hidden Mystery the Treasured Symbol, through whom the letters B and E (Be) have been joined and knit together. I testify that it is He Whose Name hath been set down by the Pen of the Most High, and Who hath been mentioned in the Books of God, the Lord of the Throne on high and the earth below. (Baha'i Prayers, 13)

Likewise continue thou to ascend through one Revelation after another, knowing that thy progress in the Knowledge of God shall never come to an end, even as it can have no beginning. (Selections from the Writings of the Bab, 91)

Christianity

Let not your heart be troubled: ye believe in God, Believe also in me. In my Father's house are many mansions: if it were not so, I would have told you. I go to prepare a place for you. And if I go and prepare a place for you, I will come again, and receive you unto myself; that where I am, there ye may be also. And whither I go ye know, and the way ye know. Thomas saith unto him, Lord, we know not whither thou goest; and how can we know the way? Jesus saith unto him, I am the way, the truth, and the life: no man cometh unto the Father, but by me. If ye had known me, ye should have known my Father also: and from hence forth ye know him, and have seen him. Philip saith unto him, Lord shew us the Father, and it sufficeth us. Jesus saith unto him Have I been so long time with you, and yet hast thou not known me, Philip? He that hath seen me hath seen the Father; and how sayest thou then, Shew us the Father? Believest thou not that I am in the Father , and the Father in me? The words that I speak unto you I speak not of myself: but the Father that dwelleth in me, he doeth the works. (John 14:1-10)

All things are delivered unto me of my Father: and no man knoweth the Son, but the Father; neither knoweth any man the Father, save the Son, and he to whomsoever the Son will reveal him. (Matthew 11:27)

But the Comforter, which is the Holy Ghost, whom the Father will send in my name, he shall teach you all things, and bring all things to your remembrance, whatsoever I have said unto you. (John 14:26)

Jesus said to him, "I am the way, the truth, and the life; no one comes to the Father, but by me. (John 14:6)

The Messengers are the signs of God in the human world—the world that is separate from God. Compared to reunion with God the world is like a prison. The Messengers provide us with a safe path to choose the presence of God that frees us from the prison of remoteness. "Thus doth the Nightingale utter His call unto you from this prison. He hath but to deliver this clear message. Whosoever desireth, let him turn aside from this counsel and whosoever desireth let him choose the path to his Lord" (Baha'i Faith. Baha'u'llah. Tablet of Ahmad). We have this place to stand, the world, which is not in the presence of God, from which we can chose to approach God. The Messengers provide the signs that provide a safe approach to God through their lives and teachings. "I swear by God, the Peerless, the Incomparable, the True One: for no other reason hath He—the supreme Testimony of God—invested Me with clear signs and tokens than that all men may be enabled to submit to His Cause" (The

Baha'i Faith. Selections from the Writings of the Bab, 12).
The Messenger is a safe approach to God to the degree
appropriate to our capacities. "All the keys of heaven God
hath Chosen to place on My right hand, and all the keys of
hell on My left..." (Baha'i Faith. Selections from the Writings of the Bab, 12). The Messenger provides the optimal
path through reward and punishment. To the person that
sincerely seeks the presence of God, He provides the measure of grace appropriate to their capacity. To the human
heart whose time to approach God is upon him but who is
negligent, the Messenger provides the motivation or grace
appropriate to the situation. Our position is shaped by our
response to the Messenger. Submission to the will of God
results in nearness to God while refusal results in remoteness
and error.

Jesus talked about His being the approach to God in a
conversation with Thomas and Philip. They were troubled
about their relationship with God.

> Let not your heart be troubled: ye believe in God, Be-
> lieve also in me. In my Father's house are many mansions:
> if it were not so, I would have told you. I go to prepare a
> place for you. And if I go and prepare a place for you, I will
> come again, and receive you unto myself; that where I am,
> there ye may be also. And whither I go ye know, and the
> way ye know. Thomas saith unto him, Lord, we know not
> whither thou goest; and how can we know the way? Jesus
> saith unto him, I am the way, the truth, and the life: no
> man cometh unto the Father, but by me. If ye had known
> me, ye should have known my Father also: and from hence
> forth ye know him, and have seen him. Philip saith unto
> him, Lord shew us the Father, and it sufficeth us. Jesus
> saith unto him Have I been so long time with you, and yet
> hast thou not known me, Philip? He that hath seen me
> hath seen the Father; and how sayest thou then, Shew us
> the Father? Believest thou not that I am in the Father, and
> the Father in me? The words that I speak unto you I speak
> not of myself: but the Father that dwelleth in me, he doeth
> the works. (Christianity. John 14:1-10)

The passage begins as an admonition not to be troubled. "Let not your heart be troubled." The conversation with Philip and Thomas is meant to assure them that Jesus is the path to God. Jesus is addressing the mystery of the nature of the Messenger that directs us toward God through our uncertainty. He tells them that God has "many mansions." The gifts associated with His presence are infinite. The Messenger is God in that He makes the presence of God known to the awareness of the individual. He does not do this just once. The approach is infinite. The Messenger provides the ever-increasing experience of the presence of God.

There is nevertheless confusion over the experience of the person of Jesus in the flesh and the experience of the presence of God that Jesus provides as the Messenger. "He that hath seen me hath seen the Father." Jesus is addressing the nature of the Messenger. He is both the person standing in front of them and the presence of God that He provides for them. But Thomas and Philip are troubled because the presence of God is not constant—awareness comes and goes. They are not in a constant state of certitude about their relationship with God through Jesus. Jesus assures them that He is the presence of God with them and that they need not fear. "If ye had known me, ye should have known my Father also: and from hence forth ye know him, and have seen him." However, Philip wants complete certitude. "Philip saith unto him, Lord shew us the Father, and it sufficeth us." Jesus instructs them that the approach to God is progressive and involves periods of distance in the relationship and He reassures them that He will always guide them. Jesus tells Philip and Thomas that although He leaves them to themselves, they will always know the way to Him. "And if I go and prepare a place for you, I will come again, and receive you unto myself; that where I am, there ye may be also." Jesus assures them that they always have the capacity to turn to God. "And whither I go ye know, and the way ye know."

Jesus is addressing two levels of separation and identity that are aspects of the mystery of the Messenger. He is differentiating between His physical presence and His presence as the word of God. Both of these aspects of the Messenger come and go. The one refers to the consciousness of society at large and to the physical nature of the Messenger—Jesus was speaking of His coming death and His eventual return. The other refers to the consciousness of the individual—Jesus was speaking of His presence as the word of God. "I am the way, the truth, and the life: no man cometh unto the Father, but by me." He is identifying Himself as the presence of God that they have experienced. Both aspects of the Messenger refer to the ongoing progression of the approach to God. He appears to humankind progressively as different Messengers. He appears progressively to the individual throughout this life and the next in response to individual efforts to follow the admonitions of the Messenger.

Jesus is the Messenger of God, the Son of God that is beyond human perception or attainment. "All things are delivered unto me of my Father: and no man knoweth the Son, but the Father; neither knoweth any man the Father, save the Son, and he to whomsoever the Son will reveal him" (Christianity. Matthew 11:27). He is the source of life. There is only one source, but the way is infinite, limitless. There is always more of God's bounty to experience. "In my Father's house are many mansions: if it were not so, I would have told you" (Christianity. John 14:2).

God is self-subsistent and we are contingent. Implicit in the relationship is that God does not make Himself known to us completely. We would need to be God to know Him completely. He does not make us His equal by somehow elevating us to the station of God nor does He provide final confirmation of His reality by becoming physical. The person of the Messenger is not God. He is the word of God. The Messenger is how God makes Himself known. The Messenger speaks as God. For all intents and purposes for human beings, the Messenger is God in that we cannot know God except as He makes Himself known. There is always more to know and therefore a longing for more.

Later in the same chapter Jesus tells Thomas and Philip that He will always be available to them through the presence or spirit of God. "But the Comforter, which is the Holy Ghost, whom the Father will send in my name, he shall teach you all things, and bring all things to your remembrance, whatsoever I have said unto you" (Christianity. John 14:26).

The signs of God that Jesus provides as well as the presence of God are the path to God. The Messenger is the outward sign and the personal proof. The Messenger is also the fulcrum through which the choice toward or away from God is realized. "I am the Primal Point from which have been generated all created things. I am the Countenance of God Whose splendor can never be obscured, the Light of God Whose radiance can never fade. Whoso recognizeth Me, assurance and all good are in store for him, and whoso faileth to recognize Me, infernal fire and all evil await him..." (Baha'i Faith. Selections from the Writings of the Bab, p 12). The presence of God provides fulfillment. Unbelief by its nature is distance from God, which is the fire of remoteness. Our approach to the Messenger is our approach to God. When we turn toward God, we find the refuge of eternal life in His presence. When we turn away, we condemn ourselves to alienation. Through the Messenger we are given the power to choose the path to God and to testify concerning what we have witnessed.

> I testify unto that whereunto have testified all created things, and the Concourse on high, and the inmates of the all-highest paradise, and beyond them the Tongue of Grandeur itself from the all-glorious Horizon, that Thou art God, that there is no God but Thee, and that He Who hath been manifested is the Hidden Mystery the Treasured Symbol, through whom the letters B and E (Be) have been joined and knit together. I testify that it is He Whose Name hath been set down by the Pen of the Most High, and Who hath been mentioned in the Books of God, the Lord of the Throne on high and the earth below. (Baha'i Faith. Baha'u'llah, Baha'i Prayers, 12-13)

As we wrestle with our choices to recognize and comply with the directives and guidance of the Messengers, our lives ebb and flow in proximity to God. The process is eternal. "Likewise continue thou to ascend through one Revelation after another, knowing that thy progress in the Knowledge of God shall never come to an end, even as it can have no beginning" (Baha'i Faith. Selections from the Writings of the Bab, p. 91).

− 5 −

SPIRITUAL CONCEPTS

Introduction

As God is beyond description, so is the reality which God sustains. Today's scientists are discovering the mysteries of the physical world and expanding the circle of knowledge at an ever accelerating rate. The circle has no size limit. It is infinite. Our conceptualizations of physical reality are not absolute. All descriptions of reality give way to ever more precise measurement. No description absolutely encompasses what it describes. This is also true of our conceptualizations of spiritual reality. All concepts of spiritual reality such as the soul, resurrection and reincarnation, rebirth, eternal life, the next life, judgment, heaven and hell are limited and subject to refinement.

Expanding our understanding of the reality sustained by God is an aspect of praising God. However, just as it is a mistake to confuse the presence of God with our understanding of Him; it is a mistake to assume our concepts of physical or spiritual reality, derived from science or scripture are reality. They are our conceptualizations and explanations of reality. The following is my layman's attempt at providing continuity to several of the more common spiritual concepts.

The Soul

Buddhism

Knowing that this body is like foam, and comprehending that it is as unsubstantial as a mirage, one should destroy the flower-tipped shafts of sensual passions [Mara], and pass beyond the sight of the King of death. (Dhammapada 46)

Baha'i Faith

Now observe that in the sensible world appearances are not repeated, for no being in any respect is identical with, nor the same as, another being. The sign of singleness is visible and apparent in all things. If all the granaries of the world were full of grain, you would not find two grains absolutely alike, the same and identical without any distinction. It is certain that there will be differences and distinctions between them. As the proof of uniqueness exists in all things, and the Oneness and Unity of God is apparent in the reality of all things, the repetition of the same appearance is absolutely impossible. (Abdul-Baha. Some Answered Questions, 283)

O ye servants of God! Verily, be not grieved if a thing ye asked of Him remaineth unanswered, inasmuch as He hath been commanded by God to observe silence, a silence which is in truth praiseworthy. We have indeed enabled Thee to truly see in Thy dream a measure of Our Cause, but wert Thou to acquaint them with the hidden Mystery, they would dispute its truth among themselves. Verily Thy Lord, the God of truth, knoweth the very secrets of hearts.... (Selections from the Writings of the Bab, 48).

Confucianism.

Ts'ai-wu said, "I have heard the names kuei and shen, but I do not know what they mean." The Master said, "The [intelligent] spirit is of the shen nature, and shows that in fullest measure; the animal soul is of the kuei nature, and shows that in fullest measure." (Book of Ritual 21.2.1)

Judaism

The body is the sheath of the soul. (Talmud, Sanhedrin 108a)

The dust returns to the earth as it was, and the spirit returns to God who gave it. (Ecclesiastes 12.7)

Then the Lord God formed man out of the dust of the ground, and breathed into his nostrils the breath of life; and man became a living being. (Judaism. Genesis 2.7)

Islam

And He originated the creation of man out of clay, then He fashioned his progeny of an extraction of mean water, then He shaped him, and breathed His spirit in Him. (Qur'an 32.8-9)

Sikhism

Man wails over the loss of what he calls his: Know, the self is not perishable. (Adi Granth, Gauri, M.5, p.188)

Hinduism

Now my breath and spirit goes to the Immortal, and this body ends in ashes; OM. O Mind! Remember. Remember the deeds. Remember the actions. (Isha Upanishad 17)

The Self cannot be pierced with weapons or burned with fire; water cannot wet it, nor can the wind dry it. The Self cannot be pierced or burned, made wet or dry. It is everlasting and infinite, standing on the motionless foundation of eternity. The Self is un-manifested, beyond all thought, beyond all change. Knowing this you should not grieve. (Bhagavad Gita 2.19-25)

The various religious traditions have commented on the nature of the soul, referring to it as primary and the body as secondary. "The body is the sheath of the soul" (Judaism. Talmud, Sanhedrin 108a). The human soul is immortal. It is the essence of human life that returns to its creator after the death of the body. "The dust returns to the earth as it was, and the spirit returns to God who gave it" (Judaism. Ecclesiastes 12.7). "Now my breath and spirit goes to the Immortal, and this body ends in ashes..." (Hinduism. Isha Upanishad 17).

The human soul is beyond comprehension. God makes Himself known to man yet exists infinitely beyond the knowledge of man. Man is in everlasting pursuit of God and is a reflection of the infinite mystery of God in that man has unlimited capacity to approach God. It is appropriate to seek an understanding of the nature of the soul as it is appropriate to seek an understanding of the nature of God. It is a mistake to think that the soul can be completely understood, characterized, or limited to description just as it is a mistake to think an understanding of God is God. Any conception of the soul is a limited view of an eternal reality.

> The Self cannot be pierced with weapons or burned with fire; water cannot wet it, nor can the wind dry it. The Self cannot be pierced or burned, made wet or dry. It is everlasting and infinite, standing on the motionless foundation of eternity. The Self is un-manifested, beyond all thought, beyond all change. Knowing this you should not grieve. (Hinduism. Bhagavad Gita 2.19-25)

A further testament to the indescribable nature of the soul is the reality of uniqueness. Conceptualization is by its nature a limited intellectual approach to understanding the uniqueness of all reality. As there are not two snowflakes alike, there are not two souls alike.

> Now observe that in the sensible world appearances are not repeated, for no being in any respect is identical with, nor the same as, another being. The sign of singleness is visible and apparent in all things. If all the granaries of the world were full of grain, you would not find two grains absolutely alike, the same and identical without any distinction. It is certain that there will be differences and distinctions between them. As the proof of uniqueness exists in all things, and the Oneness and Unity of God is apparent in the reality of all things, the repetition of the same appearance is absolutely impossible. (Baha'i Faith. Abdul-Baha. Some Answered Questions. 283)

Each being is unique and has a unique approach to God; an approach which itself contains infinite possibilities.

There are an infinite number of states of being if viewed in terms of uniqueness. It can be helpful from our human perspective, to conceptualize being in five categorical states. The first, which has been referred to in some scriptures as the animal state, is blindly subject to the cause and effect world. The animal nature does not have access to a rational or objective place to stand outside of experience. This is the realm of least resistance, where a being does what is desirable under the circumstances without conscious analysis or choice. The second state is the rational soul. This state of being enjoys a modicum of independence from experience in that it can conceptualize and objectify it. This is the realm of logic and mathematics as well as metaphor and simile. It is also the realm of conscience. Confucian scriptures refers to these two states as kuei and shen.

> Ts'ai-wu said, "I have heard the names kuei and shen, but I do not know what they mean." The Master said, "The [intelligent] spirit is of the shen nature, and shows that in fullest measure; the animal soul is of the kuei nature, and shows that in fullest measure." (Confucianism. Book of Ritual 21.2.1)

The third state is unity with reality. It is the state of the realization of reality. This is the realm of transcendence, self awareness, unity, and awareness of the reality of God. It is the realm that receives revelation. It is the state that has awareness of the eternal nature of being. "Man wails over the loss of what he calls his: Know, the self is not perishable" (Sikhism. Adi Granth, Gauri, M.5, 188).

The forth state of being is that of the Messenger of God. The Messenger is God making His own Self known. This is the realm of the word of God. It is the state that provides revelation. "The Lord your God will raise up for you a prophet like me [Moses] from among you, from your brethren—him you shall heed" (Christianity. Deuteronomy 18:15).

This state of being is available for us to perceive with our being. The Messenger speaks as God to the human soul and initiates a religious dispensation.

The fifth state of being is beyond all knowledge or access. It is the state of being God—the self-subsistent, the unknowable.

Resurrection and Reincarnation

Buddhism

The supreme, complete enlightenment is the realm of Nirvana. The realm of Nirvana is the Dharma-body of the Tathagata [the Eternal Buddha]. Attaining the absolute Dharma-body is [attaining] the absolute One Vehicle. (Lion's Roar of Queen Srimala 5).

Sooner, do I declare, would a one-eyed turtle, if he were to pop up to the surface of the sea only once at the end of every hundred years, chance to push his neck through a yoke with one hole than would a fool, who has once gone to the Downfall, be reborn as a man. (Samyutta Nikaya v.455)

The outward form, brethren, of him who has won the truth stands before you, but that which binds it to re-birth is cut in twain. (Digha Nikaya: Brahmajala Sutta)

Baha'i Faith

Moreover, this material world has not such value or such excellence that man, after having escaped from this cage, will desire a second time to fall into this snare. No, through the Eternal Bounty the worth and true ability of man becomes apparent and visible by traversing the degrees of existence, and not by returning. (Abdul-Baha. Some Answered Questions. 286)

Christianity

Jesus said to her, "I am the resurrection and the life; he who believes in me, though he die, yet shall he live, and whoever lives and believes in me shall never die." (John 11:25)

So it is with the resurrection from the dead. What is sown is perishable, what is raised is imperishable. It is sown in dishonor, it is raised in glory. It is sown in weakness, it is raised in power. It is sown in a physical body, it is raised in a spiritual body. If there is a physical body, there is also a spiritual body. (1 Corinthians 15:40-44)

In the resurrection they neither marry nor are given in marriage, but are like angels in heaven. (Matthew 22:30)

Verily, verily, I say unto thee, We speak that we do know, and testify that we have seen; and ye receive not our witness. If I have told you earthly things and ye believe not, how shall ye believe, if I tell you of heavenly things. (John 3:11-12)

Hinduism

His next birth is regulated by the deeds of the present life—the deeds which make up his character. If his character is dominated by light, he achieves a higher birth, that of a deva or of a sage; if by passion, he is returned to earth as a demon or as a man; and if by darkness he is born from the lower wombs. (Srimad Bhagavatam 11.15)

Resurrection

In the parable of the rich man and Lazarus, the rich man asked Abraham to send Lazarus back from the dead to warn his relatives not to neglect the admonitions of Moses and the prophets as he had done in his callousness to Lazarus. "And [Abraham] said unto him, If they hear not Moses and the prophets, neither will they be persuaded, though one rose from the dead" (Christianity. Luke 16:31).

The concept of resurrection is currently the focus of attention for many Christians who are expecting the return of Christ. If the resurrection is understood in terms associated with our physical nature, it would mean that resurrection refers to the physical body returning to life. In the context of the end times, it would mean the physical resurrection of the bodies of all of those who have been "saved" over all of human history. From this perspective, Jesus conquered death in a physical resurrection and those who have believed that literal statement have been "saved" and will be physically resurrected upon His return. The return of Christ is seen as a physical return of the body and person of Jesus when all of the believers from over the centuries will physically be resurrected on the earth.

If, however, resurrection refers to the state of being the Messenger of God, the word of God that conquers death; being "saved" refers to waking to the presence of God as He makes Himself known through His Messengers. "Jesus said to her, 'I am the resurrection and the life; he who believes in me, though he die, yet shall he live, and whoever lives and believes in me shall never die'" (Christianity. John 11:25). Those who have experienced the presence of God have experienced eternal life. They know the eternal nature of their own beings. They have truly believed in and given praise to God. From this perspective, resurrection for the individual is the recognition of the Messenger of God. "And no man hath ascended up to heaven, but he that came down from heaven, even the Son of man which is in heaven" (Christianity. John 3:13). Jesus is not talking about His physical body going up and down from heaven. He makes this clear by saying that He is in heaven even though He is right in front of them on the earth.

Our responsibility with respect to resurrection is to recognize the Messenger. Recognition provides eternal life. It is the state of being in the presence of God. Being "saved" in this context is the realization of eternal life in the presence of God. The human soul can have this experience in this world and the next. An individual can still be on this earth in a physical body and experience the presence of God. The death of the body is still going to happen, but the soul already knows eternal life. The sting of death is gone. The confusion between the death of the body and that of the soul has been removed. The soul is no longer dead to the presence of God.

> So it is with the resurrection from the dead. What is
> sown is perishable, what is raised is imperishable. It is sown

in dishonor, it is raised in glory. It is sown in weakness, it is raised in power. It is sown in a physical body, it is raised in a spiritual body. If there is a physical body, there is also a spiritual body. (Christianity. 1 Corinthians 15:40-44)

The body is born of passions and is perishable. The soul, born to the presence of God, is raised to a glorious station, which is the realization of its imperishable nature before the presence of God. We have a physical nature or body that is perishable, and we have a spiritual nature or body that is imperishable. Resurrection is being in the presence of the Messenger of God.

Reincarnation

Many of the concepts associated with both resurrection and reincarnation derive from applying a physical explanation to spiritual reality. As the resurrection from the grave in the end times of the bodies of all of the Christians who died over the centuries is an understanding of resurrection in physical terms, the return of an individual in another body to this world after death is a literalized, physical understanding of reincarnation.

For many, the literal concept of reincarnation is a positive, comforting one. It replaces the spiritual concept of reincarnation as cyclical attachments to temporal phenomenon with a literal interpretation—multiple lifetimes on this earth. The physical concept of reincarnation substitutes the threat of the unknown worlds after death with return to the known physical world, where a gradual approach to God can occur over many lifetimes. It is similar to the concept of a physical resurrection in that both are a preference for the material world over the spiritual world. A final resolution to the difficulties of life is imagined in physical terms.

For those that delight in the spiritual pleasure of nearness to God, the literalized concepts of resurrection and reincarnation are infinitely less comforting than the fulfillment experienced in the presence of God. The concepts of reincarnation and resurrection can be understood in spiritual terms: reincarnation as attachment to the endless cycles of desire and death associated with human appetite; resurrection as ascendance to the spiritual presence of God.

The concept of reincarnation, if viewed as a description of attachment to the lower, physical states of existence, is not a desirable state. The desired state requires freedom from cycles of attachment to objects of desire. "Whosoever seeks, by whatever means, merely the happiness of cyclic existence for personal ends, he is to be understood as a mean person" (Buddhism. Bodhipathapradipa). Reincarnation can be understood as a concept describing attachment to the temporal world over the experience of enlightenment or the presence of God. Everything in the physical world is subject to change— the death of one composition gives rise to the birth of another. For human consciousness that is fettered to the physical world, attachments are continuously cycling through birth and death as one attachment gives way to another. "On some by His Law falls grace; others by His Law are whirled around in cycles of births and deaths" (Sikhism. Adi Granth, Japuji 2, M.1, p.1).

Scripture often uses physical descriptions as metaphor for spiritual experience since the spiritual worlds are not subject to literal description. Jesus refers to the difficulty of teaching about spiritual reality when He said, "Verily, verily, I say unto thee, We speak that we do know, and testify that we have seen; and ye receive not our witness. If I have told you earthly things and ye believe not, how shall ye believe, if I tell you of heavenly things" (Christianity. John 3:11-12). Jesus refers to the difficulty of accepting His guidance concerning earthly and heavenly things. Of the two, spiritual lessons are harder to teach. It is easier to listen with the intellect than with the spirit. The intellect understands through physical experience and reason. The spirit acknowledges being. Both experience the same reality, but through different faculties. It is similar to the perception of an object through different senses. A bowl, perceived through sight and touch, is the same bowl, but the perception is very different.

The scriptures of all of the religious traditions instruct that our existence is ultimately satisfied only by knowing God. "The supreme, complete enlightenment is the realm of Nirvana. The realm of Nirvana is the Dharma-body of the Tathagata [the Eternal Buddha]. Attaining the absolute Dharma-body is [attaining] the absolute One Vehicle" (Buddhism. Lion's Roar of Queen Srimala 5). Texts from the scriptures of all of the religions encourage seeking the presence of God through the Messenger (the Tathagata) rather than pursuing material gratification. "The outward form, brethren, of him who has won the truth stands before you, but that which binds it to rebirth is cut in twain" (Buddhism. Digha Nikaya: Brahmajala Sutta). Spiritual reality transcends and is preferable to material existence. The following Buddhist passage reiterates the unenlightened nature of attachment to the concept of physical rebirth.

> Sooner, do I declare, would a one-eyed turtle, if he were to pop up to the surface of the sea only once at the end of every hundred years, chance to push his neck through a yoke with one hole than would a fool, who has once gone to the Downfall, be reborn as a man. (Buddhism. Samyutta Nikaya v.455)

It is extremely improbable that even a fool would choose to be reborn to the physical world after suffering death and being born to the spiritual world. The following Baha'i scripture reaffirms the sentiment.

> Moreover, this material world has not such value or such excellence that man, after having escaped from this cage, will desire a second time to fall into this snare. No, through the Eternal Bounty the worth and true ability of man becomes apparent and visible by traversing the degrees of existence, and not by returning. (Baha'i Faith. Abdul-Baha. Some Answered Questions, p. 286)

The concept of reincarnation also serves as a mechanism for describing justice. It is a way to explain the obvious inequities among people in the physical world. The following passage from Hindu writings is a view of reincarnation as a mechanism of justice.

> His next birth is regulated by the deeds of the present life—the deeds which make up his character. If his character is dominated by light, he achieves a higher birth, that of a deva or of a sage; if by passion, he is returned to earth as a demon or as a man; and if by darkness he is born from the lower wombs. (Hinduism. Srimad Bhagavatam 11.15)

As a concept of justice, reincarnation can be understood in terms of the consequences of choices. Our choices affect the nature of our unfolding situations. We reap what we sow. The scriptural passage above serves as a warning against unjust behavior. It presents a milder version of scriptural warning than those found in images of hell and retribution. If interpreted as metaphor, it can be understood as receiving the higher, spiritual levels of consciousness associated with the station of a sage or deva for choices dominated by light or goodness, whether in this world or the next. The levels of consciousness associated with passions are described as being human or demonic. Those dominated by darkness or evil intentions are described as animalistic. Justice is served as attachments at the various levels reveal their consequences. Loss and regret accompany attachment to the mutable realms of human and animal desires. The spiritual realms of goodness and light never perish.

Rebirth

Buddhism

> Today I indeed know that I am really a son of Buddha, born from the mouth of Buddha, evolved from the Law, and have obtained a place in the Buddha-law. (Lotus Sutra 3)

Christianity

To all who received him [Jesus], who believed in his name, he gave power to become children of God; who were born, not of blood nor of the will of the flesh nor the will of man, but of God. (John 1:12-13)

Jesus answered him, "Truly, truly, I say to you, unless one is born anew, he cannot see the kingdom of God." Nicodemus said to him, "How can a man be born when he is old? Can he enter a second time into his mother's womb and be born?" Jesus answered, "Truly, truly, I say to you, unless one is born of water and the Spirit, he cannot enter the kingdom of God. That which is born of the flesh is flesh, and that which is born of the Spirit is spirit. Do not marvel that I say to you, "'You must be born anew.'" (John 3:5-6)

Hinduism

Of him who gives natural birth and him who gives the knowledge of the Veda, the giver of the Veda is the more venerable father; for the birth for the sake of the Veda ensures eternal rewards both in this life and after death. (Laws of Manu 2.146)

Judaism

Repentance makes man a new creature; hitherto dead through sin, he is fashioned afresh. (Midrash Psalms 18)

Jesus makes it clear that being born again does not refer to physical birth.

Jesus answered him, "Truly, truly, I say to you, unless one is born anew, he cannot see the kingdom of God." Nicodemus said to him, "How can a man be born when he is old? Can he enter a second time into his mother's womb and be born?" Jesus answered, "Truly, truly, I say to you, unless one is born of water and the Spirit, he cannot enter the kingdom of God. That which is born of the flesh is flesh, and that which is born of the Spirit is spirit. Do not marvel that I say to you, 'You must be born anew.'" (Christianity. John 3:5-6)

The terms Jesus uses to describe the second birth are water and spirit. Water can be understood as the act of purification. John the Baptist baptized with water. Purification did not take place because the water cleaned the body; purification is derived from an act of repentance. Recognition of the Messenger and admission that His way is better than our way are required to realize a relationship with Him. "To all who received him [Jesus], who believed in his name, he gave power to become children of God; who were born, not of blood, nor of the will of the flesh nor the will of man, but of God" (Christianity. John 1:12-13). Repentance, submission to God, is a prerequisite to reunion—being born of the spirit. The kingdom of God is the word of God, the presence of God. Entrance requires willing submission to the will of God. "Repentance makes man a new creature; hitherto dead through sin, he is fashioned afresh" (Judaism. Midrash Psalms 18).

The metaphor of birth is also used in the Buddhist scriptures to refer to submission to the will of God. "Today I indeed know that I am really a son of Buddha, born from the mouth of Buddha, evolved from the Law, and have obtained a place in the Buddha-law" (Buddhism. Lotus Sutra 3). The word of God proceeds from the mouth of the Messenger. It is the law of God. Willingness to listen to and obey the law of God is a birth "from the mouth of Buddha."

The Hindu scriptures also use birth as a metaphor for spiritual enlightenment. "Of him who gives natural birth and him who gives the knowledge of the Veda, the giver of the Veda is the more venerable father; for the birth for the sake of the Veda ensures eternal rewards both in this life and after death" (Hinduism. Laws of Manu 2.146). Knowledge of the Veda is a birth into eternal life whether the individual is in this life or the next. The Veda is the word of God. It is the kingdom of God. It is eternal.

Eternal Life

Hinduism

From the unreal lead me to the Real! From darkness lead me to light! From death lead me to immortality! (Brihadaranyaka Upanishad 1.3.28)

The Self cannot be pierced with weapons or burned with fire; water cannot wet it, nor can the wind dry it. The Self cannot be pierced or burned, made wet or dry. It is everlasting and infinite, standing on the motionless foundation of eternity. The Self is unmanifested, beyond all thought, beyond all change. Knowing this, you should not grieve. (Bhagavad Gita 2.19-25)

Islam

Those who have faith and do righteous deeds, they are the best of creatures. Their reward is with God: Gardens of Eternity, beneath which rivers flow; they will dwell therein forever; God well pleased with them, and they with Him; all this for such as fear their Lord and Cherisher. (Qur'an 98.7-8)

Baha'i Faith

O Son of Man! Thou art My dominion and My dominion perisheth not; wherefore fearest thou thy perishing? Thou art My light and My light shall never be extinguished; why dost thou dread extinction? Thou art My glory and My glory fadeth not; thou art My robe and My robe shall never be outworn. Abide then in thy love for Me, that thou mayest find Me in the realm of glory. (Hidden Words: From the Arabic, no. 14, 7)

O Son of Worldliness! Pleasant is the realm of being, wert thou to attain thereto; glorious is the domain of eternity, shouldst thou pass beyond the world of mortality; sweet is the holy ecstasy if thou drinkest of the mystic chalice from the hands of the celestial Youth. Shouldst thou attain this station, thou wouldst be freed from destruction and death, from toil and sin. (Hidden Words: From the Persian, no. 70, 46)

Taoism

Being in accord with Tao, he is everlasting. (Tao Te Ching 16)

Birth is not a beginning; death is not an end. There is existence without limitation; there is continuity without a starting point. Existence without limitation is space. Continuity without a starting point is time. There is birth, there is death, there is issuing forth, there is entering in. That through which one passes in and out without seeing its form, that is the Portal of God. (Chuang Tzu 23)

Zoroastriansim

Then do I proclaim what the Most Beneficent spoke to me, the Words to be heeded, which are best for mortals: those who shall give hearing and reverence shall attain unto perfection and immortality by the deeds of good spirit of the Lord of Wisdom! (Avesta, Yasna 45.5)

Jainism

The supreme stage of the Soul is free from birth, old age and death; he is supreme, pure, and devoid of eight karmas; he possesses infinite knowledge, intuition, bliss, and potency; he is indivisible, indestructible, and inexhaustible. (Kundakaunda, Niyamasara 176-77)

Buddhism

Even ornamented royal chariots wear out. So too the body reaches old age. But the Dhamma of the Good grows not old. Thus do the Good reveal it among the Good. (Dhammapada 151)

All of the Messengers refer to the transcendent nature of the human soul. It is eternal. In Jainism eternal life is referred to as a stage of the soul. "The supreme stage of the Soul is free from birth, old age and death; he is supreme, pure, and devoid of eight karmas; he possesses infinite knowledge, intuition, bliss, and potency; he is indivisible, indestructible, and inexhaustible" (Jainism. Kundakaunda, Niyamasara 176-77). Realization of the soul's eternal nature is an experience available in this life and the next. The Baha'i Faith refers to the realm of being as a station free from death.

O Son of Worldliness! Pleasant is the realm of being, wert thou to attain thereto; glorious is the domain of eternity, shouldst thou pass beyond the world of mortality; sweet is the holy ecstasy if thou drinkest of the mystic chalice from the hands of the celestial Youth. Shouldst thou attain this station, thou wouldst be freed from destruction and death, from toil and sin. (Baha'i Faith. Hidden Words: From the Persian 70)

The exalted nature of the realm of being is contingent upon making an effort to attain it. The station can be attained by drinking from the "mystic chalice" provided by the Messenger—the "celestial Youth." Attainment requires a choice to forgo attachment to the mortal world for that of a relationship with the Messenger of God. Zoroastrian scripture also refers to the need for an effort to attain eternal life. We are instructed to give "hearing and reverence" to the "Words to be heeded" if we are to "attain unto perfection and immortality." (Zoroastrianism. Avesta, Yasna 45.5) The Taoist understands attainment to the eternal by "being in accord with the Tao"—which is heaven, the way (Taoism. Tao Te Ching 16). Attainment requires effort according to the Qur'an as well. "Those who have faith and do righteous deeds, they are the best of creatures. Their reward is with God: Gardens of Eternity, beneath which rivers flow; they will dwell therein forever; God well pleased with them, and they with Him; all this for such as fear their Lord and Cherisher" (Islam. Qur'an 98.7-8).

The Next Life

Islam

Wealth and sons are the adornment of the present world; but the abiding things, the deeds of righteousness, are better with God in reward, and better in hope. (Qur'an 18.46)

Hinduism

As a man passes from dream to wakefulness, so does he pass at death from this life to the next. (Brihadaranyaka Upanishad 4.3.35)

Giving no pain to any creature, a person should slowly accumulate spiritual merit for the sake of acquiring a companion in the next world....For in the next world neither father, nor mother, nor wife, nor sons, nor relations stay to be his companions; spiritual merit alone remains with him. (Laws of Manu 4.238-39)

Judaism

Better is one hour of repentance and good works in this world than all the life of the World to Come, and better is one hour of calmness of spirit in the World to come than all the life of this world. (Mishnah, Abot 4.22)

Confucianism

Tzu-lu asked how one should serve ghosts and spirits. The Master said, "Till you have learnt to serve men, how can you serve ghosts?" Tzu-lu then ventured upon a question about the dead. The Master said, "Till you know about the living, how are you to know about the dead?" (Analects 11.11)

Sikhism

O shrewd businessman, do only profitable business: deal only in that commodity which shall accompany you after death. (Adi Granth, Sri Raga, M.1, 22)

Buddhism

Relatives and friends and well-wishers rejoice at the arrival of a man who had been long absent and has returned home safely from afar. Likewise, meritorious deeds will receive the good person upon his arrival in the next world, as relatives welcome a dear one on his return. (Dhammapada 219-20)

Christianity

Do not lay up for yourselves treasures on earth, where moth and rust consume and where thieves break in and steal, but lay up for your selves treasure in heaven, where neither moth nor rust consumes and where thieves do not break in and steal. For where your treasure is, there will your heart be also. (Matthew 6:19-21)

"As a man passes from dream to wakefulness, so does he pass at death from this life to the next" (Hinduism. Brihadaranyaka Upanishad 4.3.35). We all make that transition. The scriptures advise us about the nature of the next world and its relationship to our actions in this world. The primary admonishment central to all of the scriptures with respect to following the ways of God is to treat others as we would be treated. The "golden rule" is the fulcrum for determining between good and bad action. All of the scriptures admonish us to do what is good. The benefits of following the advice of the Messengers accrue in this life and the next. "Better is one hour of repentance and good works in this world than all the life of the World to come, and better is one hour of calmness of spirit in the World to come than all the life of this world" (Judaism. Mishnah, Abot 4.22). Repentance is the act of returning to a relationship with God. It requires a willingness to admit that God's way is better than insistence on our way. "Even ornamented royal chariots wear out. So too the body reaches old age. But the Dhamma of the Good grows not old. Thus do the Good reveal it among the Good" (Buddhism. Dhammapada 151).

In the next life good works performed in this life accompany us. "Relatives and friends and well-wishers rejoice at the arrival of a man who had been long absent and has returned home safely from afar. Likewise, meritorious deeds will receive the good person upon his arrival in the next world, as relatives welcome a dear one on his return" (Buddhism. Dhammapada 219-20). "Giving no pain to any creature, a person should slowly accumulate spiritual merit for the sake of acquiring a companion in the next world....For in the next world neither father, nor mother, nor wife, nor sons, nor relations stay to be his companions; spiritual merit alone remains with him" (Hinduism. Laws of Manu 4.238-39). "Wealth and sons are the adornment of the present world; but the abiding things, the deeds of righteousness, are better with God in reward, and better in hope" (Islam. Qur'an 18.46). "O shrewd businessman, do only profitable business: deal only in that commodity which shall accompany you after death" (Sikhism. Adi Granth, Sri Raga, M.1, 22).

The scriptures warn us that our attachment to things of the earth causes anxiety and loss.

> Do not lay up for yourselves treasures on earth, where moth and rust consume and where thieves break in and steal, but lay up for your selves treasure in heaven, where neither moth nor rust consumes and where thieves do not break in and steal. For where your treasure is, there will your heart be also. (Christianity, Matthew 6:19-21)

Freedom from attachment to this world is a gift of the presence of God that serves us both in this world and the next.

Judgement

Christianity
> Do not be deceived; God is not mocked, for whatever a man sows, that he will also reap. (Galatians 6:7)

Jainism
> Men who acquire wealth by evil deeds, by adhering to principles which are wrong, fall into the trap of their own passions and fettered with karma they sink further down. (Uttaradhyayana Sutra 4.2)

Islam

And in the Hereafter there is grievous punishment, and forgiveness from God and good pleasure; whereas the present life is but the joy of delusion. (Qur'an 57.20)

Whatever affliction may visit you is for what your own hands have earned. (Qur'an 42.30)

And let not those who disbelieve imagine that the rein We give them bodes good for their souls. We only give them rein that they may grow in sinfulness. And theirs will be a shameful doom. (Qur'an 3.178)

Sikhism

Brother! Behold the Creator's justice: As are a man's actions, so is his recompense. (Adi Granth, Gauri Var, M.4, 308)

Judaism

For they sow the wind, and they shall reap the whirlwind. (Hosea 8.7)

Buddhism

As sweet as honey is an evil deed, so thinks the fool so long as it ripens not; but when it ripens, then he comes to grief.... An ignorant man committing evil deeds does not realize the consequences. The imprudent man is consumed by his own deeds, like one burnt by fire. (Dhammapada 69, 136)

Not in the sky, nor in mid-ocean, nor in a mountain cave, is found that place on earth where abiding one may escape from the consequences of one's evil deed. (Dhammapada 127)

Hinduism

Even if they attain to sovereignty, the wicked, engaged in cruel deeds, condemned by all men, do not enjoy it long, but fall like trees whose roots have been severed. O dweller in darkness, as in its proper season the tree puts forth its flowers, so in the course of time evil actions produce bitter fruit. (Ramayana, Aranya Kanda 29)

Unrighteousness, practiced in this world, does not at once produce its fruit; but, like a cow, advancing slowly, it cuts off the roots of him who committed it. (Laws of Manu 4.172)

Taoism

The net of Heaven is cast wide. Though the mesh is not fine, yet nothing ever slips through. (Tao Te Ching 73)

The scriptures warn us of an accounting for our actions. "And in the Hereafter there is grievous punishment, and forgiveness from God and good pleasure; whereas the present life is but the joy of delusion" (Islam. Qur'an 57.20). We will reap what we sow. "Do not be deceived; God is not mocked, for whatever a man sows, that he will also reap" (Christianity. Galatians 6:7). "For they sow the wind, and they shall reap the whirlwind" (Judaism. Hosea 8.7). The choice to disregard God's admonitions results in our attachment to a self-insistent, isolated existence. "Men who acquire wealth by evil deeds, by adhering to principles which are wrong, fall into the trap of their own passions and fettered with karma they sink further down" (Jainism. Uttaradhyayana Sutra 4.2).

God's justice is not always apparent in the affairs of humankind. The temporal perspective does not divulge the whole picture. Reality unfolds over time for humankind.

As sweet as honey is an evil deed, so thinks the fool so long as it ripens not; but when it ripens, then he comes to grief.... An ignorant man committing evil deeds does not realize the consequences. The imprudent man is consumed by his own deeds, like one burnt by fire. (Buddhism. Dhammapada 69, 136)

"And let not those who disbelieve imagine that the rein We give them bodes good for their souls. We only give them rein that they may grow in sinfulness. And theirs will be a shameful doom" (Islam. Qur'an 3.178). The transgressions that we are permitted to accumulate form a barrier between ourselves and God. "Unrighteousness, practiced in this world, does not at once produce its fruit; but, like a cow, advancing slowly, it cuts off the roots of him who committed it" (Hinduism. Laws of Manu 4.172).

> Even if they attain to sovereignty, the wicked, engaged in cruel deeds, condemned by all men, do not enjoy it long, but fall like trees whose roots have been severed. O dweller in darkness, as in its proper season the tree puts forth its flowers, so in the course of time evil actions produce bitter fruit. (Hinduism. Ramayana, Aranya Kanda 29)

To the degree that we disregard the counsel of the Messengers and follow inclinations that cause harm to ourselves and others we dwell in darkness. We are severed from the light. The separation becomes a bitter fruit as we are drawn toward an awareness of God and our eternal nature.

God makes it clear that there is no place to hide from His justice. "Not in the sky, nor in mid-ocean, nor in a mountain cave, is found that place on earth where abiding one may escape from the consequences of one's evil deed" (Buddhism. Dhammapada 127). "The net of Heaven is cast wide. Though the mesh is not fine, yet nothing ever slips through" (Taoism. Tao Te Ching 73).

Heaven and Hell

Christianity

> You have come to Mount Zion and to the city of the living God, the heavenly Jerusalem, and to innumerable angels in festal gathering, and to the assembly of the first-born who are enrolled in heaven, and to a judge who is God of all, and to the spirits of just men made perfect, and to Jesus, the mediator of a new covenant. (Hebrews 12:22-24)

> These are they who have come out of the great tribulation; they have washed their robes and made them white in the blood of the Lamb. Therefore they are before the throne of God, and serve him day and night within his temple; and he who sits upon the throne will shelter them

with his presence. They shall hunger no more, neither thirst any more; the sun shall not strike them, nor any scorching heat. For the Lamb in the midst of the throne will be their shepherd, and he will guide them to springs of living water; and God will wipe away every tear from their eyes. (Revelation 7:9-17)

As for the cowardly, the faithless, the polluted, as for murderers, fornicators, sorcerers, idolaters, and all liars, their lot shall be in the lake that burns with fire and sulfur, which is the second death. (Revelation 21:8)

But many that are first shall be last; and the last shall be first. (Matthew 19:30)

But as many as received Him, to them gave He power to become sons of God, even to them that believe on His name. (John 1:12)

Hinduism

Behold! Between the worlds of mortals and of gods there is no difference! To speak the truth is the world of gods; to speak untruth, the mortal world. Good works is heaven, Bad works is hell; you are the witness, O Lord. (Basavanna, Vacana 239)

Sikhism

Higher than all stands the Realm of Grace—None can have access there except heroes of supreme might, inspired by God-consciousness. In that sphere abide numberless heroines like Sita of surpassing praise and beauty indescribable. Those to God united suffer not mortality nor delusion. In that sphere abide devotees assembled from the various universes, cherishing the holy Eternal ever in their hearts. In everlasting bliss. The formless Supreme Being abides in the Realm of Eternity. Over His creation He casts His glance of grace. In that realm are contained all the continents and universes, Exceeding in number all count. Of creation, worlds upon worlds abide therein—all obedient to His Will; He watches over them in bliss, and has each constantly in mind. Says Nanak, Such is that realm's [glory] that to try to describe it is to attempt the impossible. (Adi Granth, Japuji 37 M.1, 8)

There is a stream of fire from which emerge poisonous flames. There is none else there except the self. The waves of the ocean of fire are aflame and the sinners are burning in them. (Adi Granth, Maru Solahe, M.1, 1026)

Buddhism

When a son of Buddha fulfils his course, in the world to come he becomes Buddha. (Lotus Sutra 2)

And after their lifetime's end they will enter the Avici hell, for a complete kalpa; reborn at each kalpa's end they thus go on revolving unto innumerable kalpas; when they come out of hell, they will degrade into animals, such as dogs or jackals, with lean-cheeked forms, blue-black with scabs and sores, the sport of men; moreover by men hated and scorned, ever suffering hunger and thirst, bones and flesh withered up. Alive, beaten with thorns, dead, with shards and stones; by cutting themselves off from the Buddha seed, they receive such recompense. (Lotus Sutra 3)

Then the man of unwholesome deeds boils in water infested with worms. He cannot stay still—the boiling pots, round and smooth like bowls, have no surfaces which he can get hold of. Then he is in the jungle of sword blades, limbs mangled and hacked, the tongue hauled by hooks, the body beaten and slashed. Then he is in Vetarani, a watery state difficult to get through, with its two streams that cut like razors. The poor beings fall into it, living out their unwholesome deeds of the past. Gnawed by hungry jackals, ravens and black dogs, and speckled vultures and crows, the sufferers groan. Such a state is experienced by the man of unwholesome deeds. It is a state of absolute suffering. So a sensible person in this world is as energetic and mindful as he can be. (Sutta Nipata 672-76)

Judaism

Rabbi Joseph, son of Rabbi Joshua ben Levi, was ill and fell into a coma. When he recovered, his father asked him, "What did you see?" He replied, "I beheld a world the reverse of this one; those who are on top here were below there, and vice versa." He said to him, "My son, you have seen a corrected world. But what is the position of us students of Torah there?" He answered, "We are the same as here. I heard it stated, 'Happy is he who comes here possessed of learning'; and I further heard it said that martyrs occupy an eminence which nobody else can attain." (Talmud, Pesahim 50a)

Islam

Hell is before him, and he is made to drink a festering water, which he sips but can hardly swallow. Death comes to him from every side, yet he cannot die—before him is a harsh doom. (Qur'an 14.15-16)

Hell will lurk in ambush to receive home the arrogant, who will linger there for ages. They will taste nothing cool in it nor any drink except hot bathwater and slops, a fitting compensation since they have never expected any reckoning and have wittingly rejected Our signs. Everything We have calculated in writing. "So taste! Yet We shall only increase torment for you!" (Qur'an 78.21-30)

Taoism

...The king of the dark realm...said to him, "Here the dead receive punishment for their deeds of evil. The living know not the lot that is reserved for them. They must be thrown into a bed of coals whose heat is in proportion to the extent of their crimes and to the harm they have done their fellows." (From Treatise on Response and Retribution, Appended Tales)

Heaven is not a place. It is a state of being whether in this life or the next. It is determined by our choices and the mercy of God. Good works bring us into harmony with the will of God. Self-insistent deeds separate us from the beauty of His reality.

Behold! Between the worlds of mortals and of gods there is no difference! To speak the truth is the world of gods; to speak untruth, the mortal world. Good works is heaven, Bad works is hell; you are the witness, O Lord. (Hinduism. Basavanna, Vacana 239)

Heaven is nearness to God whether in this world or the next. The Messenger is the mediator of the terms required to be in the presence of God, the covenant. Proximity to God is contingent on the terms established by the Messenger. Good works, responding to the will of the Messenger, is heaven. Bad works, following our selfish inclinations, is hell. God's terms or conditions provided by the Messengers, if followed, provide justice in the affairs of human beings. Refusal to abide by the will of God as provided by the Messengers is a denial of justice for others and self and results in the denial of and separation from God, which is hell.

> You have come to Mount Zion and to the city of the living God, the heavenly Jerusalem, and to innumerable angels in festal gathering, and to the assembly of the first-born who are enrolled in heaven, and to a judge who is God of all, and to the spirits of just men made perfect, and to Jesus, the mediator of a new covenant. (Christianity. Hebrews 12:22-24)

The perfection of the spirits of just men is accomplished with assistance provided by the Messengers. Those who recognize the Messenger and follow the guidance of His covenant are the "first-born." They are enrolled in heaven, the kingdom of the word of God.

> These are they who have come out of the great tribulation; they have washed their robes and made them white in the blood of the Lamb. Therefore they are before the throne of God, and serve him day and night within his temple; and he who sits upon the throne will shelter them with his presence. They shall hunger no more, neither thirst any more; the sun shall not strike them, nor any scorching heat. For the Lamb in the midst of the throne will be their shepherd, and he will guide them to springs of living water; and God will wipe away every tear from their eyes. (Christianity. Revelation 7:9-17)

The perfection of our spirits, changing our disposition with respect to God, is the "great tribulation." Giving up the desires of our hearts which conflict with the will of God looks completely unjust from our self-insistent positions. We generally learn how to do this through our lifetimes. God assists the process through rewards and punishments. On the one hand, He gives us glimpses of Himself and the mercy and justice of His ways. Through His Messengers, He provides us with living examples of submission to His will and the experience of His presence. On the other hand, He shows us the error of our ways by taking away those things that we have chosen over His gifts. The punishment is that we lose both the presence of God and the things that we wanted instead of God. It is the fire of loss and regret. Loss is part of the "great tribulation." Coming through the loss to repentance and the presence of God is heaven.

Most of us work out our salvation through daily battles with our insistent selves. We work our way toward the will of God through the lessons of our lives as we give and take with others. Against the tendency to blatantly give over wholeheartedly to our corrupt inclinations and desires, the scriptures provide warnings. Death will come to this life and with it an end to those things we value above God and justice. A second death will be faced in the next world as we discover the eternal nature of our being and learn about the suffering we caused.

> ...The king of the dark realm...said to him, "Here the dead receive punishment for their deeds of evil. The living know not the lot that is reserved for them. They must be thrown into a bed of coals whose heat is in proportion to the extent of their crimes and to the harm they have done their fellows. (Taoism. From Treatise on Response and Retribution, Appended Tales)

> As for the cowardly, the faithless, the polluted, as for murderers, fornicators, sorcerers, idolaters, and all liars, their lot shall be in the lake that burns with fire and sulfur, which is the second death. (Christianity. Revelation 21:8)

There is a stream of fire from which emerge poisonous flames. There is none else there except the self. The waves of the ocean of fire are aflame and the sinners are burning in them. (Sikhism. Adi Granth, Maru Solahe, M.1.p.1026)

The descriptions of hell in some of the scriptures are very graphic metaphors that tell of the consequences of evil. They act as a warning and as a hedge against our insistent selves in this world. They engage the imagination as a counter balance to the voices of desire and assist in the provision of a position from which to choose between good works and bad. "So a sensible person in this world is as energetic and mindful as he can be" (Buddhism. Sutta Nipata 676). The following Buddhist passages are further examples.

And after their lifetime's end they will enter the Avici hell, for a complete kalpa; reborn at each kalpa's end they thus go on revolving unto innumerable kalpas; when they come out of hell, they will degrade into animals, such as dogs or jackals, with lean-cheeked forms, blue-black with scabs and sores, the sport of men; moreover by men hated and scorned, ever suffering hunger and thirst, bones and flesh withered up. Alive, beaten with thorns, dead, with shards and stones; by cutting themselves off from the Buddha seed, they receive such recompense. (Buddhism. Lotus Sutra 3)

Then the man of unwholesome deeds boils in water infested with worms. He cannot stay still—the boiling pots, round and smooth like bowls, have no surfaces which he can get hold of. Then he is in the jungle of sword blades, limbs mangled and hacked, the tongue hauled by hooks, the body beaten and slashed. Then he is in Vetarani, a watery state difficult to get through, with its two streams that cut like razors. The poor beings fall into it, living out their unwholesome deeds of the past. Gnawed by hungry jackals, ravens and black dogs, and speckled vultures and crows, the sufferers groan. Such a state is experienced by the man of unwholesome deeds. It is a state of absolute suffering. So a sensible person in this world is as energetic and mindful as he can be. (Buddhism. Sutta Nipata 672-76)

These descriptions are metaphors for conditions of being. Literal, material, linear understandings do not encompass reality. For example, experience of hell in the next life is eternal. That does not mean, however, that it is forever in a linear sense. It means that the experience sees no resolution or end. There is no hope. In the next life there is a fuller realization of the eternal nature of our existence. The situation is eternal because it refers to consciousness of the eternal nature of the soul. It is eternal damnation because the soul views eternity from a position of denial. The experience is eternal in that our unrepentant state is aware of our eternal nature. It will persist until the unrepentant position is changed and that is dependent on both the justice and mercy of God.

> Hell will lurk in ambush to receive home the arrogant, who will linger there for ages. They will taste nothing cool in it nor any drink except hot bathwater and slops, a fitting compensation since they have never expected any reckoning and have wittingly rejected Our signs. Everything We have calculated in writing. "So taste! Yet We shall only increase torment for you!" (Islam. Qur'an 78.21-30)

The "arrogant," those who reject the will of God, will "linger there for ages." The duration or measure of hell is prescribed by justice according to our offenses. "Whatever affliction may visit you is for what your own hands have earned" (Islam. Qur'an 42.30). "Brother! Behold the Creator's justice: As are a man's actions, so is his recompense" (Sikhism. Adi Granth, Gauri Var, M.4, p. 308).

The next life is a "corrected world." "But many that are first shall be last; and the last shall be first" (Christianity. Matthew 19:30). Punishment is the mercy of God in that it brings about justice and repentance. To the degree that we have been busy in this life trying to live good lives by gradually conforming our ways to God's through adherence to the admonitions provided by His Messengers in the scriptures, "we are the same as here" when we arrive in the next life. Our happiness is still the pleasure of good works and the presence of God.

Rabbi Joseph, son of Rabbi Joshua ben Levi, was ill and fell into a coma. When he recovered, his father asked him, "What did you see?" He replied, "I beheld a world the reverse of this one; those who are on top here were below there, and vice versa." He said to him, "My son, you have seen a corrected world. But what is the position of us students of Torah there?" He answered, "We are the same as here. I heard it stated, 'Happy is he who comes here possessed of learning'; and I further heard it said that martyrs occupy an eminence which nobody else can attain." (Judaism. Talmud, Pesahim 50a)

In the world that Joseph beheld, the martyrs "occupy an eminence which nobody else can attain." Martyrs give their lives in support of the efforts of the Messengers to save humankind from their remoteness from God. Their love for God is stronger than their inclination to preserve their mortal lives. The "eminence which nobody else can attain" is a description indicating that the state of being is beyond description. It cannot be related to beings confined to mutable and transient realms whether in this world or the next.

Higher than all stands the Realm of Grace—None can have access there except heroes of supreme might, inspired by God-consciousness. In that sphere abide numberless heroines like Sita of surpassing praise and beauty indescribable. Those to God united suffer not mortality nor delusion. In that sphere abide devotees assembled from the various universes, cherishing the holy Eternal ever in their hearts. In everlasting bliss. The formless Supreme Being abides in the Realm of Eternity. Over His creation He casts His glance of grace. In that realm are contained all the continents and universes, Exceeding in number all count. Of creation, worlds upon worlds abide therein—all obedient to His Will; He watches over them in bliss, and has each constantly in mind. Says Nanak, Such is that realm's [glory] that to try to describe it is to attempt the impossible. (Sikhism. Adi Granth, Japuji 37 M.1, p.8)

The station of "those to God united" is reflected in the following verse from Buddhism. "When a son of Buddha fulfils his course, in the world to come he becomes Buddha" (Buddhism. Lotus Sutra 2). Those who cherish "the holy Eternal ever in their hearts" are Buddha in that they are a reflection of the will of God by submission of their own will in His. It is perhaps helpful to note that they are not in this world the person or identity of the Buddha who is the author of a particular religious dispensation. It is similar to Jesus saying that He has given us the power to become "sons of God." "But as many as received Him, to them gave He power to become sons of God, even to them that believe on His name" (Christianity. John 1:12). In the next life the veils of separation will be removed for the sons of God—the sons of Buddha. The station of unity with the Messenger in the next life is beyond comprehension and expression in terms associated with this life.

> This is the realm of full awareness, of utter self-effacement. Even love is no pathway to this region, and longing hath no dwelling here; wherefore is it said, "Love is a veil betwixt the lover and the beloved." Here love becometh an obstruction and a barrier, and all else save Him is but a curtain. The wise Saná'í hath written:
>
> > Never the covetous heart shall come to the
> >   stealer of hearts,
> > Never the shrouded soul unite with beauty's rose.
>
> For this is the realm of Absolute Command and is free of all the attributes of earth. (Baha'i Faith. Seven Valleys and the Four Valleys p. 59)

– 6 –

THE GOLDEN RULE
AND THE TEN COMMANDMENTS

The Golden Rule

Judaism
You shall love your neighbor as yourself. (Leviticus 19.18)

Christianity
Whatever you wish that men would do to you, do so to them. (Matthew 7:12)

Islam
Not one of you is a believer until he loves for his brother what he loves for himself. (Hadith of an-Nawawi 13)

Baha'i Faith
If thine eyes be turned towards mercy, forsake the things that profit thee and cleave unto that which will profit mankind. And if thine eyes be turned towards justice, choose thou for thy neighbor that which thou choosest for thyself. (Tablets of Baha'u'llah, 64)

Jainism
A man should wander about treating all creatures as he himself would be treated. (Sutrakritanga 1.11.33)

Confucianism
Try your best to treat others as you would wish to be treated yourself and you will find that this is the shortest way to benevolence. (Mencius VII.A.4)

Hinduism

One should not behave towards others in a way which is disagreeable to oneself. This is the essence of morality. (Mahabharata, Anusasana Parva 113.8)

Buddhism

Comparing oneself to others in such terms as "Just as I am so are they, just as they are so am I," he should neither kill nor cause others to kill. (Sutta Nipata 705)

The Ten Commandments

Judaism.

I am the Lord your God...you shall have no other gods before me....You shall not make for yourself a graven image....You shall not take the name of the Lord your God in vain....Remember the Sabbath day, to keep it holy.... Honor your father and your mother....You shall not kill.You shall not commit adultery.You shall not steal. You shall not bear false witness against your neighbor. You shall not covet your neighbor's house;...wife,...or anything that is your neighbor's (Exodus 20.1-17).

Hinduism.

Contentment, forgiveness, self-control, not appropriating anything unrighteously, purification, coercion of the organs, wisdom, knowledge of the Supreme, truthfulness, and abstention from anger: these constitute the tenfold law. (Laws of Manu 6.92)

Islam

Thy Lord has decreed... that you be kind to parents. Whether one or both of them attain old age in your lifetime, do not say to them a word of contempt, nor repel them, but address them in terms of honor. And, out of kindness, lower to them the wing of humility, and say, "My Lord! Bestow on them Thy mercy even as they cherished me in childhood." (Qur'an 17.23)

Jainism.

Forgiveness, humility, straightforwardness, purity, truthfulness, self-restraint, austerity, renunciation, non-attachment and chastity are the ten duties. (Tatthvarthasutra 9.6)

Buddhism.

Not killing, no longer stealing, forsaking the wives of others, refraining completely from false, divisive, harsh and senseless speech, forsaking covetousness, harmful intent and the views of Nihilists—these are the ten white paths of action, their opposites are black. (Nagarjuna, Precious Garland 8-9)

Those who wish to be born in [the Pure Land] of Buddha...should act filially towards their parents and support them, and should serve and respect their teachers and elders. (Meditation on Buddha Amitayus 27)

They will practice these virtues: abstain from taking life, abstain from taking what is not given, abstain from adultery, abstain from lying, abstain from evil speaking, abstain from abuse and from idle talk, abstain from covetousness, from ill will, from false opinions, abstain from the three things—incest, wanton greed, and perverted desires—be filial towards their mothers and fathers, be pious toward holy men, and respect heads of clans. (Buddhism. Digha Nikaya iii.74, Cakkavatti-Sihanada Suttanta)

Zoroastrianism

This I ask Thee. Tell me truly, Lord. Who fashioned esteemed piety in addition to rule? Who made a son respectful in his attentiveness to his father? (Avesta, Yasna 44.7)

Confucianism

Now filial piety is the root of all virtue, and the stem out of which grows all moral teaching....Our bodies—to every hair and bit of skin—are received by us from our parents, and we must not presume to injure or wound them: this is the beginning of filial piety. When we have established our character by the practice of the filial course, so as to make our name famous in future ages, and thereby glorify our parents; this is the end of filial piety. It commences with the service of parents; it proceeds to the service of the ruler; it is completed by the establishment of [good] character. (Classic on Filial Piety 1)

Love Thy Neighbor as Thyself

The human spirit has integrity, authority, and power to fruitfully shape events in this world to the degree that it aligns itself to the truth rather than the inclinations of its own designs and desires. "He that findeth his life shall lose it: and he that loseth his life for my sake shall find it" (Christianity. Matthew 10:39). We must die to our insistent selves if we want to find spiritual life in proximity to the will of God. This is generally done in the context of considering the needs of others rather than only ourselves. The prophets educate us in the ways of service to God and our neighbors. The golden rule is central to all of the world's great religions. Each of the faith traditions provides an iteration of the injunction to love one another and do unto others, as we would have them do unto us. Our responses to this eternal dictate determine the course of our individual lives and that of our collective social history. Our capacities as individuals or collectively unfold from our affirmations of this law of reality. Our failures are a result of our negations of this teaching.

Those who sacrifice their own advantage for the love of God and their neighbor are the builders of civilization and are the foundation upon which a healthy social order is dependent. Their character and actions are the reminders to the rest of us of our higher nature. They are the "salt of the earth" that stimulates our taste for life. The selfless act punctures the illusion of the finite by providing evidence of the eternal reality of our nature. Selflessness allows us to touch unbounded life and provides the energy for constructive human activity. Material civilization rises from all the arts, sciences, crafts, and industry that have their origin in this spiritual energy.

Human beings without spiritual guidance rely on an adversarial and competitive physical nature when needed or desired resources are limited. Resources are shared only to the point that the return on the relationship is beneficial. Alliances depend on perceived advantages. All plans and designs derived from this adversarial and competitive center are petty no matter how seemingly grandiose and complex. They all have their consummation in death. They are tied to the limited self, which denies its unity with the whole. This is not a pleasant place for human consciousness to live, nor is it the foundation for the building of a bountiful human civilization. It does not even provide for coherent material civilization. It sabotages visions that are not its own and squanders resources in the relentless drive to satisfy its self-defined purposes. Its most poignant expression is war.

It would be reasonable at this point to acknowledge that we are all a mixture of the physical and spiritual aspects of human motivation. We are all the builders and the destroyers of human well-being and happiness. This human world is not the realm of perfection. The wheat and the weeds grow together. There is an innate tendency in the human situation to hear first the imperative demands of one's own body and mind over the distant, second-hand sounds of someone else's expressed needs. The golden rule provides the mechanism by which we articulate justice into our affairs. It is not that we are ever certain that we know precisely what justice requires in any given situation; all sides in a situation can know the truth to some degree. Truth is bigger than anyone's perspective, save God's. It is our willingness to forgo our own advantage in favor of the dictates of the truth that allows us to be susceptible to decisions that are closer in proximity to justice than our independent and rather biased perspectives otherwise permit. This willingness to forgo our own advantage is at the heart of successful life for the individual and for civilization, rather than our ability to force our will or perspective on others. The golden rule "is the essence of morality" (Hinduism. Mahabharata, Anusasana Parva 113.8). It is the prerequisite of justice. "...[I]f thine eyes be turned towards justice, choose thou for thy neighbor that which thou choosest for thyself" (Baha'i Faith. Tablets of Baha'u'llah, p. 64).

The Fear of God

The essence of morality is the selfless love of our neighbor. It has its impetus in our experience of the love of God. We do not, however, live most of our conscious existence in this pure state. Most of our lives are a complex mixture of sentiments and motivations that range from angelically and bountifully selfless to wretchedly and aggressively self-centered. Our behaviors towards each other rely most often on a pragmatic foundation—the fear of God. On the higher end of this motivational paradigm is the experience of awe, a realization of the beauty and power of God and the counterpart realization of the insignificance of our narrow and selfish perspective. In this arena, the possibility of the loss of proximity to God informs the experience of fear. The practical steps taken to check our selfish inclinations are moved by a desire to stay within reasonable proximity to the pleasure of God's presence.

Our personal covenant with God, our personal agreement with Him, rests on our willingness to comply with His will. We can only have His presence if we abide by His law. In daily routine, the fear of God is in evidence in the little motivational flash of conscience that briefly appears before we do something we suspect to be in opposition to the will of God.

The lower end of fear's motivational hold on our behavior is the self-centered preoccupation with our well-being. God could punish us. We fear an image of God that we possess. Compliance with societal laws from this vantage point is based on the fear of being caught and punished by agents of the law or ultimately by what we imagine to be God. Outward observance of propriety is the primary focus, even preoccupation, at this level of fear.

The Ten Commandments

Regardless of the particular motivational position from which we, at any given moment, individually view the will of God, the scriptures of the varying religious traditions provide guidance for how we are to behave with respect to each other. This guidance generally provides the moral bedrock of the world's cultures for the construction of laws aimed at providing social justice.

For Judaism and Christianity, the Ten Commandments are a scriptural summary of behavioral guidance.

> I am the Lord your God...you shall have no other gods before me....
> You shall not make for yourself a graven image....
> You shall not take the name of the Lord your God in vain....
> Remember the Sabbath day, to keep it holy....
> Honor your father and your mother....
> You shall not kill.
> You shall not commit adultery.
> You shall not steal.
> You shall not bear false witness against your neighbor.
> You shall not covet your neighbor's house;...wife,...or anything that is your neighbor's. (Judaism. Exodus 20.1-17)

The passage from Exodus begins with the fundamental basis of the law—serving God rather than our image of God. We are advised not to follow the image of God that we create from the corrupt inclinations of a selfish nature. Nor are we to use His name in vain and insist in our prayers that God conform to our will. We are advised to observe religious orthodoxy—the safe approach to God provided by his Messengers. Respect for parental authority and by implication, obedience to the institutions of society is prescribed over anarchy. The remaining commandments admonish us against killing, adultery, stealing, lying, and covetousness.

Commandments from Other Scriptures

All of the faith traditions, in a manner similar to the Ten Commandments of Exodus, afford essential moral guidance. They provide warnings against our tendency to construct an image of God to our own liking and worship it rather than submit to the will of God (See chapter 3). The various scriptures also prescribe observance of religious orthodoxy as in the admonitions for prayer and fasting as an aid to following the path of God (See chapter 7). And all of the scriptures provide guidance for how we should treat each other as is evidenced in the provision of the golden rule in all of the scriptures. The teaching for us to honor our father and mother is also a common theme of religion. The admonition is central to the maintenance of social order. The following are examples from Islam, Buddhism, Confucianism, and Zoroastrianism.

Thy Lord has decreed... that you be kind to parents. Whether one or both of them attain old age in your lifetime, do not say to them a word of contempt, nor repel them, but address them in terms of honor. And, out of kindness, lower to them the wing of humility, and say, "My Lord! Bestow on them Thy mercy even as they cherished me in childhood." (Islam. Qur'an 17.23)

Those who wish to be born in [the Pure Land] of Buddha...should act filially towards their parents and support them, and should serve and respect their teachers and elders. (Buddhism. Meditation on Buddha Amitayus 27)

Now filial piety is the root of all virtue, and the stem out of which grows all moral teaching....Our bodies—to every hair and bit of skin—are received by us from our parents, and we must not presume to injure or wound them: this is the beginning of filial piety. When we have established our character by the practice of the filial course, so as to make our name famous in future ages, and thereby glorify our parents; this is the end of filial piety. It commences with the service of parents; it proceeds to the service of the ruler; it is completed by the establishment of [good] character. (Confucianism. Classic on Filial Piety 1)

The Zoroastrian scriptures make the case for filial piety rhetorically. "This I ask Thee. Tell me truly, Lord. Who fashioned esteemed piety in addition to rule? Who made a son respectful in his attentiveness to his father?" (Avesta, Yasna 44.7). The rule of law is conditioned on piety which is conditioned on filial respect which is fashioned through the grace of God—the "who" in the question.

The Rest of the Ten Commandments

The scriptures of the various religious traditions provide admonitions against lying, stealing, killing, adultery, and covetousness. The following are Buddhist commandments.

> They will practice these virtues: abstain from taking life, abstain from taking what is not given, abstain from adultery, abstain from lying, abstain from evil speaking, abstain from abuse and from idle talk, abstain from covetousness, from ill will, from false opinions, abstain from the three things—incest, wanton greed, and perverted desires—be filial towards their mothers and fathers, be pious toward holy men, and respect heads of clans. (Buddhism. Digha Nikaya iii.74, Cakkavatti-Sihanada Suttanta)

Some scriptures express the admonitions mostly in terms of good behaviors rather than bad. For instance, the Laws of Manu from Hinduism are framed mostly in positive terms. "Contentment, forgiveness, self-control, not appropriating anything unrighteously, purification, coercion of the organs, wisdom, knowledge of the Supreme, truthfulness, and abstention from anger: these constitute the tenfold law" (Hinduism. Laws of Manu 6.92). The basic guidance for successful human society is articulated in all of the world's scriptures in iterations of both the golden rule and the Ten Commandments.

− 7 −

RELIGIOUS PRACTICES

Religious Practices

Buddhism

Not by sacred water is one pure, although many folk bathe in it. In whom is truth and dhamma, he is pure; he is a Brahmin. (Udana 6)

Abstaining from fish or flesh, nakedness, shaving of the head, wearing the hair matted, smearing with ashes, wearing rough deerskins, attending the sacrificial fire, all the various penances performed for immortality, neither incantations, oblations, sacrifices, nor observing seasonal feasts will cleanse a man who has not overcome his doubt. (Sutta Nipata, 249)

Even three times a day to offer three hundred cooking pots of food does not match a portion of the merit acquired in one instant of love. (Nagarjuna, Precious Garland 283)

If your kingdom exists for the doctrine and not for fame or desire, then it will be extremely fruitful. If not, its fruit will be misfortune. (Nagarjuna, Precious Garland 327)

One thing, when it comes to pass, does so to the loss, to the unhappiness of many folk...to the misery of the gods and humankind. What is that one thing? Schism in the order of monks. (Itivuttaka 11)

Confucianism

Ch'un-yu K'un said, "Is it prescribed by the rites that, in giving and receiving, man and woman should not touch each other? "It is," said Mencius. "When one's sister-in-law is drowning, does one stretch out a hand to help her?" "Not to help a sister-in-law who is drowning is to be a brute. It is prescribed by the rites that, in giving and receiving, man and woman do not touch each other, but in stretching out a helping hand to the drowning sister-in-law one uses one's discretion." (Mencius IV.A.17)

The Master said, "A man who is not humane, what can he have to do with ritual." (Analects 3.3)

Christianity

Hear and understand, not what goes into the mouth defiles a man, but what comes out of the mouth, this defiles a man....Do you not see that whatever goes into the mouth passes into the stomach, and so passes on? But what comes out of the mouth proceeds from the heart, and this defiles a man. For out of the heart come evil thoughts, murder, adultery, fornication, theft, false witness, slander. These are what defile a man. (Matthew 15:11-20)

[Jesus] went on from there, and entered their synagogue. And behold, there was a man with a withered hand. And they asked him, "Is it lawful to heal on the Sabbath?" so that they might accuse him. He said to them, "What man of you, if he has one sheep and it falls into a pit on the Sabbath, will not lay hold of it and lift it out? Of how much more value is a man than a sheep! So it is lawful to do good on the Sabbath." Then he said to the man, "Stretch out your hand." And the man stretched it out, and it was restored, whole like the other. But the Pharisees went out and took counsel against him, how to destroy him. (Matthew 12:9-14)

Hinduism

May your counsel be common, your assembly common, common the mind, and the thoughts of these united. A common purpose do I lay before you, and worship with your common oblation. Let your aims be common, and your hearts of one accord, and all of you be of one mind, so you may live well together. (Rig Veda 10.191.2-4)

Concerned alone with the upholding of the world, you should act. Whatever the best man does, others do that also. The world follows the standard he sets for himself. (Bhagavad Gita 3.20-21)

Look, you brothers, who bathe in the holy waters, Look, you monks, who bathe in the stream. Give up, give up, your unholy thoughts; Give up lustful thoughts for another man's wife, Give up coveting after another man's wealth. If you bathe in the waters without giving up these, it is as if bathing in a stream that has run dry. (Basavanna, Vacana 642)

Finite and transient are the fruits of sacrificial rites. The deluded, who regard them as the highest good, remain subject to birth and death....Attached to works, they know not God. Works lead them only to heaven, whence, to their sorrow, their rewards quickly exhausted, they are flung back to earth. Considering religion to be observance of rituals and performance of acts of charity, the deluded remain ignorant of the highest good. Having enjoyed in heaven the reward of their good works, they enter again into the world of mortals. But the wise, self-controlled, and tranquil souls, who are contented in spirit, and who practice austerity and meditation in solitude and silence, are freed from all impurity, and attain by the path of liberation the immortal, the truly existing, the changeless Self. (Mundaka Upanishad. 1.2.7-11)

Islam

It is not piety that you turn your faces [in prayer] to the East and to the West. True piety is this: to believe in God, and the Last Day, the angels, the Book, and the Prophets, to give of one's substance, however cherished, to kinsmen, and orphans, the needy, the traveler, beggars, and to ransom the slave, to perform the prayer, to pay the alms. And they who fulfill their covenant, when they have engaged in a covenant, and endure with fortitude misfortune, hardship, and peril, these are they who are true in their faith, these are the truly God-fearing. (Qur'an 2.177)

Maintain religion, and do not stir up any divisions within it. (Qur'an 42.13)

And when a company meets together in one of the houses of God to pore over the Book of God and to study it together among themselves, the Shechinah comes down to them and mercy overshadows them, the angels surround them, and God remembers them among them that are His. (Forty Hadith of an-Nawawi 36)

Judaism

If two sit together and the words between them are of Torah, then the Shechinah is in their midst. (Mishnah, Abot 3.2)

The world stands upon three things: upon the Law, upon worship, and upon showing kindness. (Mishnah, Abot 1.2)

Religious Practices

"The world stands upon three things: upon the Law, upon worship, and upon showing kindness" (Judaism. Mishnah, Abot 1.2). Worship is the uplifted human response to proximity to God. As we recognize or remember God, our joy over the glimpse of His Beauty is worship. The effectiveness of our efforts to assist human social well-being is supported by the experience of worship. It frees us from the concerns of our physical natures, sensitizes us to the reality of others, and provides the basis for the cooperative action required for community. All of the world's religions teach us to obey the will of God, to make efforts to improve our character through worship, and to treat others as we wish to be treated. The integrity of our efforts is supported through communion with God.

The result of observing the admonitions of the Messengers with respect to worship and good works is both proximity to God and the establishment of justice in the affairs of humankind. Spiritual practices are meant to provide an approach to God. The purpose of the admonitions of the Messengers in the context of this world is to assist individuals to progress spiritually and to live in harmony with others. Spiritual practices as ritual observance or as a means to establish self-righteousness are of little value to us or others.

> It is not piety that you turn your faces [in prayer] to the East and to the West. True piety is this: to believe in God, and the Last Day, the angels, the Book, and the Prophets, to give of one's substance, however cherished, to kinsmen, and orphans, the needy, the traveler, beggars, and to ransom the slave, to perform the prayer, to pay the alms. And they who fulfill their covenant, when they have engaged in a covenant, and endure with fortitude misfortune, hardship, and peril, these are they who are true in their faith, these are the truly God-fearing. (Islam. Qur'an, 2.177)

The following Buddhist scripture admonishes that, the "various penances performed for immortality" as external observances will not provide salvation. Asceticism without trust in God will not satisfy the desire for forgiveness. The individual must change an internal disposition of doubt into knowledge of God.

> Abstaining from fish or flesh, nakedness, shaving of the head, wearing the hair matted, smearing with ashes, wearing rough deerskins, attending the sacrificial fire, all the various penances performed for immortality, neither incantations, oblations, sacrifices, nor observing seasonal feasts will cleanse a man who has not overcome his doubt. (Buddhism. Sutta Nipata, 249)

The waters of redemption flow from proximity to God. The presence of God is only available to those who overcome their estrangement. The following passage from Hindu scripture provides a similar admonition. Adhering to the prescribed, outward observances of God's directives does not result in cleanliness. Suspending the internal attachment to things forbidden by God is prerequisite to attaining His presence.

> Look, you brothers, who bathe in the holy waters,
> Look, you monks, who bathe in the stream. Give up, give
> up, your unholy thoughts; Give up lustful thoughts for
> another man's wife, Give up coveting after another man's
> wealth. If you bathe in the waters without giving up these,
> it is as if bathing in a stream that has run dry. (Hinduism.
> Basavanna, Vacana 642)

Many of the passages of scripture set spiritual practices in
the context of priorities. They explicate by comparison the
preferred order of religious practices like ritual, good works,
love of one's neighbor, and communion with God. "Even
three times a day to offer three hundred cooking pots of
food does not match a portion of the merit acquired in one
instant of love" (Buddhism. Nagarjuna, Precious Garland
283). Ritual works performed out of fear of punishment or
for social recognition are a shadow of those performed out of
love.

Jesus instructs the Pharisees that the ritual observance of
the Sabbath is not as important as good works. He thereby
instructs us that consideration for the needs of others is more
important to our relationship with God than external observance of religious orthodoxy.

> [Jesus] went on from there, and entered their syna-
> gogue. And behold, there was a man with a withered hand.
> And they asked him, "Is it lawful to heal on the Sabbath?"
> so that they might accuse him. He said to them, "What
> man of you, if he has one sheep and it falls into a pit on the
> Sabbath, will not lay hold of it and lift it out? Of how
> much more value is a man than a sheep! So it is lawful to
> do good on the Sabbath." Then he said to the man,
> "Stretch out your hand." And the man stretched it out,
> and it was restored, whole like the other. But the Phari-
> sees went out and took counsel against him, how to de-
> stroy him. (Christianity. Matthew 12:9-14)

Confucius expresses the underlying purpose of ritual as
support for human compassion in a brief statement. "A man
who is not humane, what can he have to do with ritual"

(Confucianism. Analects 3.3). Additional Confucian scripture on the topic clarifies the teaching with a hypothetical example.

> Ch'un-yu K'un said, "Is it prescribed by the rites that, in giving and receiving, man and woman should not touch each other? "It is," said Mencius. "When one's sister-in-law is drowning, does one stretch out a hand to help her?" "Not to help a sister-in-law who is drowning is to be a brute. It is prescribed by the rites that, in giving and receiving, man and woman do not touch each other, but in stretching out a helping hand to the drowning sister-in-law one uses one's discretion." (Confucianism. Mencius IV.A.17)

The passage admonishes us against holding external observance of religious laws and rituals as more important than human need. The use of discretion or reason associated with selfless consideration of another's need is above brutish observance of ritual and religious law.

Good works are more important than the observance of ritual. However, when good works are done for benefit in this world, they are tied to the rewards of material life and have little spiritual, eternal benefit. Good works are not always free from the vagaries and uncertainties of selfishness in this life. Such actions may be clouded by associated attachments to social, emotional, or material benefit. Under these conditions, "good" actions are a form of attachment.

> Finite and transient are the fruits of sacrificial rites. The deluded, who regard them as the highest good, remain subject to birth and death....Attached to works, they know not God. Works lead them only to heaven, whence, to their sorrow, their rewards quickly exhausted, they are flung back to earth. Considering religion to be observance of rituals and performance of acts of charity, the deluded remain ignorant of the highest good. Having enjoyed in heaven the reward of their good works, they enter again into the world of mortals. But the wise, self controlled,

and tranquil souls, who are contented in spirit, and who practice austerity and meditation in solitude and silence, are freed from all impurity, and attain by the path of liberation the immortal, the truly existing, the changeless Self. (Hinduism. Mundaka Upanishad. 1.2.7-11)

Heaven in this context may be understood as the self-righteous pleasure associated with observing religious practices. It is not a reference to heaven as the presence of God. Spiritual practices are provided by the Messengers of God as a safe approach to His presence and as methods to assist in the establishment of love and justice in our affairs. They are integral to the maintenance of social order and a safe approach to God. They are not established as an end in themselves.

Worship

Buddhism

Every son and every daughter of a family ought with their whole mind to make fervent prayer for [rebirth in] the Pure Land of Buddha Amitayus. (Smaller Skhavativyuha Sutra 10)

One thing, when it comes to pass, does so to the loss, to the unhappiness of many folk...to the misery of the gods and humankind. What is that one thing? Schism in the order of monks. (Itivuttaka 11)

Hinduism

Worship me through meditation in the sanctuary of the heart. (Srimad Bhagavatam 11.5)

Judaism

Always let a man test himself: if he can direct his heart, let him pray; if he cannot, let him not pray. (Talmud, Berakot 30b)

My house shall be called a house of prayer for all peoples. (Isaiah 56.7)

Christianity

> Pray constantly. (1 Thessalonians 5:17)

> We know that God does not listen to sinners, but if anyone is a worshipper of God and does his will, God listens to him. (John 9:31)

Islam

> Prayer restrains one from shameful and unjust deeds; and remembrance of God is the greatest thing in life, without doubt. (Qur'an 29.45)

Worship is the mechanism by which individuals are motivated to abide by the law of God. The spiritual nature of worship pertains to the remembrance and recognition of God. It is the presence of God—His voice, His beauty. Worship is the experience of the eternal word of God, which is the essential gift of all religions. "My house shall be called a house of prayer for all peoples" (Judaism. Isaiah 56.7). Turning to God in prayer and meditation is mentioned in all of the religious traditions. "Pray constantly" (Christianity. 1 Thessalonians 5:17). "Worship me through meditation in the sanctuary of the heart" (Hinduism. Srimad Bhagavatam 11.5). "Prayer restrains one from shameful and unjust deeds; and remembrance of God is the greatest thing in life, without doubt" (Islam. Qur'an 29.45). "Every son and every daughter of a family ought with their whole mind to make fervent prayer for [rebirth in] the Pure Land of Buddha Amitayus" (Buddhism. Smaller Skhavativyuha Sutra 10). "Always let a man test himself: if he can direct his heart, let him pray; if he cannot, let him not pray" (Judaism. Talmud, Berakot 30b). The admonition to pray requires that it be sincerely directed from the selfless heart. There is a similar admonition in the Gospel of John. "We know that God does not listen to sinners, but if anyone is a worshipper of God and does his will, God listens to him" (Christianity. John 9:31). Remembrance of God in prayer is conditioned on a sincere willingness to respond to His will.

Worship energizes altruistic human behavior through the love of God. It also provides for the establishment of socially benevolent behavior. Observance of prayers, rituals, and procedures that express spiritual, intellectual, emotional, and social consciousness of God provide support for social order. It admonishes through the love and fear of God. Fear of the governance structures of society will restrain some outward behavior, but most people monitor their own behavior through a complex set of internalized values that are integrally related to their belief in God. It is a mixture of the love of God, a desire to do good, fear of losing the good pleasure of God, and fear of the wrath of God. The worship associated with religious institutions binds people together in their common commitment to promote the well-being of the community.

However, the amount of incredibly vicious and brutal conflict initiated in the name of God is the obvious caveat to human solidarity provided by religion. Human history is replete with religious persecutions and warfare. The inhuman behavior is generally directed at non-believers or those who appear to violate the rules of the believers. Before the convergence of disparate religious groups into a global community, geographic isolation buffered conflict between members of different religions. Religious persecutions were mostly internal affairs. In this age, the global neighborhood has increased tensions between adherents of the world's religions. Religious intolerance and fanaticism have become significant barriers to social stability and advances in social justice for the peoples of the world. Religious fanaticism is in direct opposition to the purpose of religion. "One thing, when it comes to pass, does so to the loss, to the unhappiness of many folk...to the misery of the gods and humankind. What is that one thing? Schism in the order of monks" (Buddhism. Itivuttaka 11). The Messengers are our connection to God. They bring personal salvation. They also provide social laws for the welfare of the individual and society. When religion is corrupted, it becomes a source of contention and conflict and no longer serves its purpose.

Kindness—Unity

Christianity

There is neither Jew nor Greek, there is neither slave nor free, there is neither male nor female; for you are all one in Christ Jesus. (Galatians 3:28)

Every kingdom divided against itself is laid waste, and no city or house divided against itself will stand. (Matthew 12:25)

Jainism

Consider the family of humankind one. (Jinasena, Adipurana)

Sikhism

Let all mankind be thy sect. (Adi Granth, Japuji 28, M.1 6)

All jealousies have vanished in the society of the Saints. All are my friends now, there being no enemy or stranger. (Adi Granth, Kanara, M.5, 1299)

Judaism

Behold, how good and pleasant it is when brothers dwell in unity!....for there the Lord has commanded the blessing, life for evermore. (Psalm 133)

Separate yourself not from the community. (Mishnah, Abot 2.4)

The world stands upon three things: upon the Law, upon worship, and upon showing kindness. (Mishnah, Abot 1.2)

Have we not all one father? Has not one God created us? (Malachi 2.10)

Baha'i Faith

O contending peoples and kindreds of the earth! Set your faces toward unity, and let the radiance of its light shine upon you. Gather ye together, and for the sake of God resolve to root out whatever is the source of contention among you. Then will the effulgence of the world's great Luminary envelop the whole earth, and its inhabitants become the citizens of one city, and the occupants of one and the same throne. (Gleanings 111)

Beware lest the desires of the flesh and of a corrupt inclination provoke divisions among you. Be ye as the fingers of one hand, the members of one body. Thus counsels you the Pen of Revelation, if ye be of them that believe. (Gleanings, 72)

Buddhism

Happy is the unity of the Sangha. Happy is the discipline of the united ones. (Dhammapada 194)

Human community is supported by the grace of God that flows through worship. Experience of the love and bounty of God frees us from the concerns of self-preservation and permits acts of selflessness and kindness. "All jealousies have vanished in the society of the Saints. All are my friends now, there being no enemy or stranger" (Sikhism. Adi Granth, Kanara, M.5, 1299). "Behold, how good and pleasant it is when brothers dwell in unity!....for there the Lord has commanded the blessing, life for evermore" (Judaism. Psalm 133). Worship supports community through the recognition of the underlying unity and security of being. Human community is the living expression of the golden rule to love others as ourselves. "Let all mankind be thy sect" (Sikhism. Adi Granth, Japuji 28, M.1 6). "Consider the family of humankind one" (Jainism. Jinasena, Adipurana). "Every kingdom divided against itself is laid waste, and no city or house divided against itself will stand" (Christianity. Matthew 12:25).

Religion is fundamentally a unifying force for humankind. It revolves around the law of love and kindness. The eternal nature of kindness rests on the realization of the self of another as one's own self. It is a transcendent unity. "Happy is the unity of the Sangha. Happy is the discipline of the united ones" (Buddhism. Dhammapada 194). Peace and happiness are supported by the preference of this unity over the inclinations of self-preservation.

The roots of cooperation are both spiritual and biological. Cooperation is the practical outcome of the higher levels of consciousness i.e. faith, love, and self-actualization. It is also as fundamental a part of nature as competition or survival of the fittest. In the human social environment, cooperation is supported by reason; all of the participants benefit. The temporal benefit of kindness accrues from the mutual benefits associated with cooperation. Adaptation is as much successful cooperation with an environment as it is defeat of a competitor. Cooperative relationships can be seen throughout nature i.e. herds, hives, flocks, and the cells that work cooperatively as organisms. The spiritual energy associated with the underlying reality of our unity helps to integrate the benevolent aspects of the body, mind, and spirit of humankind.

> O contending peoples and kindreds of the earth! Set your faces toward unity, and let the radiance of its light shine upon you. Gather ye together, and for the sake of God resolve to root out whatever is the source of contention among you. Then will the effulgence of the world's great Luminary envelop the whole earth, and its inhabitants become the citizens of one city, and the occupants of one and the same throne. (Bahai' Faith. Gleanings 111)

Equality and Justice

Christianity

There is neither Jew nor Greek, there is neither slave nor free, there is neither male nor female, for you are all one in Christ Jesus. (Galatians 3:28)

Islam

For the white to lord it over the black, the Arab over the non-Arab, the rich over the poor, the strong over the weak or men over women is out of place and wrong. (Hadith of Ibn Majah)

Judaism

I call heaven and earth to witness: whether Jew or Gentile, whether man or woman, whether servant or freeman, they are all equal in this: that the Holy Spirit rests upon them in accordance with their deeds! (Seder Eliyyahu Rabbah 10)

Proclaim liberty throughout the land to all its inhabitants. (Leviticus 25.10)

Take away from me the noise of your songs; To the melody of your harps I will not listen. But let justice roll down like waters, and righteousness like an ever-flowing stream. (Amos 5.23-24)

Buddhism

Not by matted hair, nor by family, nor by birth does one become a Brahmin. But in whom there exists both truth and righteousness, pure is he, a Brahmin is he. (Dhammapada 393, 396)

Hinduism

I look upon all creatures equally; none are less dear to me and none more dear. (Bhagavad Gita 9.29)

All those who take refuge in me, whatever their birth, race, sex, or caste, will attain the supreme goal; this realization can be attained even by those whom society scorns. Kings and sages, too seek this goal with devotion. (Bhagavad Gita 9.32-33)

The realization of the equality of humanity is a corollary to the golden rule. Treat others as you would treat yourself. The directive does not discriminate based on race, nationality, class, or gender.

I look upon all creatures equally; none are less dear to me and none more dear. (Hinduism. Bhagavad Gita 9.29)

There is neither Jew nor Greek, there is neither slave nor free, there is neither male nor female, for you are all one in Christ Jesus. (Christianity. Galatians 3:28)

All those who take refuge in me, whatever their birth, race, sex, or caste, will attain the supreme goal; this realization can be attained even by those whom society scorns. Kings and sages, too seek this goal with devotion. (Hinduism. Bhagavad Gita 9.32-33)

For the white to lord it over the black, the Arab over the non-Arab, the rich over the poor, the strong over the weak or men over women is out of place and wrong. (Islam. Hadith of Ibn Majah)

Not by matted hair, nor by family, nor by birth does one become a Brahmin. But in whom there exists both truth and righteousness, pure is he, a Brahmin is he. (Buddhism. Dhammapada 393, 396)

The theme of equality before God is well established throughout the world's scriptures. Biased treatment based in the human heart and/or in the institutions of society demonstrates, at this stage in the evolution of human social order on this planet, a denial of spiritual guidance. God's view establishes the norm. As He regards us all equally, therefore, we are equal. This is not the static equality of sameness. It is the equality of the essence of human worth and dignity. It is the transcendent, eternal equality of our being. The equality of our essential nature is the reality which our behaviors as well as our laws and social institutions should endeavor to reflect. "I call heaven and earth to witness: whether Jew or Gentile, whether man or woman, whether servant or freeman, they are all equal in this: that the Holy Spirit rests upon them in accordance with their deeds!" (Judaism. Seder Eliyyahu Rabbah 10).

The equality of the peoples of the world requires that the institutions and governance structures of our world promote social justice. The scriptures recognize that we are different. We are not the same, but we are equal. The promotion of social justice does not require that everyone be treated the same. We do not all wear the same size shoes, like the same colors, or have the same capacities. Equality of treatment means we all should have equal respect for each other's needs and perspectives under the governance structures of society. In today's world it also requires that we have representation in governing the affairs of the community. "Proclaim liberty throughout the land to all its inhabitants." (Judaism. Leviticus 25.10)

The political process produces social justice to the degree that it converts prejudiced perspectives into consensus. Prejudice is part ignorance of an alternate understanding and part dismissal of the holder of a different view. It derives from our living separate experiences in separate bodies. If I have a headache, I suffer. If you have a headache, I can feel and express my sympathy, but I do not feel your pain. Our separate human experiences are bridged by our ability to transcend our isolation through communication. We have the ability to acknowledge the reality of another as if it were ours, experience ourselves in others, and stretch to understand another's experience. It is more than the emotional or psychological identification with the image of the other. It is based on the experience of the other as we experience ourselves. It is an acknowledgement of their being with our being.

Political processes are aided to the degree that the participants afford each other respect for their varied positions and perspectives. Prejudice violates and obscures recognition of the value of the holder of a different perspective. The elimination of prejudice does not require the elimination of differences nor of preferences for differences. It requires developing the human capacity to see the inherent equality of the other and to be unified within differences, to seek consensus of what to do about a situation, to find agreement, or to compromise. We must make a decision before we can enter the realm of action. To the degree that the processes used to form a decision are informed by the open and respectful exchange of ideas and positions, they are likely to produce more effective solutions to problems or conflicts. Equality and justice in the affairs of global society will become realized through the evolution of governance structures that promote agreement rather than dominance of one group over another that is based in prejudice.

Spiritual Education

Buddhism

By degrees, little by little, from time to time, a wise person should remove his own impurities as a smith removes the dross from silver. (Dhammapada 239)

Confucianism

The Master said, "At fifteen I set my heart upon learning. At thirty, I had planted my feet upon firm ground. At forty, I no longer suffered from perplexities. At fifty, I know what were the biddings of Heaven. At sixty, I heard them with a docile ear. At seventy, I could follow the dictates of my own heart; for what I desired no longer overstepped the boundaries of right." (Analects 2.4)

Wang-sun Chia asked about the saying, "Better pay court to the stove than pay court to the shrine". Confucius said, "It is not true. He who has put himself in the wrong with Heaven has no means of expiation left." (Analects 3.13)

Christianity

Woe unto you, scribes and Pharisees, hypocrites! For ye compass sea and land to make one proselyte, and when he is made, ye make him twofold more the child of hell than yourselves. (Matthew 23:15)

Islam

O man! Verily you are ever toiling on toward your Lord—painfully toiling—but you shall meet Him.... You shall surely travel from stage to stage. (Qur'an 84.6, 19)

I was a secret treasure, and I created the creatures in order that I might be known. (Hadith)

Baha'i Faith

Briefly, the journey of the soul is necessary. The pathway of life is the road which leads to divine knowledge and attainment. Without training and guidance the soul could never progress beyond the conditions of its lower nature, which is ignorant and defective. (Promulgation of Universal Peace, 296)

The purpose of the one true God, exalted be His glory, in revealing Himself unto men is to lay bare those gems that lie hidden within the mine of their true and inmost selves. (Gleanings, 132)

Taoism

Do not try to develop what is natural to man; develop what is natural to Heaven. He who develops Heaven benefits life; he who develops man injures life. (Chuang Tzu 19)

Progress is everywhere apparent in the natural world. Nothing stands still. Everything in nature begins, unfolds, and dies. The cumulative process is also not stagnant, but is evolving from simpler to more complex forms. The purpose of human evolution is found in the knowledge and love of God. "O man! Verily you are ever toiling on toward your Lord—painfully toiling—but you shall meet Him.... You shall surely travel from stage to stage" (Islam. Qur'an 84.6, 19). Anyone who has consciously experienced the love of God has some knowledge of this truth. "I was a secret treasure, and I created the creatures in order that I might be known" (Islam. Hadith). Society is evolving or maturing to more complex forms and within it human beings are evolving their individual capacity to know and love God. "The purpose of the one true God, exalted be His glory, in revealing Himself unto men is to lay bare those gems that lie hidden within the mine of their true and inmost selves" (Baha'i Faith. Gleanings, 132). The purpose of civilization is to aid in the fulfillment of this human purpose. Everything in the universe has been created for the education of humanity in the ways of God.

The processes of civilization are evolutionary but they are directed by purpose. The evolving nature of society as a whole can be viewed as a reflection of the development of individual capacity through the life cycle. Individual responsibility in this process begins and ends with the refinement of self. This world is made for our learning, and we learn by degrees through both success and failure. "By degrees, little by little, from time to time, a wise person should remove his own impurities as a smith removes the dross from silver" (Buddhism. Dhammapada 239).

> The Master said, "At fifteen I set my heart upon learning. At thirty, I had planted my feet upon firm ground. At forty, I no longer suffered from perplexities. At fifty, I know what were the biddings of Heaven. At sixty, I heard them with a docile ear. At seventy, I could follow the dictates of my own heart; for what I desired no longer overstepped the boundaries of right." (Confucianism. Analects 2.4)

The first priority for education is the heart and soul and secondarily, the intellect and talent. If you educate a person in the sciences and arts but do not educate his character, he will likely produce things that are harmful to himself and others. If the first priority in education is the advancement of spiritual perception and sensitivities to life and second the education of the intellect, education will benefit the individual and society. "Do not try to develop what is natural to man; develop what is natural to Heaven. He who develops Heaven benefits life; he who develops man injures life" (Taoism. Chuang Tzu 19). "Wang-sun Chia asked about the saying, 'Better pay court to the stove than pay court to the shrine.' Confucius said, 'It is not true. He who has put himself in the wrong with Heaven has no means of expiation left'" (Confucianism. Analects 3.13).

Excess in religious education can become as harmful as no religious education. The rhetoric and theology of religious instruction can become shrill and negative to the degree that it lacks the compassion born of a relationship with God. An individual genuinely sharing a valued treasure does not need to scare or force the receiver into taking the gift. Children who are abused by religious zealotry are not being given a gift. Further barriers to their experience of the bounties of God are being set before them. "Woe unto you, scribes and Pharisees, hypocrites! For ye compass sea and land to make one proselyte, and when he is made, ye make him twofold more the child of hell than yourselves" (Christianity. Matthew 23:15). Character education must proceed from the inside out. It must be chosen by the individual. The student must be attracted to the benefits of spiritual perception and proximity to the remembrance of God.

Society and Spiritual Maturity

The advancement of individual capacity and of society are integral to each other. The progress of society is dependent upon the maturation of the individual, which in turn is dependent upon the progress of society.

> Briefly, the journey of the soul is necessary. The pathway of life is the road which leads to divine knowledge and attainment. Without training and guidance the soul could never progress beyond the conditions of its lower nature, which is ignorant and defective. (Baha'i Faith. Promulgation of Universal Peace, 296)

Feral children are an extreme example of the impact of a lack of education on an individual. Children who have been deprived of social interaction with other humans, beyond a certain level of physical development, will even be unable to develop adequate language skills. In the normal processes of human social development, we learn to interact within a framework of social conventions and develop our capacities through our personal proclivities and choices. The forces of the individual and those of the social environment contribute to the development of each other. On the one hand, individuals can dramatically impacted society—i.e. celebrated philosophers, scientists, industrialists, entrepreneurs, and educators. On the other, those celebrated individuals could not have developed their potential without the processes of socialization.

Individuals find their purpose in this world in the service of others. "All men have been created to carry forward an ever-advancing civilization" (Baha'i Faith. Gleanings, 58).

The purpose of society is the ongoing development of human capacity. Society progresses by developing the capacities of individuals, who in turn contribute to the progress of the whole. Our efforts to contribute to the unfolding capacities of human society are provided motivation and given direction by our glimpses of the beauty of God. The love of God fortifies and enriches the human heart for service to the world of humanity. "The world stands upon three things: upon the Law, upon worship, and upon showing kindness" (Judaism. Mishnah, Abot 1.2).

– 8 –

RELIGIOUS AND CIVIL LAW

The Law

Christianity

And they sent some of the Pharisees and some of the Herodians, to entrap Jesus in his talk. And they came and said to him, "Teacher, we know that you are true, and care for no man; for you do not regard the position of men, but truly teach the way of God. Is it lawful to pay taxes to Caesar, or not? Should we pay them, or should we not?" But knowing their hypocrisy, he said to them, "Why put me to the test? Bring me a coin, and let me look at it." And they brought one. And he said to them, "Whose likeness and inscription is this?" They said to him, "Caesar's." Jesus said to them, "Render to Caesar the things that are Caesar's, and to God the things that are God's." (Mark 12:13-17)

Confucianism

The moral law is to be found everywhere, and yet it is a secret. The simple intelligence of ordinary men and women of the people may understand something of the moral law; but in its utmost reaches there is something which even the wisest and holiest men cannot understand. The ignoble natures of ordinary men and women of the people may be able to carry out the moral law; but in its utmost reaches even the wisest and holiest of men cannot live up to it. (Doctrine of the Mean 12)

Jainism

The Law is that which leads to welfare and salvation. It forms conduct and character distinguished by the sense of equality among all beings. (Somadeva, Nitivakyamrita 1.1)

Islam

Hearing and obeying [those in government] are the duty of a Muslim both regarding what he likes and what he dislikes, as long as he is not commanded to perform an act of disobedience to God, in which case he must neither hear nor obey. (Hdith of Bukhari)

Ibn 'Umar reported the Prophet as saying, "The sultan is God's shade on earth to which each one of His servants who is wronged repairs. When he is just he will have a reward, and it is the duty of the common people to be grateful; but when he acts tyrannically the burden rests on him, and it is the duty of the common people to show endurance." (Hadith of Baihaqi)

Maintain religion, and do not stir up any divisions within it. (Qur'an 42.13)

Sikhism

By Divine Law are all forms manifested; Inexpressible is the Law. By Divine Law are beings created; by Law are some exalted. By Divine Law are beings marked with nobility or ignominy; by the Law are they visited with bliss or bale. On some by His Law falls grace; others by His Law are whirled around in cycles of births and deaths. All by the Law are governed, none is exempt. Says Nanak, should man realize the power of the Law, he would certainly disclaim his ego. (Adi Granth, Japuji 2, M.1, 1)

Judaism

If two sit together and the words between them are of Torah, then the Shechinah is in their midst. (Mishnah, Abot 3.2)

Rabbi Hanina the deputy of the priests, said, "Pray for the peace of the government; for, except for the fear of that, we should have swallowed each other alive." (Mishnah, Abot 3.2)

Buddhism

Then the people gathered together and lamented, saying, "Evil ways are rife among the people—theft, censure, false speech, and punishment have appeared among us. Let us choose one man from among us, to dispense wrath, censure, and banishment when they are right and proper, and give him a share of our rice in return." So they chose the most handsome, attractive, and capable among them and invited him to dispense anger, censure, and banishment. He consented and did so, and they gave him a share of their rice. (Dgha Nikaya iii.92-93, Agganna Suttanta)

Hinduism

May your counsel be common, your assembly common, common the mind, and the thoughts of these united. A common purpose do I lay before you, and worship with your common oblation. Let your aims be common, and your hearts of one accord, and all of you be of one mind, so you may live well together. (Rig Veda 10.191.2-4)

One should not behave towards others in a way which is disagreeable to oneself. This is the essence of morality. (Mahabharata, Anusasana Parva 113.8)

Taoism

The net of Heaven is cast wide. Though the mesh is not fine, yet nothing ever slips through. (Tao Te Ching 73)

The Messengers of God reveal the social and spiritual laws that provide the basis for harmonious human interactions. These are not just a set of guidelines and procedures for human activity. The Messengers express the eternal law, the word of God. The human spirit can receive the reflections of divine law, but the human mind cannot fully comprehend or in turn express them. "By Divine Law are all forms manifested; Inexpressible is the Law" (Sikhism. Adi Granth, Japuji 2, M.1, 1).

The moral law is to be found everywhere, and yet it is a secret. The simple intelligence of ordinary men and women of the people may understand something of the moral law;

but in its utmost reaches there is something which even the wisest and holiest men cannot understand. The ignoble natures of ordinary men and women of the people may be able to carry out the moral law; but in its utmost reaches even the wisest and holiest of men cannot live up to it. (Confucianism. Doctrine of the Mean 12)

Divine law is the will of God that creates and sustains the particulars of all of creation. "By Divine Law are beings created; by Law are some exalted. By Divine Law are beings marked with nobility or ignominy; by the Law are they visited with bliss or bale. On some by His Law falls grace; others by His Law are whirled around in cycles of births and deaths. All by the Law are governed, none is exempt" (Sikhism. Adi Granth, Japuji 2, M.1, p.1).

With respect to society, divine law is the will of God as it pertains to maintaining our relationship with Him and each other. Our relationships with God and others are linked. The conditions placed on maintaining our relationship with God involve how we behave in our relationships to each other. The primary agreement with God, the covenant with him, requires submission to His will particularly as it pertains to how we treat each other. "The Law is that which leads to welfare and salvation. It forms conduct and character distinguished by the sense of equality among all beings" (Jainism. Somadeva, Nitivakyamrita 1.1).

The implications for this directive to the people of God throughout the world are fairly clear at least in the abstract. Most of us, for example, would agree that we prefer freedom and equality over oppression, education over ignorance, empowerment over helplessness, and wealth over poverty. Difficulties arise with the movement from the abstract to the particular. The world community is very complex. Cultural norms, religious practices and theologies, political allegiances, traditional animosities, geographic limitations, and a host of social circumstances militate against agreement on the best way to implement equal treatment and fairness in political, economic, and social terms. This is generally the case even among those who dedicate their lives to the service of God and humanity within the construct of a particular faith tradition.

Agreement about the directives for human behavior found in scripture is difficult within a given culture, much less across cultures. The admonition against killing, for instance, for some Hindus who cultivate sensitivity to all life, includes insects. In the United States, the implications of the commandment not to kill is culturally manifest in the struggles over the use of capital punishment, the legal right to end one's life, and discussions regarding whether abortion is murder. The diversity of scriptural interpretation reveals the temporal nature underlying the human situation. This is not the realm of the absolute. Our physical natures and everything pertaining to them are temporal. They are imperfect, conditional, and subject to change. The human mind cannot express the will of God. The human spirit or soul may glimpse the perfect beauty of God, but we can only respond imperfectly in the context of human situations.

Assumptions of the legitimacy of absolute positions of right and wrong in the context of the temporal world is a significant barrier to constructive consultation and a cause of considerable conflict among peoples and nations. The problem is exacerbated when political and religious leaders use allegiance to theological or moral absolutes to accomplish personal and political agendas. It results in the division of people over issues that have temporal not absolute solutions.

The primary requirement for effective participation in deliberations aimed at resolving human conflict is that the participants admit their fallibility. None speak for God. We do not know the eternal will of God. "God knows, and you know not" (Islam. Qur'an 16.74). "For that which is esteemed among men is abomination in the sight of God" (Christianity. Luke 16:15). If we are to engage hearts and minds in pursuit of justice, we cannot dictate absolutes to each other as though they are pronouncements of the will of God. Our decisions pertain to the realm of the contingent, the finite. Only God determines reality with absolute decisions. We must trust that God's law will not be threatened by our inadequacies and missteps in the processes of decision-making. "The law and the prophets were until John: since that time the kingdom of God is preached, and every man presseth into it. And it is easier for heaven and earth to pass, than one tittle of the law to fail" (Christianity. Luke 16:16-17). Each person must turn to God for guidance in the processes of negotiating solutions to human problems. God's dominion is not threatened by our imperfect perceptions and actions. For each of us, the pleasure of God's company is conditioned on our willingness to submit to His will and not by our ability to enforce a rigid understanding of it upon our neighbor.

The unity of the peoples of the planet derived from processes of consensus is a higher good than the forced dominance of a particular interpretation of scripture no matter how sophisticated or enlightened. Submission to the will of God and the law of love are primary. "Therefore all things whatsoever ye would that men should do to you, do ye even so to them: for this is the law and the prophets" (Matthew. 7:12). We will learn through choice, consequence, and prayerful effort the ways of building consensus for the maintenance of an increasingly more just, peaceful, and bountiful human community.

Arriving at consensus for action in the context of diverse views and agendas is a proactive expression of the golden rule. In most circumstances, unified human action is more likely to be an expression of the will of God than conflict and warfare. In order to arrive as best we can at the justice implicit in the commandment to love one another, we must develop processes for finding agreement or consensus. Fighting about how to be just in the context of global community is antithetical to the purposes of justice. Agreement about how to integrate the commandments of God into practice for global community requires peaceful deliberations. Overt force and coercion may produce external compliance, but the optimal path to justice requires the independence of hearts and minds to pursue the will of God.

Peer Review

Consensus permits unified action within the infinite reality God has provided for us. Whether establishing consensus through science or scripture, it requires willingness and openness to accept the truth, regardless of predispositions or biases going into the search. "Says Nanak, should man realize the power of the Law, he would certainly disclaim his ego" (Sikhsim. Adi Granth, Japuji 2, M.1, p.1).

Selfless objectivity is required of anyone researching some aspect of the physical world as well as seeking an understanding of the law of God. Good science as well as good spiritual understanding requires a selfless perspective. Allegiance to the truth is productive for both science and religion. Reality is unified; science and religion are reflections of that unity in the realms of the human mind and spirit respectively.

In the scientific realm, consensus is achieved through experimentation and reporting processes that employ mechanisms of peer review. The models, concepts, and theories developed regarding the ways things work are based on integrity in experimentation and reporting that is repeatable and can be examined by other scientists. All individual efforts are submitted to the scrutiny of other researchers.

The underlying unity of science and religion, the mind and the spirit, provides a basis for religionists in their efforts to find consensus for scriptural interpretation. Peer review processes and conceptual frameworks similar to those used in scientific discovery are also productive for the resolution of practical conflicts associated with scriptural interpretation. The unified nature of reality dictates the holistic integration of mind and spirit—science and religion. Religious understanding must be in harmony with reason and the findings of science. For the institutions of religion, the use of processes similar to peer review can assist articulation of spiritual principles into the institutions of society, regardless of particular cultural or theological biases and predispositions.

For the researcher, personal commitment to the truth, regardless of bias, is required for the integrity of research and reporting. In religious discussions, concepts of theology and right and wrong behavior need to be subject to a personal commitment to the truth as understood through scripture as well as through scientific observation. Humility before God and His creation permits parity with others in discussions concerning scriptural interpretation. An individual's understanding of scripture must bear open discussion just as an individual's research is subject to evaluation by other researchers. Individuals participating in resolution of human conflict must acknowledge that they do not speak for God or His Messengers with any finality, even as a scientist cannot claim ownership of an absolute description of reality. Nor are religionists responsible for insuring compliance with a particular view of the will of God just as individual scientists are not responsible for enforcing a particular view of reality.

Religionists and scientists must, in the context of this contingent reality, rely on processes of consensus-building. The prerogatives associated with revealing absolute reality to human beings belong to God. Individuals need not take over this responsibility for God and act in His stead. Consensus requires finding agreement despite diverse perspectives rather than conforming or forcing conformance to one inflexible concept of reality.

In this day, as science and religion must both be employed for the benefit of society, all participants need to admit that they do not speak as the author of reality, concede that God speaks to every human heart, and not assume to know how well someone is listening. Ours is but to construct decisions through consultation that reflect our best efforts at finding justice in the temporal realms of reality. Acceptance of this basic rule for pursuance of the will of God releases individuals to participate whole-heartedly with peers in arriving at the best solutions available. It also permits the integrated use of science and religion, reason and spiritual insight, in the pursuit of a healthier more just human community.

Unity as a Primary Value

Unity provides the most efficient political mechanism for problem-solving in the social, political, and economic aspects of society. The primacy of unity in processes of consultation can be extrapolated from the golden rule. Basing decision-making on the ability to value others as we value ourselves is a spiritual perspective. It is also a practical perspective. An underlying principle associated with effective consultation is the value placed on unity, even more than being "right." This principle derives from recognizing the value of human life over the assumption of absolutely right or wrong positions. The selection of peaceful over bellicose methods of resolving conflict is based on the value of human life and well being over dominance in the resolution of conflicting opinions.

The principle is reflected in the use of majority rule; however, voting is a fairly crude mechanism for arriving at agreements. Consensus of opinion is preferable to an up or down vote in the resolution of most problems. Arriving at consensus through deliberations obviates the need to choose between or among conflicting solutions to a problem. The actual articulation of justice into the processes of governance is aided by frank discussion of issues that results in a consensus of opinion that includes all of the perspectives. If, however, consensus does not evolve from deliberations and a vote must be taken, the majority position is the next best alternative. If a consensus solution is not available, the fallback position requires a willingness to abide by the majority perspective.

The individuals who hold a minority perspective must abide in good faith by the majority view even if they truly believe that it is not the best way to proceed. Avoidance of anarchy or armed rebellion is the obvious reason to go along, but the principle has further practical outcomes. Supporting a position with which you disagree affords an opportunity for the proposal to succeed or fail on its own merit. If it succeeds, the end is accomplished. If it fails, the group will need to take another look at alternative solutions. The group will likely waste less time in making a course correction if there was wholehearted support of implementation rather than resistance. Resistance increases the difficulty of determining if the proposal failed because it was faulty or because it was sabotaged.

The limits to the practical benefits of majority rule are reached with decisions that result in more destruction to human life and well being than resistance would impart. Tyranny of the majority will be avoided to the extent that the minority perspective has a respected and effective voice. Social order is based on justice and equality. The processes of governance will be successful at providing harmonious and productive environments to the degree that they provide for the discovery of consensus solutions to social, political, and economic conflicts. "Take away from me the noise of your songs; To the melody of your harps I will not listen. But let justice roll down like waters, and righteousness like an ever-flowing stream" (Judaism. Amos 5.23-24).

Render Unto Caesar

Basing civil law in the will of God requires that none of the participants in consultation assumes the ability to speak for God. Realization of the relative nature of scriptural interpretation with respect to human understanding provides the central argument for the separation of church and state. It is a mechanism for protecting the independence of the individual to pursue truth in both the spiritual and temporal realms. Separation of church and state is an integral component of an environment of consensus-building because it ensures the independent investigation of truth. The laws of society must be based on political consensus-building processes that require the freedom of the individual to participate independently. Political freedom has its roots in religious freedom. This principle is acknowledged in the modern world in the context of societies that are evolving democratic institutions. It is by no means completely resolved as an issue for global community, even in modern democratic societies. For this reason, it needs continued support as a tenet of global community.

Sanction for the separation of church and state and its corollary, the independent investigation of truth, can be derived from the guidance of the Messengers of the various faith traditions. It is seen in their advice with respect to the relationship of their followers to civil law. For example, Jesus was confronted by the Pharisees over the issue of paying taxes. His response to them is instructive with respect to resolving the tension between religious and civil authorities.

> And they sent some of the Pharisees and some of the Herodians, to entrap Jesus in his talk. And they came and said to him, "Teacher, we know that you are true, and care for no man; for you do not regard the position of men, but truly teach the way of God. Is it lawful to pay taxes to Caesar, or not? Should we pay them, or should we not?" But knowing their hypocrisy, he said to them, "Why put me to the test? Bring me a coin, and let me look at it." And they brought one. And he said to them, "Whose likeness and inscription is this?" They said to him, "Caesar's." Jesus said to them, "Render to Caesar the things that are Caesar's, and to God the things that are God's." (Christianity. Mark 12:13-17)

The Pharisees were interested in discrediting Jesus by pitting Him against Rome. The Romans were an occupying force. Many Jews were expecting a Messiah who would conquer the Romans. Jesus would lose credibility among the more militant population if He were to side with obedience to civil law. He would be in trouble with the Herodians if He spoke against paying taxes to Caesar. Jesus' statements support civil authority. However, He put it in the context of the will of God. The inscription on the coin was Caesar's. It, therefore, came under the authority of Caesar. However,

God is the all possessing. Caesar and everything within his domain belong to God. However, Jesus was not just trying to keep both sides happy. He was making a distinction between the civil and religious authority. He instructed the Pharisees that, in this contingent world, respect for civil law is required.

Jesus provided another equally important teaching concerning religious and civil law in this interaction. He reproved the Pharisees for putting Him to the test. Religious leaders should not put people in conflict with civil authority. Nor should they use the religion of God to foster disunity in the furtherance of their short-sighted agendas. "Maintain religion, and do not stir up any divisions within it" (Islam. Qur'an 42.13). The litmus test for measuring the legitimacy of those who would advance the will of God and prosperity of humankind is whether they provide constructive guidance. Jesus addressed the Pharisees at a time of conflict between the Roman Empire and the Jewish people. He promoted love and unity between Jew and Gentile and thereby established a path for the eventual reconciliation of the conflict. Through His followers over the next few hundred years, that solitary, humble Jew conquered Rome with His message of conciliation and established western civilization as we understand it today. Many in the Jewish community at the time who rejected His message of peace went on to promote armed rebellion against the Roman Empire. They did not succeed.

Submission to Civil Law

The Messengers of God have always submitted to civil law and instructed their followers to do the same. They have promoted harmonious cooperation. None have promoted anarchy. The following passage from Buddhism refers to the benefits and methods of governance.

> Then the people gathered together and lamented, saying, "Evil ways are rife among the people—theft, censure, false speech, and punishment have appeared among us.

Let us choose one man from among us, to dispense wrath, censure, and banishment when they are right and proper, and give him a share of our rice in return." So they chose the most handsome, attractive, and capable among them and invited him to dispense anger, censure, and banishment. He consented and did so, and they gave him a share of their rice. (Buddhism. Dgha Nikaya iii.92-93, *Agganna Suttanta*)

In the following verse from Hinduism, the common purpose set before human society is the harmony of the community.

May your counsel be common, your assembly common, common the mind, and the thoughts of these united. A common purpose do I lay before you, and worship with your common oblation. Let your aims be common, and your hearts of one accord, and all of you be of one mind, so you may live well together. (Hinduism. *Rig Veda* 10.191.2-4)

Support for government as distinct from the functions of religious institutions is in evidence in the following passages from Judaism and Islam.

Rabbi Hanina the deputy of the priests, said, "Pray for the peace of the government; for, except for the fear of that, we should have swallowed each other alive." (Judaism. Mishnah, *Abot* 3.2)

Hearing and obeying [those in government] are the duty of a Muslim both regarding what he likes and what he dislikes, as long as he is not commanded to perform an act of disobedience to God, in which case he must neither hear nor obey. (Islam. Hdith of Bukhari)

Obedience to governance is conditioned on the will of God in the above quote from Islamic texts. The individual is first responsible to God and then to civil authorities. This is not a statement of the prerogatives of the institutions of religion with respect to civil authorities. The institutions of religion must submit to civil authority. It is a statement referring to the responsibilities of the individuals in listening to their consciences. The independent investigation of truth is established in the conscience of the individual before God, not the institutions of religion.

Religious freedom as expressed in the individual's pursuit of truth is required for fruitful civil governance. The prerequisite to fruitful outcomes for human interaction is the submission of the individual to the will of God. God provides access to His guidance for any individual who humbly submits his own self before Him. No human being could be held accountable before God if this were not the case. It follows that the individual should listen first to guidance from God while considering the needs of the community. The corollary to the independence of the individual in seeking the truth before God is the responsibility of the individual in the processes of governance. It is the process that flows from sublimating self-insistence in problem-solving first to God and then to the well being of the community. It is the basis for effective consultation and consensus-building.

Conflict and contention can best be resolved through earnest and straightforward discussion in which the individuals risk their own ideas and agendas in the pursuit of justice. The key requirement is to resist taking over the prerogatives of God with respect to the other individuals in the process. The guidance obtained from communion with God is personal. It is not necessarily appropriate for another individual. We are not the intermediaries of the relationship between God and anyone else. Creative solutions are forged from the fire of conflict to the degree that the participants detach themselves from their positions for the sake of God. "God knows, and you know not" (Islam. Qur'an 16.74).

Submission to God in the context of conflict resolution assists in letting go of the tendency to view our positions as absolutes and opens our perspective to the realization of the other as we realize our selves. It provides a glimpse of the primary value of our being—a glimpse of unity. A particular solution is always temporal. When there is a conflict between our positions and unity of action, unity is preferable because it is a reflection of the value of our underlying unity in reality. The act of submission to God in the processes of consultation has the power to transform the contrary positions of opponents into cooperative solutions. It interjects selfless sincerity and respect into the conversation. In the context of the current global community, sincere consultation is a powerful tool for the resolution of conflict at every level of human endeavor in the political, economic, social, and religious spheres. The actions, positions, and statements of individuals are likely to be fruitful to the degree that self-insistence is submitted to the will of God in the context of consultation. Selfless sincerity is a compelling force for opening hearts and minds to alternative solutions. "You will know them by their fruits" (Christianity. Matthew 7:20).

Religious Unity

Global social order requires the assistance of religion at spiritual and practical levels. Religion as articulated by the Messengers of God is a mechanism for unity and cooperation. It provides the underlying structures for human social order at every level of consciousness and activity. Religion advances the truest interests of humankind. It is the upholder of human progress, advancement, and fulfillment. Religions throughout history have provided the social mainspring for cooperative order. The purpose of religion is human well being and prosperity, not conflict and destruction.

Religions have advanced the social organization of human society through stages of cooperation. Tribal ways of social life gave way to those of the city-state, which in turn gave way to those of the nation. We are now in the process of building global governance structures. The process requires the assistance of religion. It is in its unifying, cooperative nature rather than the condemnatory, insular, and defensive proclivities of some of its adherents that religion will assist this final stage of social unity on the earth. Religious leadership should promote inclusion rather than exclusion and reach for common ground rather than promote alienation and conflict. Inclusion brings individuals under the protection of the cooperative mechanisms of religion. Exclusion sets a course toward mistrust, fear, and hostility. The prerequisite to the use of religion's civilizing influence in today's multi-religious world is the recognition of the underlying unity of religions.

Happy is the unity of the Sangha. Happy is the discipline of the united ones. (Buddhism. Dhammapada 194)

One thing, when it comes to pass, does so to the loss, to the unhappiness of many folk...to the misery of the gods and humankind. What is that one thing? Schism in the order of monks. (Buddhism. Itivuttaka 11)

O contending peoples and kindreds of the earth! Set your faces toward unity, and let the radiance of its light shine upon you. Gather ye together, and for the sake of God resolve to root out whatever is the source of contention among you. Then will the effulgence of the world's great Luminary envelop the whole earth, and its inhabitants become the citizens of one city, and the occupants of one and the same throne. (Baha'i Faith. Gleanings, 111)

Now is the gracious Lord's ordinance promulgated, no one shall cause another pain or injury; all mankind shall live in peace together, under a shield of administrative benevolence. (Sikhism. Adi Granth, Sri Raga, M.5, 74)

When the right principles of man operate, the growth of good government is rapid, and when the right principles of soil operate, the growth of vegetables is rapid. Indeed, government is comparable to a fast-growing plant. Therefore the conduct of government depends upon the men. The right men are obtained by the ruler's personal character. The cultivation of the person is to be done through the Way, and the cultivation of the Way is to be done through benevolence. (Confucianism. Doctrine of the Mean 20)

The Temporal and Eternal Aspects of the Law

To the degree that the adherents of the various religions of the world use their view of religious orthodoxy to condemn those who profess a different faith, religion becomes the cause of disunity. The directives for human behavior in the various scriptures of the world's religions that are most likely to come into conflict are those addressing the particular needs of their respective cultures. If religious social laws and observances are absolutes, then one set of laws given through one Messenger is right, all the rest are wrong, and conflict over which is the right one is inevitable. The other possibility is that all of the Messengers are harbingers of the same eternal truth and provide particular guidance, not in absolute terms, but relative to the social needs of the times. The Messengers provide both an articulation of the eternal verities like the golden rule, which are in agreement in all of the scriptures, and guidance that was particular to the requirements of the day. The differences in the laws have to do primarily with the exigencies of the times and cultures that the Messengers addressed.

For instance, the laws associated with the dispensation of Moses applied to a people wandering in the desert. A nomadic people cannot build prisons. Responses to criminal activity like stealing would need to take this into consideration. Religious dispensations address the particular social circumstances of evolving human civilization. There are cultural and behavioral differences in the particulars of what constitutes social justice in the context of evolving human society. Though important, the differences are not absolutes and are not worth fighting over given the agreement in the world's scriptures over the fundamental verities which are mutually supportive.

When viewed in the context of a shared evolution of humanity on this planet, the religious and cultural differences associated with the last ten thousand years constitute a thin veneer. They are even less significant than the genetic variations that show up in skin, hair, and eye color. The superficial differences that we associate with biological differences do not constitute enough genetic difference to predict the similarity of the DNA belonging to any two individuals on the planet. For example, a woman in sub-Saharan Africa might have less in common genetically with her next door neighbor with whom she shares a cultural history than a woman living in China.

Though science can demonstrate the inconsequential nature of our "racial" differences in the context of their numerical and biological insignificance compared to the rest of our DNA, racially based prejudice and discrimination are rampant in human society. Religious differences that derive from the exigencies of the times that their respective Messengers were addressing are also not significant when compared to our underlying religious and spiritual unity.

While the attitudes associated with both racial and religious prejudices may resist change, the civil institutions of society must be based on equality before the law and need to guard the individual from all manner of discrimination including religious. The resolution of conflict in the affairs of the peoples of the various religious traditions requires submission to civil law as separate from submission to religious law. The institutions associated with civil law provide the mechanism for building consensus concerning truths derived from both physical and spiritual laws. The individual's freedom of religion and the right to the independent investigation of truth are the underlying principles that argue for the submission of religious institutions to civil law. The institutions of religion need to respect the rights of individuals to search for truth and choose their religious affiliation and therefore must accept the separation of church and state.

However, the need for the separation of religious and civil institutions is lessened and potentially obviated to the degree that the institutions of religion promote the individual's right to the independent investigation of truth with respect to both science and religion. Similar to the requirement for an open dialog between scientific and spiritual perception for the development of a healthy society, there should be a similar ongoing discussion over the relationship between civil and religious institutions.

– 9 –

CHANGING NEEDS

Marriage: An Example

Buddhism

Now she who's called: a mistress, slayer, thief, who's harsh, immoral, lacking in respect, when death comes will wander in the miseries of hell. But mother, sister or companion, slave, in precept long established and restrained, when death comes will wander in the happy heaven world. These, Sujata, are the seven kinds of wives a man may have; and which of them are you? "Lord," said Sujata, "let the Exalted One think of me as a handmaid from this day forth." (Anguttara Nikaya iv.91, Sujata Sutta)

If fearless of the lash and stick, unmoved, all things enduring, calm, and pure in heart, she bear obedience to her husband's word, from anger free—call that wife a handmaid! (Anguttara Nikaya iv.91, Sujata Sutta)

Confucianism

The moral man finds the moral law beginning in the relation between man and woman, but ending in the vast reaches of the universe. (Doctrine of the Mean 12)

In the family women's appropriate place is within; men's without. When men and women keep their proper places they act in accord with Heaven's great norm. Among the members of the family are the dignified master and mistress whom we term father and mother. When father, mother, sons elder and younger brothers all act in a manner suited to their various positions within the family, when husbands play their proper role and wives are truly wifely, the way of that family runs straight. It is by the proper regulation of each family that the whole world is stabilized. (I Ching 37: The Family)

Christianity

He who loves his wife loves himself. For no man ever hates his own flesh, but nourishes it and cherishes it, as Christ does the church, because we are members of his body. "For this reason a man shall leave his father and mother and be joined to his wife, and the two shall become one flesh." This mystery is a profound one, and I am saying that it refers to Christ and the church; however, let each one of you love his wife as himself, and let the wife see that she respects her husband. (Ephesians 5:27-33)

It is well for a man not to touch a woman. But because of the temptation to immorality, each man should have his own wife and each woman her own husband. (1 Corinthians 7:1)

Be subject to one another out of reverence for Christ. Wives, be subject to your husbands, as to the Lord. For the husband is the head of the wife as Christ is the head of the church, his body, and is himself its Savior. As the church is subject to Christ, so let wives also be subject in everything to their husbands. (Ephesians 5:21-23)

Hinduism

The possession of many wives undermines a man's moral nature. (Srimad Bhagavatam 11.3)

The husband who wedded her with sacred texts always gives happiness to his wife, both in season or out of season. Though he may be destitute of virtue, or seek his pleasure elsewhere, or devoid of good qualities, yet a husband must be constantly revered as a god by a faithful wife. Women need perform no sacrifice, no vow, no fast; if she obeys her husband, she will for that reason alone be exalted in heaven. A faithful wife, who desires to dwell after death with her husband, must never do anything that might displease him who took her hand, whether he be alive or dead....She who, controlling her thoughts, words, and deeds, never slights her lord, resides after death with her husband in heaven, and is called a virtuous wife. (Laws of Manu 5.153-65)

I am He, you are She; I am Song, you are Verse, I am Heaven, you are Earth. We two shall here together dwell, becoming parents of children. (Atharva Veda 14.2.71)

Islam

All of you are guardians and are responsible for your wards. The ruler is a guardian; the man is a guardian of his family; the lady is a guardian and is responsible for her husband's house and his offspring; and so all of you are guardians and are responsible for your wards. (Hadith of Bukhari)

"Your wife has rights over you," said the Prophet, according to Abu Juhaifa. (Hadith of Bukhari)

Your wives are as a tilth to you; so approach your tilth when or how you will; but do some good act for your souls beforehand, and fear God. (Qur'an 2.223)

You will not be able to deal equally between your wives, however much you wish to do so. (Qur'an 4.129)

Among His signs is that He created spouses for you among yourselves that you may console yourselves with them. He has planted affection and mercy between you. (Qur'an 30.21)

Judaism

A man is forbidden to compel his wife to her marital duty. (Talmud, Erubin 100b)

He who loves his wife as himself; who honors her more than himself; who rears his children in the right path, and who marries them off at the proper time of their life, concerning him it is written: "And you will know that your home is at peace." (Talmud, Yebamot 62)

The Lord God said, "It is not good that the man should be alone; I will make him a helper fit for him." (Genesis 2.18)

Sikhism

Not those are true husband and wife that with each other [merely] consort: Truly wedded are those that in two frames, are as one light. (Adi Granth, Var Suhi, M.3. 788)

Native American Religions

Do not abuse your wife. Women are sacred. If you make your wife suffer, you will die in a short time. Our grandmother, Earth, is a woman, and in abusing your wife you are abusing her. By thus abusing our grandmother, who takes care of us, by your action you will be practically killing yourself. (A Winnebago Father's Precepts)

African Traditional Religions

Whoever has many wives will have troubles in surfeit. He will be deceitful, he will lie, he will betray [some of them] to have them together; It is not certain that he can have peace to pray well. (Yoruba Poem. Nigeria)

Marriage: an Example

In the current transition to global culture, a great deal of conflict is generated by the changing roles of women in the social order and its impact on societal institutions and individual marital relationships. One of the characteristics of the economically and technologically advanced environs of global community is the ascendancy of women in the social order. As the world's diverse cultures integrate into the modern world, the roles of women tend toward equity with men in the institutions of society including marriage. The cultural norms and expectations for marriage are a pivotal example of the difficulties likely to be encountered as globalization intrudes with accelerating frequency on local cultural mores. The change in customs involves religion because it appears to clash with the specific scriptural guidance from the major faith traditions.

Gender roles are intimately related to the particulars of scriptural advice within the various religious dispensations represented in the modern world. The encroachment of modern social advances like gender equity on cultural terrain once ruled by age-old religious orthodoxies is an example of the challenge that globalization presents to the institutions of religion and vice versa. As a step toward understanding the role of religion in the transition to global community, the following is an examination of the nature of the guidance received from the Messengers of the various faiths concerning men and women.

As has been addressed earlier, the various scriptures articulate two types of guidance—the eternal unchanging verities and the more practical directives appropriate to the needs of the times. They all provide practical laws particular to the circumstances of the people being addressed. For example, Judaic law provided guidance for how thieves were to be treated in the context of nomadic societies that could not build prisons—under certain circumstances a hand might be removed. It was not guidance intended for modern societies but guidance particular to the limitations of an earlier stage of social development.

From the vantage point of today's societal and political requirements, the specific advice of the Messengers addressing the needs of the past may appear to be defective. The modern sensibilities associated with gender equity, as another example, are offended by the harsh realities that were seemingly condoned by the Messengers of past religious dispensations. The particular laws appropriate to the past could be considered defective if articulated for these times. Messengers have provided guidance for the various stages of human social development. If human society were static, only one Messenger would have been required. Since it is progressive, Messengers appear periodically to address the exigencies of evolving cultures. The essential spiritual teachings remain the same. An examination of the guidance concerning marriage from the various dispensations provides an example of the difference between the practical and essential guidance and also points out the need for new guidance for the changing gender roles relevant to the current needs of a global community.

The fundamental teachings from which the particulars emerge are common to all the scriptures. The Messengers rearticulate the eternal spiritual laws. As discussed earlier, each dispensation has an iteration of the golden rule as the central tenet governing human behavior. The core directive for the relationship of marriage is an iteration of the golden rule. The participants should love each other as they love themselves. "Not those are true husband and wife that with each other [merely] consort: Truly wedded are those that in two frames, are as one light" (Sikhism. Adi Granth, Var Suhi, M.3.p.788). "The moral man finds the moral law beginning in the relation between man and woman, but ending in the vast reaches of the universe" (Confucianism. Doctrine of the Mean 12).

Although the central tenet of all of the faith traditions direct men and women to love in their personal relationships, the parameters of gender roles in society and the nature of the institution of marriage have been addressed by the various faith traditions with a variety of culturally specific injunctions. Different societal circumstances have dictated very different arrangements for marriages and the provisions for children. Monogamy is the preferred relationship articulated in the context of most of the faith traditions in the modern world, but other arrangements have been sanctioned. Though polygamy has been common, having multiple husbands has also been sanctioned in some societies. Even within traditions prescribing or preferring monogamy, views on the relationship have been very different. The following scriptural passages support monogamy but they do it from very different perspectives.

> The possession of many wives undermines a man's moral nature. (Hinduism. Srimad Bhagavatam 11.3)

> You will not be able to deal equally between your wives, however much you wish to do so. (Islam. Qur'an 4.129)

> It is well for a man not to touch a woman. But because of the temptation to immorality, each man should have his own wife and each woman her own husband. (Christianity. 1 Corinthians 7:1)

Male Dominance

Most of the religious institutions over recorded history have been dominated by male proclivities, values, and perspectives. Modern sensibilities concerning gender equity view the apparent sanction by religious institutions of male dominance as backward. For many in today's modern societies, this casts a shadow on the integrity of the Messengers of God through whom those institutions claim their legitimacy. The following passages are examples of the scriptural description of gender roles that support male superiority.

> Be subject to one another out of reverence for Christ. Wives, be subject to your husbands, as to the Lord. For the husband is the head of the wife as Christ is the head of the church, his body, and is himself its Savior. As the church is subject to Christ, so let wives also be subject in everything to their husbands. (Christianity. Ephesians 5:21)

> All of you are guardians and are responsible for your wards. The ruler is a guardian; the man is a guardian of his family; the lady is a guardian and is responsible for her husband's house and his offspring; and so all of you are guardians and are responsible for your wards. (Islam. Hadith of Bukhari)

> In the family women's appropriate place is within; men's without. When men and women keep their proper places they act in accord with Heaven's great norm. Among the members of the family are the dignified master and mistress whom we term father and mother. When father, mother, sons elder and younger brothers all act in a manner suited to their various positions within the family, when husbands play their proper role and wives are truly wifely, the way of that family runs straight. It is by the proper regulation of each family that the whole world is stabilized. (Confucianism. I Ching 37: The Family)

> I am He, you are She; I am Song, you are Verse, I am Heaven, you are Earth. We two shall here together dwell, becoming parents of children. (Hinduism. Atharva Veda 14.2.71)

The nature of the developmental stages of social order and its relationship to the obvious dominance of men in the institutions of society is a very complex phenomenon and will likely be a subject of interest and of scholarly exploration for a long time to come. The nature of the guidance of the Messengers in this regard is even more abstruse.   It is, nevertheless, reasonable to attempt a tentative understanding by viewing the guidance from the Messengers of God as particular to the capacities of the times.

The relationship of male and female has a long complex evolutionary history. They have separate evolutionary paths because their biological roles are different. Yet the developmental paths are integrally related. Their separate evolutions are dependent on each other and the physical differences between male and female are integral to the development of social roles. For example, men generally have stronger upper body strength and have therefore been physically dominant. It could be argued that this physical dominance is the primary cause of male dominance in most of the institutions of society. Regardless of the particulars of the origins of dominance in the structures of society, the world's spiritual Messengers have prescribed social behaviors that were appropriate for the various stages of cultural maturation.

It is further helpful to realize that the guidance does not cause or excuse the apparent injustice and abuse associated with gender differences. The Messengers do not sanction injustice. Their lives and primary teachings are a template for justice. However, their guidance is not always followed. Guidance from God is limited by the hearer not the speaker. We are given a degree of freedom in this world to accept or reject the guidance of the Messengers.

The primary guidance from the Messengers has never condoned abusive relationships. The core teachings of all of the Messengers concern love and respect. The advice given has always optimized the benevolent outcomes prescribed for the limitations of the times. Some of the world's scriptures specifically address the abuse that is likely in the male dominated stages of societal evolution. They acknowledge the plight of women in the social order and recognize the possibilities of oppression integral to their situations.

The *Sujata Sutta* is an example from Buddhist scripture. It tells the story of a young woman recently married who is not happy in her new role in her husband's household. She rebels against the situation. She has a conversation with the Blessed One, the Buddha, who instructs her in the seven types of wives: mistress, slayer, thief, mother, sister, companion, and slave. After describing their characteristics He assigns the seven types to two groups—those who would be happy in the next life and those that would be miserable and asks her which of the seven types of wives she would choose to be.

> Now she who's called: a mistress, slayer, thief, who's harsh, immoral, lacking in respect, when death comes will wander in the miseries of hell. But mother, sister or companion, slave, in precept long established and restrained, when death comes will wander in the happy heaven world.

> These, Sujata, are the seven kinds of wives a man may have; and which of them are you? "Lord," said Sujata, "let the Exalted One think of me as a handmaid from this day forth." (Buddhism, Anguttara Nikaya iv.91, Sujata Sutta)

Sujata responded by acknowledging that she was a slave and would be contented. This description of the handmaid or slave is that of a martyr. The Buddha describes her as "fearless of the lash and stick, unmoved, all things enduring, calm, and pure in heart, she bears obedience to her husband's word, from anger free—call that wife a handmaid!" (Buddhism, Anguttara Nikaya iv.91, Sujata Sutta). The Buddha was acknowledging the limits of her situation and instructing her in the outcomes of the choice that was before her. The type of husband a woman ended up with was dependent on her family situation. If she were married to an abusive man whose family contributed to her pain and suffering, she was a slave. Her choice was what she would do about it—rebel or submit. The situation was not just, particularly from the vantage point of modern social sensibilities. It was brutal. If she wanted to be independent, her options were that of a prostitute, a thief, or a murderer. This path was prone to anger and hate and would be carried with her into the next life. The Buddha presented her with her options. She decided to make the best of a bad situation.

Some might interpret these passages of the scriptures as permission for men to abuse their wives because the Buddha had acknowledged the situation and put the onus on the woman to "correct" her behavior. Comparing this particular advice from the Buddha to His primary advice as articulated in the golden rule argues for a different interpretation. The husband should treat his wife with the love and respect which he would want to have. He chose to be abusive. The Buddha provided the woman with the optimal path for her own happiness given the limits of her situation. In the context of modern societies, social activism would seem to be better advice. In the context of Sujata's times, social activism was not a realistic option. This passage of scripture was instructing women in the optimal path for their own happiness under the circumstances.

Jesus offers similar advice to His followers concerning how to respond to people who are their enemies and treat them unjustly. His directive to love our enemies does not condone injustice. It is advice on how to effectively address it.

Passages from Hindu scripture provide another example of the harsh reality for women within the institutions of male dominated societies. No matter what kind of husband a woman has, she must treat him as her lord. The situation again is described in the terms of martyrdom. Obedience on the part of a wife to her husband is reason alone for admission to heaven. This is no small accomplishment. It is again similar to the injunction of Christ to "love your enemies" and "turn the other cheek."

The husband who wedded her with sacred texts always gives happiness to his wife, both in season or out of season. Though he may be destitute of virtue, or seek his pleasure elsewhere, or devoid of good qualities, yet a husband must be constantly revered as a god by a faithful wife. Women need perform no sacrifice, no vow, no fast; if she obeys her husband, she will for that reason alone be exalted in heaven. A faithful wife, who desires to dwell after death with her husband, must never do anything that might displease him who took her hand, whether he be alive or dead....She who, controlling her thoughts, words, and deeds, never slights her lord, resides after death with her husband in heaven, and is called a virtuous wife. (Hinduism. Laws of Manu 5.153-65)

The Centrality of Marriage to Society

The relationship of the husband and wife is at the base of the social order and is of central concern to religion. For example, in the Christian dispensation, the marital relationship is used as a metaphor for the relationship of Christ to His church. Paul calls the relationship between a man and a woman similar to that of the Messenger to His followers. The religion of a particular culture is its source of order and well being. Christ referred to Himself as the "Bread of Life." He gives sustenance to the individual personally through prayer and meditation and by creating social institutions optimal for the development of human capacity.

He who loves his wife loves himself. For no man ever hates his own flesh, but nourishes it and cherishes it, as Christ does the church, because we are members of his body. "For this reason a man shall leave his father and mother and be joined to his wife, and the two shall become one flesh." This mystery is a profound one, and I am saying that it refers to Christ and the church; however, let each one of you love his wife as himself, and let the wife see that she respects her husband. (Christianity. Ephesians 5:21-33)

The focus of the mystery is selfless love. Love is the central requirement for the relationship to be just in this temporal world. The spiritual relationship is the union of equals at their essence, but they are not the same in the context of the temporal world. Paul admonishes them to different roles as provider and supporter. The one gives sustenance; the other is submissive.

Where Do We Go from Here?

The acceptance of subservient social and marital roles for women in the former dispensations is one of the many signs that humankind is in need of new guidance. The changes evident in every aspect of human life as the world's separate cultures converge into a global culture beg for guidance from God. Among the myriad changes in today's world that cause the souls of humankind to seek understanding from God, the changing role of women is one of the most significant and urgent. The greater physical strength associated with male dominance in the earlier stages of social development loses its primacy in the new environs of global cultural. Technology has obviated any advantage that bodily strength once provided for the security of society. Intellectual, organizational, and communication skills become far more significant to the security of society in the complex economic and political provinces of global community. In these arenas, women compete favorably with men as is evidenced in modern society by the greater number of women taking advantage of higher education and succeeding in business ventures as well as their increasing ascendancy in the political realms. The independence gained by these advances results in the restructuring of the marital relationship and with it the structure and function of the family as the primary unit responsible for social continuity and order.

Part II of this work directs attention to the Baha'i dispensation as the fulfillment of the needs of these times for spiritual guidance. The Baha'i Faith reaffirms the spiritual verities articulated in all of the world's religions and provides guidance specific to these times. The guidance includes specific directives addressing the equality of men and women in the institutions of society and in the marital relationship.

In the Baha'i dispensation, marriage is described as a "fortress for well being." The two individuals are equal partners who independently and willingly initiate and sustain the relationship through frank, open, and loving consultation in submission to the will of God. Equality in the relationship is integral to their equality and independence in the context of the greater institutions of society.

The Baha'i marriage vow, "we will all verily abide by the will of God," places the relationship on the foundation of trust in God. Willing submission to the will of God is the underlying prerequisite to human well being. The bounty and beauty of God are available to us to the degree that we accept His terms for its provision. This is true for the individual and for human society at large and particularly the basic societal unit, the family.

Before discussing some of the other teachings of the Baha'i Faith, the next chapter examines passages of the world's scriptures that address the cataclysmic changes occurring in modern times.

– 10–

THE END OF CHILDHOOD

The End of Childhood

Judaism

> For the windows of heaven are opened,
> and the foundations of the earth tremble.
> The earth is utterly broken,
> the earth is rent asunder,
> the earth is violently shaken.
> The earth staggers like a drunken man,
> it sways like a hut;
> its transgression lies heavy upon it,
> and it falls, and will not rise again.
> On that day the Lord will punish
> The hosts of heaven, in heaven,
> And the kings of the earth, on the earth.
> They will be gathered together as prisoners in a pit;
> They will be shut up in a prison,
> And after many days they will be punished.
> The moon will be confounded,
> And the sun ashamed;
> For the Lord of hosts will reign on Mount Zion and
> in Jerusalem
> And before its elders he will manifest his glory.
> (Isaiah 24.18-23)

Islam

When the Trumpet shall sound one blast and the earth with its mountains shall be lifted up and crushed with one crash, then, on that day, will the Event befall. Heaven will split asunder, for that day it will be frail, the angels will be on its sides, and eight will uphold the Throne of their Lord that day above them, On that day you will be exposed; not a secret of yours will be hidden. Then, as for him who is given his record in his right hand, he will say, "Take, read my book! Surely I knew that I should have to meet my reckoning." Then he will be in blissful state in a high Garden whose clusters are in easy reach. [They will say to him,] "Eat and drink at ease for that you sent on before you in past days." But as for him who is given his record in his left hand, he will say, "Oh, would that I had not been given my book and know not what my reckoning! Oh, would that it had been death! My wealth has not availed me, my power has gone from me." "Take him and fetter him and then expose him to hellfire. Then insert him in a chain of seventy cubits' length. Lo! He used not to believe in God the Tremendous, and urged not on the feeding of the wretched, therefore has he no lover here this day, nor any food save filth which none but sinners eat." (Qur'an 69. 13-37)

Buddhism

In the evil age to come, living beings will decrease in good qualities and increase in utter arrogance, coveting gain and honors, developing their evil qualities, and being far removed from deliverance. (Lotus Sutra 13)

Christianity

For our knowledge is imperfect and our prophecy is imperfect; but when the perfect comes, the imperfect will pass away. When I was a child, I spoke like a child, I thought like a child, I reasoned like a child; when I became a man, I gave up childish ways. For now we see in a mirror dimly, but then face to face. Now I know in part; then I shall understand fully. (1 Corinthians 13:9-12)

The kingdom of Heaven is like a net which was thrown into the sea and gathered fish of every kind; when it was full, men drew it ashore and sat down and sorted the good into vessels but threw away the bad. So it will be at the close of the age. The angels will come out and separate the evil from the righteous, and throw them into the furnace of fire; there men will weep and gnash their teeth. (Matthew 13:47-50)

But understand this, that in the last days there will come times of stress. For men will be lovers of self, lovers of money, proud, arrogant, abusive, disobedient to their parents, ungrateful, unholy, inhuman, implacable, slanderers, profligates, fierce, haters of good, treacherous, reckless, swollen with conceit, lovers of pleasure rather than lovers of God, holding the form of religion but denying the power of it. (2 Timothy 3.1-5)

Jesus said to them, "No one puts new wine into old wineskins; if he does, the new wine will burst the skins and will be spilled, and the skins will be destroyed. But new wine must be put into fresh wineskins. And no one after drinking old wine desires new; for he says, 'The old is good.'" (Luke 5:37-39)

The Heavens Are Cleft Asunder

Krishna, Moses, Buddha, Jesus, and Muhammad are among the Messengers of God who have established religions. They are the central animating forces of the world's major cultures, providing both the spiritual and practical guidance for harmonious, productive society. They ensure a safe approach to God and the essential guidance for the establishment of the laws for social order. Individuals find their relationship with God—their salvation—as well as guidance for human fellowship within the context of their respective religions. The heavens of this physical world are above the earth. The heavens of the human spirit are the thoughts, inspirations, and states of being that are above the plane of the material body. The word of God, as provided through the Messengers, is heaven.

In this day, the "heavens are cleft asunder" in that the religions created by the Messengers of the past as the safe approach to God have fallen from their positions of prominence in human society. In the world of human beings, the ascendancy of science and reason along with the global proximity of competing religious systems has removed the world's great religions from their positions of unquestioned authority. The degree to which the institutions of religion do not accommodate science and each other, they violate their allegiance to the truth for reasonable minds. They lose their integrity and with it their capacity to help guide the institutions of society in this global age.

The Close of the Age

Rather than interpreting the scriptural references to the end times as the literal, cataclysmic end of the physical world, it can be understood as "the close of the age."

> The kingdom of Heaven is like a net which was thrown into the sea and gathered fish of every kind; when it was full, men drew it ashore and sat down and sorted the good into vessels but threw away the bad. So it will be at the close of the age. The angels will come out and separate the evil from the righteous, and throw them into the furnace of fire; there men will weep and gnash their teeth. (Christianity. Matthew 13:47-50)

The "kingdom of Heaven" in this passage is described in the context of "the close of the age." If heaven is understood as a place where spirits reside after the death of the body, then "the close of the age" means the end of the physical world. If, however, heaven is understood as the word of God and as the approach to God through His Messengers, then the "close of the age" means a significant change in religion. The "kingdom of Heaven" refers to a religious dispensation. It is like a net. Over time it fills with many adherents. At the close of the dispensation, a new religion is born with the return of the Messenger. Those who recognize the new Messenger have the gift of the presence of God and His guidance in the context of the new world order—the new heaven and earth—the new covenant. Those who reject the Messenger and the new guidance are left struggling with a world which has lost its order, continuity, and integrity.

The latter part of the passage in Matthew provides some insight into the nature of the change. "The angels will come out and separate the evil from the righteous, and throw them into the furnace of fire; there men will weep and gnash their teeth." Images passed down through centuries of artists depicting these horrendous times provide a picture of angels as physical beings who have wings and carry swords with which to force the separation of the evil doers from the righteous. The reference to angels, rather than being the "winged" sort derived from mythology, is more likely a reference to people who live their lives in close proximity to the will of God and who have recognized the Messenger in His new physical appearance. The adherents of the new dispensation bring the gift of a new heaven and earth through their recognition of the Messenger. They are the builders of the new "kingdom of Heaven" through their efforts to live in the presence of God and abide by the admonitions of the new Messenger. By example, they assist others in their search for God in the context of the new dispensation.

To the degree that we reject the guidance of God as He provides for us in the modern world, we find these times particularly trying. Our current world provides plenty of occasions for the "weeping and gnashing" of teeth when viewed without the assurance of the presence and guidance of God. The individual struggling to make sense of a world that appears beyond the reach of faith and reason is left in doubt and anguish. The wars of the twentieth century provide the most poignant example of the chaotic nature of these times. Cataclysms of the magnitude of global war cause many to lose the assurance of the guidance of God. The twentieth century has seen significant levels of cynicism, depression, and despair in political, social, and economic upheavals. Much of its art, literature, and music bear witness as emanations resembling the wailing and gnashing of teeth.

It is difficult to accept God's plan for our lives and times when it conflicts with our own concepts of justice. One way to avoid facing our differences with God over the nature of the world is to deny that we have contributed in any way to its problems. Self-righteousness follows to the degree that we take over the role of judge for who is at fault for the suffering. We can take refuge in condemning those who we decide are responsible for the state of affairs, those who do not share our view of the world. Another way to avoid dealing with the difficult truth of our situation is to dismiss the whole thing as nonsense and try to hide from it in whatever comfort we can find in the diversions available in this life.

The passage from Isaiah addresses these two different aspects of the "furnace of fire" in which "men will weep and gnash their teeth" (Christianity. Matthew 13:50). Isaiah describes the self righteous "hosts of heaven" and the materialistic "kings of the earth" as being in the same pit with each other in the end times when the earth "falls, and will not rise again."

> For the windows of heaven are opened, and the foundations of the earth tremble. The earth is utterly broken, the earth is rent asunder, the earth is violently shaken. The earth staggers like a drunken man, it sways like a hut; its transgression lies heavy upon it, and it falls, and will not rise again. On that day the Lord will punish The hosts of heaven, in heaven, And the kings of the earth, on the earth. They will be gathered together as prisoners in a pit; They will be shut up in a prison, And after many days they will be punished. The moon will be confounded, And the sun ashamed; For the Lord of hosts will reign on Mount Zion and in Jerusalem And before its elders he will manifest his glory. Isaiah 24.18-23

Both the world's religious hosts and secular leaders have been brought together and have been struggling for dominance for over two centuries in both the kingdoms of heaven and earth. That the world has been "violently shaken" by the opening of the "windows of heaven" can be understood as the ascendance of science (reason) and the convergence of the world's people and religions. Narrow interpretations of the scriptures use religion to cause division, strife, and warfare. They are actions that also cause the adherents of fanaticism to experience some of the harshest self-inflicted suffering. Their actions bring destruction upon themselves and confound them. Their actions also cause the illumined souls of the world's religious traditions to be ashamed. "Then the moon will be confounded and the sun ashamed."

To the religious leaders who are attached to literal interpretations of scripture, the passages from Isaiah provide details for an imagined apocalyptic end to human society on the earth. They take solace in the belief that God will intervene and punish all those who did not see things their way. However, the very scriptures used to condemn the world can be viewed as a vision of the fate of those who assume the ability to judge in place of God.

The Kings of the Earth

In the pit that Isaiah describes as the prison, the "kings of the earth" are also confined. The kings of the earth are those who have power and wealth in this life. The technical, political, social, and economic systems of the current world have created a large, materially wealthy population in the first world. The New Testament provides a graphic depiction of the materialism rampant in "the last days ."

> But understand this, that in the last days there will come times of stress. For men will be lovers of self, lovers of money, proud, arrogant, abusive, disobedient to their parents, ungrateful, unholy, inhuman, implacable, slanderers, profligates, fierce, haters of good, treacherous, reckless, swollen with conceit, lovers of pleasure rather than lovers of God, holding the form of religion but denying the power of it. (Christianity. 2 Timothy 3:1-5)

Buddhism also refers to the darkness of these times. "In the evil age to come, living beings will decrease in good qualities and increase in utter arrogance, coveting gain and honors, developing their evil qualities, and being far removed from deliverance" (Buddhism. Lotus Sutra 13).

As the institutions of religion lose their credibility through denial of the truths brought to light through science and the convergence of the world's faith traditions, the reigns of discipline for human behavior slacken. The result is the ascendancy of materialism—the pursuit of meaning, comfort, and pleasure within the confines of the material world. Thus limited to temporary existence, our connection with the spiritual, eternal nature of our existence is obscured and with it our spiritual bonds to others. We become more restricted by our selfish desires and less able to see our love and concern for others. We also become less able see their concern for us or each other. The increased isolation leaves us spiritually empty and more vulnerable to anxiety and guilt. "On that day you will be exposed; not a secret of yours will be hidden....therefore has he no lover here this day, nor any food save filth which none but sinners eat" (Islam. Qur'an 69. 13-37).

The demise of a coherent and intelligent integration of religion into the fabric of social order gives rise to an alliance between the otherwise contrary forces of materialism and religious orthodoxy. The end of the passage from Timothy refers to the allegiance of the "lovers of pleasure" to the "form of religion." For example, the Godlessness of materialism as expressed in both self-righteous nationalism and excessive pursuit of wealth joins with religious institutions whose mission becomes self promotion. In its most virulent expression, tyranny and religious extremism join as partners to further exacerbate the suffering of a world in need of faith, reason, and unity.

Responding to God

In our relationship with God, it is not uncommon for us to turn to God and ask or demand that He fix the problems associated with our lives and times. It is not uncommon to entertain the idea that if there is something wrong with the current situation, it follows that since God is in control, He must be completely responsible. In the nagging concern over our suffering and our apparent separation from God, there is a tendency to think and feel that it is God who is responsible for the parting. We cannot see our capacity to turn to God. In order to avoid a confrontation with God or ourselves, we often do not face the situation head on. Several options are available. We can try to avoid the question through denying the relevance of God to our lives and pursuing materialistic diversions instead. We can blame the problems on the people who do not hold the same concepts, values, or theologies we do. We can try to fix the problems by doing battle with those we have decided are responsible. Or, we can wait for miraculous intervention—i.e. winged angels appearing to the sound of trumpets as the old world is literally rolled up and dumped into oblivion and replaced by a new world, which God physically spreads in its place without the need for us to do anything.

An adult has an increased responsibility for his or her own response to God. The future of our individual lives as well as the collective world order will only proceed productively with our willingness to take on the responsibilities of an adult faith that fully integrates mature reason and self awareness in the presence of God. It will not be instantaneously provided without our effort. Humankind will build a just, peaceful, and bountiful world order over the coming centuries as we articulate into the context of our lives the virtues prescribed by all of Messengers of God.

The Cataclysm of Adolescence

> For our knowledge is imperfect and our prophecy is imperfect; but when the perfect comes, the imperfect will pass away. When I was a child, I spoke like a child, I thought like a child, I reasoned like a child; when I became a man, I gave up childish ways. For now we see in a mirror dimly, but then face to face. Now I know in part; then I shall understand fully. (1 Corinthians 13.9-12)

In this day, the consequences of the successes and failures of society's collective search for God are heavier than in earlier, less advanced stages in our social evolution. When children at the ages of eight or nine fight each other with the full force available to their bodies, there might not be a scratch to show for the engagement. At twenty-two or twenty-three, if they give full vent to their anger through the developed strength of their bodies and minds, death is a possible outcome.

Childhood is a time of innocence and acceptance of parental authority. It is a literal world with a simple understanding of good guys and bad guys, right and wrong. The higher reasoning faculties are not yet engaged. With the end of childhood and the onset of adulthood, parents and authority figures are challenged. Real limits replace dictates imposed from above. The rational faculty engages reality and tests it, often with assertions of independence. A search for real limits can involve rash behavior and serious mistakes. Youthful angst at the introduction to human suffering and the inevitability of death results in radical mood shifts as fear wrestles with unrestrained passions. The literal, fixed world gives way to experiences of an endless, infinite reality bursting with possibilities, ambiguities, and uncertainties.

The human race is, in a sense, going through adolescence. This is a significant juncture in the evolution of human social order. This is not change at the pace normal to the human race over any earlier period. The fifteenth and sixteenth centuries reflected the early signs of the development of these new capacities for humankind. The familiar and comfortable experiences of home and self were traded for glimpses of other worlds as cultures increased the level of interaction with each other. The first pimples on the face of societal self-assertion appeared back in the seventeenth and eighteenth centuries during the Age of Reason and the Scientific Revolution. By the nineteenth century the sounds of independence were echoed in the pronouncement of some of the world's intelligencia that God was dead. Reason had been engaged to ask the fundamental questions of life on a global, cultural scale. The initial expressions of reason and self-assertion replaced childhood faith in authoritative political and social institutions, which had earlier given structure and order to society. The twentieth century gave rise to excessive passions and demonstrated the power of the vastly strengthened body and mind of humankind. More than seventy million people died as a result of military conflict during the century. Humankind, like the individual, faces consequences magnified by new powers with the transition to adulthood—i.e. global war as an act of self-annihilation for humankind becomes possible.

In the end, no earthly power will contain the awakening capacity of the human soul. Adulthood requires the discovery of reality for itself. It will not, finally, be subject to limits imposed by someone else. Adulthood requires spiritual independence. The institutions of society, including those of religion, must accommodate this new human potential. This is the day promised in all of the world's scriptures as the day of fulfillment. The institutions of society must eventually be reshaped by the grace of God and by responsive human effort to raise structures that can accommodate and are integral to the new capacities unfolding in human experience.

Science, Religion, and Adolescents

An adolescent seeks real limits as he discards those that were imposed by his parents. Spiritual awakenings are common as a teenager engages new powers in the search for identity in reality. Spiritual experiences shape the ongoing development of adult capacity and are integral to the process. Choices toward or away from God profoundly affect the nature of the process of maturation into productive adulthood. Reason alone cannot provide an ark of security within the throes of this ever-changing sea of reality. Reason provides useful explanations associated with physical phenomenon. However, the meaning of life, trust in reality, and awareness of the value of human life are within the sphere of the spirit. Reason and faith in God must both be engaged if the adolescent is to successfully and gracefully integrate into the fabric of society.

For the greater transition of humankind through adolescents this requires the integration of the institutions of science and religion. At this juncture in the arena of global culture, they are often not mutually supportive. The literal cosmologies associated with the various religious systems of the world come under direct attack by the more dynamic, effective, and believable understandings presented through science and technology. The growing existence of religious diversity within the populations of the world also mitigates maintenance of an authoritative view by any single religious institution. The various religious systems no longer hold monolithic sway over the cosmologies presented to their populations.

The institutions of science on the other hand have achieved ubiquitous, global acceptance and include a common disposition toward rejection of consideration of the existence of God. This is seen by many as a denial of the existence of God when it is primarily admission that it cannot conclusively address the topic. Scientific methodology does not permit examination of the question because it cannot, using observation, prove or disprove with certitude, God's existence. Faith is the knowledge of God that provides certitude. Science does not undermine faith in God, though it may threaten faith in particular theologies or concepts of God. The conflict between science and religion stems from a clash of cosmologies.

The quaint cosmologies of the past are not likely to halt the ascendancy of science and technology. Proponents of the failing cosmologies often take refuge in the hope of miraculous intervention. The manner of the expected intervention generally derives from literal interpretations of the various scriptures. Although the imagined resolutions to the conflict vary dramatically, the reactionary religionists together attack the scientists as atheists and destroyers of all that is good and holy, citing as evidence the growing materialism and declining moral order of the population. Scientists often react to this condemnation by dismissing all things religious as the worst kind of backward and destructive superstition.

> One of the outcomes of this conflict between science and religion is the continuing decay of the moral foundation essential to the functioning of a benevolent human social order. As the conflict proceeds, the institutions of religion lose credibility and therefore their effectiveness at guiding people to God. "Heaven will split asunder, for that day it will be frail" (Islam. Qur'an 69. 13-37).

The social ramifications are apparent in the rampant materialism that encourages self-indulgence and indifference to the suffering of others. The increased suffering of humankind is not limited to the materially disadvantaged of the world's populations. A fair measure of suffering is associated with the denial of God on the part of those who enjoy the outward benefits of materialism. The well being associated with the assurance of the love of God and the gifts of fellowship associated with the love of each other is replaced by cynicism and alienation.

The Promise

Judaism

It shall come to pass in the latter days That the mountain of the house of the Lord Shall be established as the highest of the mountains, And shall be raised above the hills; And all the nations shall flow to it; And many peoples shall come, saying, "Come, let us go up to the mountain of the Lord, to the house of the God of Jacob; that he may teach us his ways and that we may walk in his paths." For out of Zion shall go forth the law, And the word of the Lord from Jerusalem. He shall judge between the nations, And shall decide for many peoples; And they shall beat their swords into ploughshares, And their spears into pruning hooks; Nation shall not lift up sword against nation Neither shall they learn war any more. (Isaiah 2.2-4)

For the Lord of hosts will reign on Mount Zion and in Jerusalem And before its elders he will manifest his glory. (Isaiah 24.23)

Christianity

Let the dead bury their dead. (Matthew 8:22)

Islam

On the day when We shall roll up heaven as a scroll is rolled for the writings; as We originated the first creation, so We shall bring it back again—a promise binding on Us; so We shall do. For We have written in the Psalms, after the Remembrance, "The earth shall be the inheritance of My righteous servants." (Qur'an 21.104-5)

Buddhism

They will practice these virtues: abstain from taking life, abstain from taking what is not given, abstain from adultery, abstain from lying, abstain from evil speaking, abstain from abuse and from idle talk, abstain from covetousness, from ill will, from false opinions, abstain from the three things—incest, wanton greed, and perverted desires—be filial towards their mothers and fathers, be pious toward holy men, and respect heads of clans. And because of the good they do they will increase in length of life, and in comeliness, so that the sons of them who lived but forty years will come to live eighty years; their sons to 160- years; their sons to 310 years; their sons to 640 years...2,000 years... 4,000 years... 8,000 years... 20,000 years... 40,000 years; and the sons of those that lived 40,000 years will come to live 80,000 years.

Among such humans there will be only three kinds of disease; appetite, non-assimilation, and old age. Among such humans, this world will be mighty and prosperous, the villages, towns, and royal cities will be so close that a cock could fly from each one to the next. Among such humans this India—one might think it a Waveless Deep—will be pervaded by mankind even as a jungle is by reeds and rushes. (Digha Nikaya iii.74-75, Cakkavatti-Sihanada Suttanta)

Zoroastrianism

The victorious World-renovator and his helpers... shall make the existence renovated—ageless, deathless, un-putrefying, un-corruptible, ever-living, ever benefiting, ruling at will. The dead shall rise up, life shall prevail indestructible, and existence shall be renovated at the will of God!

The worlds shall be deathless, by the will of Right, benefiting all! Evil will stand against, but will flee away, here and there causing death to the holy and his progeny and creatures, but running to its death and destruction at the will of the Judge! (Avesta, Zamayad Yasht 19.11-12)

And then when retribution Shall come for their offenses, Then, O Wise One, Thy Kingdom Shall be established by Good Thought, For those who, in fulfillment, Deliver evil into the hands of Truth! And then may we be those Who make life renovated, O Lord, Immortals of the Wise One, And O Truth, bring your alliance, That to us your minds may gather Where wisdom would be in dispute! Then indeed, shall occur The collapse of the growth of evil, Then they shall join the promised reward: Blessed abode of Good Thought, Of the Wise One, and of Right, They who earn in good reputation! (Avesta, Yasna 30.8-10)

Hope is essential to individual and collective human life. The world's scriptures provide apocalyptic visions, but they also provide glimpses of a resolution to the conflicts associated with humankind's life in this world. These passages bolster our spirits with the reassurance of the benevolent nature of God and His ultimate plan for the provision of a bountiful outcome to our struggles. The progression of human life on the planet is given a resolution worthy of the struggle. The passages concerning the end times provide hope that humankind will conquer its selfish nature and construct a just society through obedience to the will of God. "For the Lord of hosts will reign on Mount Zion and in Jerusalem and before its elders he will manifest his glory." (Judaism. Isaiah 24.23) The will of God will permeate the affairs of humankind. "It shall come to pass in the latter days that the mountain of the house of the Lord shall be established as the highest of the mountains and shall be raised above the hills and all the nations shall flow to it" (Judaism. Isaiah 2.2-4).

The guidance of God will illuminate the governance of the world through the choice of its people to articulate into their lives the admonitions of the prophets.

> And many peoples shall come, saying, 'Come, let us go up to the mountain of the Lord, to the house of the God of Jacob that he may teach us his ways and that we may walk in his paths.' For out of Zion shall go forth the law, and the word of the Lord from Jerusalem. He shall judge between the nations and shall decide for many peoples. (Judaism. Isaiah 2.2-4)

The text specifies that fulfillment of the promise for humankind will come through the prophetic line of Abraham, those religions that trace their lineage to Abraham. Jews will recognize the reference to the fulfillment of the Law of Zion. For Christians, the Lord of Jerusalem is a reference to the fulfillment of the Christian dispensation. For Moslems it is the victory of Islam. To Baha'is it is a reference to the dispensation of Baha'u'llah and the fulfillment of the promise for these times reflected in all of the world's scriptures.

The references from Isaiah need not be understood as excluding the fulfillment of the prophetic pronouncements of the other religions. It is a promise reflected in all of the major religious traditions. Buddhism links a future outcome for human social evolution to mature spiritual behavior.

> They will practice these virtues: abstain from taking life, abstain from taking what is not given, abstain from adultery, abstain from lying, abstain from evil speaking, abstain from abuse and from idle talk, abstain from covetousness, from ill will, from false opinions, abstain from the three things—incest, wanton greed, and perverted desires—be filial towards their mothers and fathers, be pious toward holy men, and respect heads of clans. (Buddhism. Digha Nikaya iii.74-75, Cakkavatti-Sihanada Suttanta)

Righteousness results in long life and the elimination of disease albeit with some exceptions. "Among such humans there will be only three kinds of disease; appetite, non-assimilation, and old age" (Buddhism. Digha Nikaya iii.74-75, Cakkavatti-Sihanada Suttanta). This world will still not be the realm of perfection. Humans will continue to want what they do not have, rebel against what they do not like, and eventually succumb to physical death. However, the prophecy looks to a future without disease where the higher capacities of the human spirit have overcome the baser instincts.

In the Zoroastrian scriptural vision of humankind's eventual fate, the "World-renovator" will rule over evil.

> The victorious World-renovator and his helpers... shall make the existence renovated—ageless, deathless, un-putrefying, un-corruptible, ever-living, ever benefiting, ruling at will. The dead shall rise up, life shall prevail indestructible, and existence shall be renovated at the will of God!
>
> The worlds shall be deathless, by the will of Right, benefiting all! Evil will stand against, but will flee away, here and there causing death to the holy and his progeny and creatures, but running to its death and destruction at the will of the Judge! (Avesta, Zamayad Yasht 19.11-12)

Three different kinds of death are referenced. The first is spiritual death—"death to the holy." The second kind of death is the death of the body—"his progeny and creatures." Jesus made reference to the difference between spiritual death and physical mortality when he instructed Andrew to "Let the dead bury their dead" (Christianity. Matthew 8:22). The third kind of death is the death of evil. The "World-renovator," the Messenger of God, brings humankind eternal life. The life of the human spirit in the presence of God is indestructible. Spiritual life is not contingent on the body. It is the realization of the eternal gift of life from God. In the context of humankind's ongoing habitation in this world, this is a reference to the changed nature of the human situation after existence is "renovated." The differences between this life and the next will be blurred when they are sustained by "the will of the Judge." Evil will cause spiritual death to the holy but only "here and there." "[T]he will of the Judge"—the will of God—will exercise the dominant influence over humankind, blurring the distinction between this life and the next by sustaining the realization of their eternal nature and making "existence renovated—ageless, deathless, un-putrefying, un-corruptible, ever-living, ever benefiting ruling at will" (Zoroastrianism. Avesta, Zamayad Yasht 19.11-12).

The Return of the Messenger

Christianity

Beware of false prophets, which come to you in sheep's clothing, but inwardly they are ravening wolves. Ye shall know them by their fruits. Do men gather grapes of thorns, or figs of thistles? Even so every good tree bringeth forth good fruit; but a corrupt tree bringeth forth evil fruit....Wherefore by their fruits ye shall know them. (Matthew 7:15-17, 20)

He who looks into the perfect law, the law of liberty, and perseveres, being no hearer that forgets but a doer that acts, he shall be blessed in his doing (James 1:25)

But seek ye first the kingdom of God, and His righteousness; and all these things shall be added unto you. (Matthew 6:30)

Then answered Jesus and said unto them, "Verily, verily, I say unto you, The Son can do nothing of himself, but what he seeth the Father do: for what things soever he doeth, these also doeth the Son likewise....For as the Father hath life in himself; so hath he given to the Son to have life in himself; And hath given him authority to execute judgment also, because he is the Son of man." (John 5:19...26-27)

The Sabbath was made for man, and not man for the Sabbath. (Mark 2:27)

For had ye believed Moses, ye would have believed me: for he wrote of me. (John 5:46)

By this shall all men know that ye are my disciples, if ye have love one to another. (John 13:35)

For had ye believed Moses, ye would have believed me: for he wrote of me (John 5:46).

A wicked and adulterous generation seeketh after a sign; and there shall no sign be given unto it, but the sign of the prophet Jonas. (Matthew 16:4)

Baha'i Faith

Since there can be no tie of direct intercourse to bind the one true God with His creation, and no resemblance whatever can exist between the transient and the Eternal, the contingent and the Absolute, He hath ordained that in every age and dispensation a pure and stainless Soul be made manifest in the kingdoms of earth and heaven. Unto this subtle, this mysterious and ethereal Being He hath assigned a twofold nature; the physical, pertaining to the world of matter, and the spiritual, which is born of the substance of God Himself. He hath, moreover, conferred upon Him a double station. The first station, which is related to His innermost reality, representeth Him as One whose voice is the voice of God Himself....The second station is the human station. (Gleanings, 66-67)

Buddhism

Because perfect wisdom tames and transforms him, wrath and conceit he does not increase. Neither enmity nor ill-will take hold of him, nor is there even a tendency towards them. He will be mindful and friendly. (Perfection of Wisdom in Eight Thousand Lines 3.51-54)

The perfume of flowers blows not against the wind, nor does the fragrance of sandalwood, tagara, and jasmine, but the fragrance of the virtuous blows against the wind; the virtuous man pervades every direction. (Dhammapada 54)

Judaism

To him who orders his way aright, I will show the salvation of God! (Psalm 50.23)

There are [always] thirty righteous men among the nations, by whose virtue the nations of the world continue to exist. (Talmud, Hullin 92a)

The Lord your God will raise up for you a prophet like me [Moses] from among you, from your brethren—him you shall heed. (Deuteronomy 18.15)

Sikhism

Liberation comes from living the holy Word. (Adi Granth, Sri Raga Ashtpadi, M.1, 62)

African Traditional Religion

The God of old bids us all abide by his injunctions. Then shall we get whatever we want, be it white or red. (Akan Prayer on Talking Drums)

Zoroastrianism

Then do I proclaim what the Most Beneficent spoke to me, the Words to be heeded, which are best for mortals: those who shall give hearing and reverence shall attain unto Perfection and Immortality by the deeds of good spirit of the Lord of Wisdom! (Avesta, Yasna 45.5)

Taoism

What Tao plants cannot be plucked, what Tao clasps cannot slip. By its virtue alone can one generation after another carry on the ancestral sacrifice. Apply it to your self and by its power you will be freed from dross. (Tao Te Ching 54)

Hinduism

The earth is upheld by the veracity of those who have subdued their passions, and, following righteous practices, are never contaminated by desire, covetousness, and wrath. (Vishnu Purana 3.12)

Whenever truth is forgotten in the world, and wickedness prevails, the Lord of Love becomes flesh to show the way, the truth, and the life to humanity. Such an incarnation is an avatar, an embodiment of God on earth. (Srimad Bhagavatam 1.1)

Whenever the Law declines and the purpose of life is forgotten, I manifest myself on earth. I am born in every age to protect the good, to destroy evil, and to re-establish the Law. (Bhagavad Gita 4. 7-8)

Examining the appearance of Jesus as the fulfillment of scriptural expectations for the Messiah is generally instructive concerning the nature of the return—the periodic appearance of the Messenger—i.e. Buddha, Moses, Krishna. Jesus addressed the nature of His station as the return of the Messenger by equating Himself with Moses. In response to those who accused Him of breaking the Law of Moses because He had cured a man on the Sabbath, He identified Himself with Moses by stating that He had the "authority to execute judgment."

> Then answered Jesus and said unto them, "Verily, verily, I say unto you, the Son can do nothing of himself, but what he seeth the Father do: for what things soever he doeth, these also doeth the Son likewise....For as the Father hath life in himself; so hath he given to the Son to have life in himself; And hath given him authority to execute judgment also, because he is the Son of man." (Christianity. John 5:19...26-27)

In telling them that He does only as the Father does and that He had authority to execute judgment, He was equating Himself with the law of God. He equated Himself with Moses. Jesus was saying that He was speaking as Moses. He was in the place of Moses. Later in the same discussion, Jesus refers directly to Moses. "For had ye believed Moses, ye would have believed me: for he wrote of me" (Christianity. John 5:46). He again makes an identity statement with Moses, this time as the word of God—"he wrote of me." It can be understood as a reference to Himself as the fulfillment of the statement in Deuteronomy that promises the return of prophetic guidance. "The Lord your God will raise up for you a prophet like me [Moses] from among you, from your brethren—him you shall heed." (Judaism. Deuteronomy 18.15)

Jesus provides a parable to shed light on the nature of the return of a Messenger. "Jesus said to them, 'No one puts new wine into old wineskins; if he does, the new wine will burst the skins and will be spilled, and the skins will be destroyed. But new wine must be put into fresh wineskins. And no one after drinking old wine desires new; for he says, "The old is good"'" (Christianity. Luke 5:37-39; see also

Mark 2:22). This was an elegant and culturally effective way for Jesus to say that He brought a new message, an update on the word of God—a new dispensation.

The Messengers of God bring teachings that are appropriate to the exigencies of the times in which they appear. The needs of human society change progressively. "The Sabbath was made for man, and not man for the Sabbath" (Christianity. Mark 2:27). Jesus fulfilled the promises latent in the Law of Moses. The way of life set up under the dispensation of Moses including all of its institutions and cultural boundaries could not continue to carry humanity forward. For example, the institutions of Judaism were not capable of conquering the Romans. Jesus brought a heightened spiritual energy and new social teachings that would provide the impetus for the evolution of western civilization out of the Roman Empire and the tribes of Europe. Revelation is not redundant. It is progressive. The institutions of Judaism would split from the intensity and vigor of the new wine.

The development of all aspects of the phenomenal world, the temporal and spiritual aspects of the social life of human beings has been and will continue to be progressive. The prophets continue to appear giving us ever more out of the treasuries of reality. "Whenever the Law declines and the purpose of life is forgotten, I manifest myself on earth. I am born in every age to protect the good, to destroy evil, and to re-establish the Law" (Hinduism. Bhagavad Gita 4.7-8). Religion addresses both the soul and body of the human situation. The Messengers give both the impetus and the direction for the unfolding of human capacity, addressing both the spiritual and material needs of humankind.

The whole of the evolutionary process of the universe is purposeful. It is like a seed unfolding its potential by inherent design. As God, through evolution, has brought humankind to consciousness, life offers the added dimension of purposeful participation. Human beings participate in evolution by choosing between their will and the will of reality. Social evolution on this planet is an open-ended, organic process dependent upon both the will of God and of humans. The possibilities available to the aggregate of human beings at this juncture in human history encompass the full spectrum: self-annihilation on one end and participation in an ever-advancing, bountiful, and peaceful global civilization on the other.

The Messengers play the pivotal roll in the social evolution of humans. They bring the "new heaven and new earth," the renewed and increased spiritual insight as well as a continually expanding framework for the evolution of social order. They are like the DNA of human culture. The responses of individuals to the guidance of the Messengers are like the responses of the chemistry of the cell to DNA. The human choice to follow the instructions, unlike biochemistry, provides the open-ended array of possibilities available to human culture.

You Will Know Them by Their Fruits

> Beware of false prophets, which come to you in sheep's clothing, but inwardly they are ravening wolves. Ye shall know them by their fruits. Do men gather grapes of thorns, or figs of thistles? Even so every good tree bringeth forth good fruit; but a corrupt tree bringeth forth evil fruit....Wherefore by their fruits ye shall know them (Christianity. Matthew 7:15-17, 20).

One of the most obvious fruits proffered by the Messengers of God is bountiful human civilization. Peaceful and bountiful civilization is a fruit that proceeds from the Messengers of God. The false prophets bring destruction. Their bitter fruit is hatred, conflict, and war.

If the Messenger brings us to the presence of God, the proof of His identity is provided. Secondarily, guidance from the presence of God has an effect on the behavior of the suppliant. To stay in the grace of God requires obedience to His commands. "To him who orders his way aright, I will show the salvation of God!" (Judaism. Psalm 50.23). A primary command of the Messengers is the golden rule. "By this shall all men know that ye are my disciples, if ye have love one to another" (Christianity. John 13:35). The admonitions of God to love one another imply articulation of the virtues required for loving relationships. "Because perfect wisdom tames and transforms him, wrath and conceit he does not increase. Neither enmity nor ill-will take hold of him, nor is there even a tendency towards them. He will be mindful and friendly" (Buddhism. Perfection of Wisdom in Eight Thousand Lines 3.51-54).

A fundamental fruit of obedience to the ordinances of God is community. Through recognition of the Messenger and submission to the guidance He brings, human beings participate in the unfolding potential of human society. Human reality is guided by intention and choice. The Messenger of God provides for the evolutionary aspects of human progression. The Messenger is the fulcrum for creation on the part of God and free will on the part of human beings. Human evolution does not devolve around the survival of the fittest but rather progresses through conscious allegiance to the will of reality as articulated by the Messengers. Intelligence is not evolving through natural selection from absolute nothingness. The Messengers of God are guiding, nurturing, and unfolding potential in an infinitely flexible plan. Submission to the will of God and not dominance of our neighbor assists in the evolution of individual and societal capacity.

The ability to see, hear, and respond to the Messenger of God provides the optimal path for human evolution. Dominance in the natural world achieves a short-lived survival, which always perishes in defeat to the next survivor. The actions, portrayed in the New Testament, of Pontius Pilot and Jesus of Nazareth are examples of the two motivational centers.

In His day, Jesus was not a winner by the standards of all of the powers and authorities of His environment. He had no wealth, no armies; He didn't make anything, write anything, or build anything that appeared consequential to most of those who witnessed some part of His short life. His followers consisted of a handful of seemingly unexceptional and unimportant people. The authorities disposed of Him the way they rid themselves of anyone who cast a shadow on their survival. His times took little note of Him. Jesus does not receive even a footnote in the writings of the dominant culture of the time.

The account of Pontius Pilot in the New Testament shows the administrator as a man of distinction in his times. He was successful. He displayed a fair amount of power and influence in his day. One of the primary messages of the New Testament has to do with who succeeds—Jesus or Pontius. Which of the two men has had more effect on the last two thousand years? Just recently, archaeological evidence of the existence of the man identified in the New Testament as Pontius Pilot has been discovered. Other than through the success of Jesus, Pontius Pilot does not have a footnote. The Christian religion gave spirit, shape, and direction to the unfolding power of western civilization. We would not have western civilization as we know it without the seemingly quiet, unpretentious, hardly noticed life of Jesus of Nazareth.

The return of the Messenger is the pattern of history. It is the evidence that the spirit is stronger than the flesh. Life is more powerful than death. Death is the struggle for physical and temporal dominance. The spirit that provides for human civilization issues from submission to the will of reality, the will of God. One of the primary lessons of religion is that there are consequences to our choices and actions. Those consequences have everything to do with the renewal of social order and the ongoing development of civilization. "Wherefore by their fruits ye shall know them" (Christianity. Matthew 7:20).

The End of War

The cessation of warfare is among the promises given for these times. Under the guidance of God, the warfare that has plagued humankind will give way to peaceful endeavors. "And they shall beat their swords into ploughshares and their spears into pruning hooks. Nation shall not lift up sword against nation. Neither shall they learn war any more" (Judaism. Isaiah 2.2-4).

The Qur'an echoes, via a reference to Psalms, the assurance found in Isaiah that the earth will one day be governed by those who adhere to the admonitions of God. "The earth shall be the inheritance of My righteous servants" (Islam. Qur'an 21.104-5). The guarantee is embedded in language referring to the end times. "On the day when We shall roll up heaven as a scroll is rolled for the writings as We originated the first creation, so We shall bring it back again—a promise binding on Us; so We shall do" (Islam. Qur'an 21.104-5). The end times does not refer to the end of creation. It does, however, refer to a significantly difference world. After the end times, the will of God will be more in evidence through human choice than before.

> It shall come to pass in the latter days That the mountain of the house of the Lord Shall be established as the highest of the mountains, And shall be raised above the hills; And all the nations shall flow to it; And many peoples shall come, saying, "Come, let us go up to the mountain of the Lord, to the house of the God of Jacob; that he may teach us his ways and that we may walk in his paths." For out of Zion shall go forth the law, And the word of the Lord from Jerusalem. He shall judge between the nations, And shall decide for many peoples; And they shall beat their swords into ploughshares, And their spears into pruning hooks; Nation shall not lift up sword against nation Neither shall they learn war any more. (Judaism. Isaiah 2.2-4)

Isaiah also assures us that when the Messenger returns, "the government shall be upon his shoulder" (Judaism. Isaiah 9.6).

PART TWO

THE BAHA'I FAITH

– 11 –

Baha'u'llah, the Return of the Messenger

Progressive Revelation

Each Messenger leaves his followers with the hope that
He will return. Through the life cycle of a dispensation, the
processes associated with the rise of the institutions of religion solidify expectations of the return into particular images
and concepts associated with the scriptural references to the
event and the signs of its coming. The expectations are also
generally defined within the context of the continuation of
the particular religious institutions that forecast the event.
For example, it is common for many Christians to see the
return of the Messenger in the end times as the return of the
person of Jesus who will extend the authority of the institutions of Christianity to the governance of the earth. Some
Jews in the time of Jesus had a similar expectation for the
coming of the Messiah and their independence from Rome.
The Messiah would come with a sword and defeat the Romans. It would be grandiose and obvious to everyone, and it
would extend the authority of the institutions of Judaism
over the Romans. New dispensations generally do not meet
the literal expectations articulated by the institutions of the
former dispensation. The Messenger brings a new message
that exceeds the capacity and expectations of the former dispensation.

In the parable of the new wine and old wine skins (Luke 5:37-39), Jesus instructs about the heightened level of spirituality and insight brought by the Messenger and the inability of the institutions of the former dispensation to contain it. The parable ends with the added note that individuals who are used to the old wine will generally prefer it to the new wine. "And no one after drinking old wine desires new; for he says, 'The old is good'" (Luke 5:39). The Messenger and His new teachings are not welcomed by most of the adherents of the former dispensation who are awaiting His arrival with expectations for the continuance of the old institutions.

The Messengers come to renew the essential spiritual guidance from God for a maturing capacity and provide particular guidance for the continued advancement of civilization. The return of the Messengers, like the coming of spring after winter, is ongoing and progressive. Nature is not stagnant. It progresses, unfolding ever more varied expressions of life.

> Among the bounties of God is revelation. Hence revelation is progressive and continuous. It never ceases. It is necessary that the reality of Divinity with all its perfections and attributes should become resplendent in the human world. The reality of Divinity is like an endless ocean. Revelation may be likened to the rain. Can you imagine the cessation of rain? Ever on the face of the earth somewhere rain is pouring down. Briefly, the world of existence is progressive. It is subject to development and growth. Consider how great has been the progress in this radiant century. Civilization has unfolded. Nations have developed. Industrialism and jurisprudence have expanded. Sciences, inventions and discoveries have increased. All of these show that the world of existence is continuously progressing and developing; and therefore, assuredly, the virtues characterizing the maturity of man must, likewise, expand and grow.
>
> The greatest bestowal of God to man is the capacity to attain human virtues. Therefore, the teachings of religion

must be reformed and renewed because past teachings are not suitable for the present time. For example, the sciences of bygone centuries are not adequate for the present because sciences have undergone reform. The industrialism of the past will not ensure present efficiency because industrialism has advanced. The laws of the past are being superseded because they are not applicable to this time. All material conditions pertaining to the world of humanity have undergone reform, have achieved development, and the institutes of the past are not to be compared with those of this age. The laws and institutes of former governments cannot be current today, for legislation must be in conformity with the needs and requirements of the body politic at this time....

Therefore, Baha'u'llah appeared from the horizon of the Orient and reestablished the essential foundations of religious teachings of the world. The worn-out traditional beliefs current among men were removed. He caused fellowship and agreement to exist between the representatives of varying denominations so that love became manifest among the contending religions. He created a condition of harmony among hostile sects and upheld the banner of the ones of the world of humanity. (Promulgation of Universal Peace, 378-79)

Four Methods of Knowing

Abdul'Baha, the son of Baha'u'llah—the prophet founder of the Baha'i Faith, spoke of four methods of acquiring knowledge as it relates to our search for God—the senses, reason, tradition, and the Holy Spirit. The first three are not essentially worthy of the absolute trust of the human soul. They pertain to temporal phenomenon. All measurement, reason, and scriptural interpretation are limited descriptions of human existence that cannot provide certitude to questions of being. Since the human spirit is self-aware and seeks eternal answers to the nature of its being, temporal methods of knowing cannot ultimately satisfy its nature.

The endowments which distinguish the human from all other forms of life are summed up in what is known as the human spirit; the mind is its essential quality. These endowments have enabled humanity to build civilizations and to prosper materially. But such accomplishments alone have never satisfied the human spirit, whose mysterious nature inclines it towards transcendence, a reaching towards an invisible realm, towards the ultimate reality, that unknowable essence of essences called God. (The Universal House of Justice, Promise of World Peace, 17)

The human spirit is inclined to seek the eternal, because it is eternal. Resolution of the search for certitude concerning existence can only be found in the experience of God by the individual. Sensory, rational, or traditional proofs are ephemeral, arbitrary, or vicarious with respect to the nature of reality. Only God can prove His existence. "Be swift in the path of holiness, and enter the heaven of communion with Me. Cleanse thy heart with the burnish of the spirit, and hasten to the court of the Most High" (Baha'u'llah, Hidden Words, p. 24). All other proofs are contingent. No individual can assure any other nor take primary responsibility for anyone other than herself with respect to a relationship with God. We are required by our contingent nature to bear witness to the reality of God as He makes Himself known. The Messengers are the personal realization of God to the individual and guidance to society at large. The Baha'i writings also refer to the Messengers as Manifestations of God. They are human and Divine.

Know that the Holy Manifestations, though They have the degrees of endless perfections, yet, speaking generally, have only three stations. The first station is the physical; the second station is the human, which is that of the rational soul; the third is that of the divine appearance and the heavenly splendor.

The physical station is phenomenal; it is composed of elements, and necessarily everything that is composed is subject to decomposition. It is not possible that a composition should not be disintegrated.

The second is the station of the rational soul, which is the human reality. This also is phenomenal, and the Holy Manifestations share it with all mankind...

The third station is that of the divine appearance and heavenly splendor: it is the Word of God, the Eternal Bounty, the Holy Spirit. (Abdul'Baha, Some Answered Questions, 151)

Sensory Proof of the Truth of the Messenger

Miracles are the most obvious sensory proof for the truth of a Messenger of God. There are accounts of Buddha, Moses, Jesus, Muhammad, the Bab and Baha'u'llah intervening in the natural order in a supernatural way. However, sensory proof through miracles is only effective for the beholder. A secondhand hearing of the event is not a sensory proof. Even for those who witness the miracle, there is not necessarily any advancement of spiritual perception. For example, most of the people in the stories of the ministry of Jesus apparently ignored the evidence of their senses when they observed miracles. Miracles are also not emphasized by the Manifestations as having primary value. Jesus advised against reliance on miracles. "A wicked and adulterous generation seeketh after a sign; and there shall no sign be given unto it, but the sign of the prophet Jonas" (Christianity. Matthew 16:4). The sign of Jonas refers to the resurrection. For the individual, resurrection is the realization of eternal life that the Messenger brings to those who recognize Him. This is the resurrection that is available for all to witness. For society at large, the resurrection is the return of the Messenger with the power to revitalize and redirect the ongoing evolution of society. The transforming message that addresses the needs of humanity is the "sign of the prophet Jonas."

Abdul'Baha, a central figure in the Baha'i Faith (see page 186), when asked about the miracles that the Messengers or Manifestations of God performed, clarified the role of miracles in the search for God.

But in the Holy Books an especial terminology is employed; and for the Manifestations these miracles and wonderful signs have no importance; they do not even wish to mention them. For, if we consider miracles a great proof, they are still only proofs and arguments for those who are present when they are performed, and not for those who are absent....But in the day of the Manifestations the people with insight see that all the conditions of the Manifestation are miracles, for they are superior to all others, and this alone is an absolute miracle. Recollect that Christ, solitary and alone, without a helper or protector, without armies and legions, and under the greatest oppression, uplifted the standard of God before all the people of the world, and withstood them, and finally conquered all, although outwardly he was crucified. Now this is a veritable miracle which can never be denied. There is no need of any other proof of the truth of Christ....The meaning is not that the Manifestations are unable to perform miracles, for they have all power. But for them inner sight, spiritual healing, and eternal life are the valuable and important things. (Abdul'Baha, Some Answered Questions, 100-102)

Many of today's religious practitioners focus on expectations of miraculous signs for the end times. They expect the sky to open up to heaven where angels with wings and swords issue forth and begin separating the believers from the non-believers and where the earth opens to hell for the non-believers. The person, Jesus, in this vision appears on clouds in the sky where He will rule the new heaven on earth. These would be spectacular sensory proofs of the legitimacy of the appearance of the return of Christ. Physical recognition would certainly be hard to avoid but would not necessarily enhance the spiritual disposition of any of the observers.

Another type of physical proof for the return of the Messenger is the appropriateness of the guidance He brings. For example, Jesus directed His followers to love and include everyone in the covenant, even the Romans. The guidance was both spiritual and practical for the creation of western civilization.

Logical Proofs of the Truth of the Messenger

When speaking of how to determine a false prophet from one sent by God, Jesus said, "Ye shall know them by their fruits" (Christianity. Matthew 7:16). You will know them by the results of their teachings and actions. Reason is not a conclusive proof of the validity or nature of the Messenger. It does, however, provide a method of approach. Reason can read the signs of legitimacy. It can perceive consistency with respect to values and actions.

For example, Baha'u'llah teaches that God has provided Messengers to all peoples and therefore all religions are essentially one religion presented by different Messengers who addressed the various needs of the peoples of their times. Reason provides four possibilities for the nature of religious revelation in this regard. First, one of the Messengers is true and the rest are false. Second, all of them are false. Third, some of them are true and some are false. Fourth, all of them are true. Given a belief in the justice and benevolence of God, the forth option is the most reasonable. If God provided guidance from and access to Himself for one of the populations of the earth, it is reasonable to expect that He would also provide it for the others. The third option is true is false prophets are included in the analysis. Since there are individuals who claim to be prophets of God who are not, it is also reasonable to expect that God has endowed us with the capacity to discern the difference.

Traditional Proof of the Messenger

Traditional proofs of the legitimacy of a Messenger rest upon interpretation of scripture. This, as in the case of sensory and rational proofs, is not the realm of perfection. It is the domain of both personal and institutional (historical) expectations of the return that are derived from scripture. Baha'u'llah, in the *Book of Certitude*, explains a passage of the Gospel of Matthew that addresses the signs that will appear announcing the return of Christ.

Immediately after the oppression of those days shall the sun be darkened, and the moon shall not give her light, and the stars shall fall from heaven, and the powers of the earth shall be shaken: and then shall appear the sign of the Son of man in heaven: and then shall all the tribes of the earth mourn, and they shall see the Son of man coming in the clouds of heaven with power and great glory. And he shall send his angels with a great sound of a trumpet. (Matthew 24: 29-31)

He dedicates the first half of the book to explanations of this verse. His explication is not intended to be a comprehensive treatment even of this passage of scripture but is a demonstration of the nature of scriptural interpretation particularly with respect to understanding the return of the Messenger. Scripture, in general, is infinitely meaningful. Every individual derives her own understanding and inspiration from scripture that corresponds to her unique approach to God. This also applies to our individual expectation concerning the return of a Messenger.

Spiritual Proof of the Truth of the Messenger

Certitude for an individual concerning the return is arrived at through communication with God over the signs He presents to us personally. The dialog is a question and answer session. The question is generally in the form of a doubt or a discrepancy that we hold with respect to scriptural expectations. Communion and certitude result to the degree we submit to whatever God intends and we listen with the sincerity of our being for guidance.

The requirement of confirmation from the Spirit of God to establish certitude and the fact that the knowledge it provides is above reason leads some to conclude that faith may violate reason. However, spiritual certitude, though beyond conceptual understanding does not contradict reason. The concept of blind faith is sometimes used to rationalize theologies that contradict science and reason. Some see their willingness to give up reason in their tenacious hold on particular ideologies or dogmas as a sign of faith. Abdul'Baha states that, "By faith is meant, first, conscious knowledge, and second, the practice of good deeds" (The Divine Art of Living, 48).

The admonishments to "know thyself" and "to thine own self be true" are references to conscious knowledge. Self-knowledge is not fundamentally the intellectual or emotional knowledge we hold about our selves. It is awareness of our selves. Faith in God is likewise knowledge of God as He makes Himself known to us. Faith in God is similar to the knowledge of others that we refer to as love. Love is aware-ness of another, a profound respect and appreciation, a cel-ebration of the soul. Faith in God is knowing God.

With respect to Baha'u'llah's claim to be the Messenger of God, an individual does not need to abandon reason to acknowledge its truth. In a letter written on behalf of Shoghi Effendi, a leading figure in the Baha'i Faith (see page 187), he advocates the use of reason in the search for faith.

> He does not ask us to follow Him blindly....God has endowed man with a mind to operate as a torchlight and guide him to the truth. Read His Words consider His Teachings and measure their value in the light of contem-porary problems and the truth will surely be revealed to you...and you will appreciate the truth of His Mission, as well as the true spirit He creates in whosoever follows His ways. (Lights of Guidance, 474)

Those who earnestly seek God find Him. "Ask and it shall be given you; seek and ye shall find; knock and it shall be opened unto you" (Christianity. Matthew 7:7).

> That which is preeminent above all other gifts, is incor-ruptible in nature, and pertaineth to God Himself, is the gift of Divine Revelation. Every bounty conferred by the Creator upon man, be it material or spiritual, is subservi-ent unto this. It is, in its essence, and will ever so remain, the Bread which cometh down from Heaven. It is God's supreme testimony, the clearest evidence of His truth, the sign of His consummate bounty, the token of His all-en-

compassing mercy, the proof of His most loving providence, the symbol of His most perfect grace. He hath, indeed, partaken of this gift of God who hath recognized His Manifestation in this Day. (Baha'u'llah, Gleanings, 195)

The Story of the Woman with the Stone

Baha'u'llah was taken to a prison in Tehran. It was an early episode among the many persecutions He experienced throughout His life. A crowd had gathered to jeer at Him. His response to one of those who wanted to inflict injury on Him is reminiscent of the attitude Jesus had toward the ignorance of similar behavior directed toward Him.

Among the crowd, which hurled abuse at Baha'u'llah and pelted Him with stones, was an old woman. She stepped forward with a stone in her hand to strike at Him. Although frenzied with rage, her steps were too weak for the pace of the procession. "Give me a chance to fling my stone in His face," she pleaded with the guard. Baha'u'llah turned to them and said, "Suffer not this woman to be disappointed. Deny her not what she regards as a meritorious act in the sight of God." Such was the measure of His compassion. (Balyuzi, The King of Glory, 78)

This story from the life of Baha'u'llah expresses the patience and humility with which the Messengers of God articulate the Message of a new dispensation into the fabric of the expectations of individuals and institutions. Our rejection of the grace and guidance of the Messengers results in unnecessary suffering for Them and us. The Messengers respond with the boundless forgiveness and love of God.

– 12 –

THE COVENANT

The central defining characteristic that distinguishes these times from the past is the approach of the age of maturity for humankind—its globalization. Its fundamental need is the establishment of a peaceful, global society that promotes the development of societal and individual capacity through the independent investigation of truth and an abiding respect for diversity.

The Greater and the Lesser Covenants

The covenant between humankind and God has been articulated by all of the Messengers of God.

> Contemplate with thine inward eye the chain of successive Revelations that hath linked the Manifestation of Adam with that of the Bab. I testify before God that each one of these Manifestations hath been sent down through the operation of the Divine Will and Purpose, that each hath been the bearer of a specific Message, that each hath been entrusted with a divinely-revealed Book and been commissioned to unravel the mysteries of a mighty Tablet. The measure of the Revelation with which every one of them hath been identified had been definitely fore-ordained. (Baha'u'llah. Gleanings, 74)

The greater covenant is the way that God accomplishes His purpose for humankind. "The purpose of God in Creating man hath been, and will ever be, to enable him to know his Creator and to attain His Presence" (Baha'u'llah, *Glean-*

ings, 70). God sustains all of reality for our instruction in His ways. He is always available to us.

> There can be no doubt whatever that if for one moment the tide of His mercy and grace were to be withheld from the world, it would completely perish. For this reason, from the beginning that hath no beginning the portals of Divine mercy have been flung open to the face of all created things, and the clouds of truth will continue to the end that hath no end to rain on the soil of human capacity, reality and personality their favors and bounties. Such hath been God's method continued from everlasting to everlasting. (Baha'u'llah. Gleaning*s*, 68-69)

God's primary commandment to us is to recognize the Messenger of God, to love Him above the things of the world, and to observe His ordinances.

> The first duty prescribed by God for His servants is the recognition of Him Who is the Day Spring of His Revelation and the Fountain of His laws, Who representeth the Godhead in both the Kingdom of His Cause and the world of creation. Whoso achieveth this duty hath attained unto all good; and whoso is deprived thereof, hath gone astray, though he be the author of every righteous deed. It behoveth every one who reacheth this most sublime station this summit of transcendent glory, to observe every ordinance of Him Who is the Desire of the world. These twin duties are inseparable. Neither is acceptable without the other. Thus hath it been decreed by Him Who is the Source of Divine inspiration. (Baha'u'llah. Gleanings, 330-31)

God is always available to every individual. He has also been available to the collective groupings of individuals throughout history, from family groupings to empires and nations, through His Messengers i.e. Krishna, Zoroaster, Abraham, Moses, Buddha, Jesus, Muhammad, and, most recently, the Bab and Baha'u'llah. The Messenger of God is the Manifestation of God in both the spiritual and material worlds. The succession of Messengers is the greater covenant of God. The Messenger provides the presence of God to those who recognize Him and abide by His guidance. He is also the physical person who through the actions of His life articulates the guidance for the well being of a specific or lesser covenant i.e. the Buddhist, Hindu, Mosaic, Islamic, and Christian covenants. The lesser covenant refers to the dispensation associated with a particular Messenger. The dispensation of Baha'u'llah addresses the exigencies of this age.

The Bab

Ali Muhammad announced His Mission to His first follower on May 23, 1844. He assumed the title of the Bab (the Gate or Door). His earthly ministry ended in martyrdom on July 9, 1850. The Bab occupies a two-fold station. He is the divinely appointed forerunner of Baha'u'llah's dispensation much as John the Baptist is for Christ's. And He occupies the station of inaugurator of a separate religious dispensation, which ends the prophetic religious cycle that began with Adam. In a letter addressed to Mulla Husayn, the first person to recognize Him as a Manifestation of God, He writes:

> Bear thou witness that verily He is I, Myself, the Sovereign, the Omnipotent. He is the One Who ordaineth life and death and unto Him shall all return. Indeed there is none other God but Him and all men bow down in adoration before Him. Verily Thy Lord, God, shall presently recompense every one as He ordaineth, even swifter than uttering the words 'Be thou, and it is'. (Selections from the Writings of the Bab, 9)

The Bab attracted a large following with His Message of the oneness of the prophets and of hope for the fulfillment of the promise of the prophets for the unity of mankind. The hostile reaction of many of the Muslim clergy and government officials to the new faith provided one of the most dramatic series of events in the annals of religious history. Shortly after the Bab's execution before a firing squad, more than twenty thousand of His followers were massacred in an attempt to completely abolish His faith.

The primary scripture of the dispensation of the Bab are His writings called the Bayan. The focus of the Bayan is the announcement of the appearance of Baha'u'llah "in the Day of the Latter Resurrection," which He indicates will occur after "a respite of nineteen years."

> This is a letter from God, the Help in Peril, the Self-Subsisting, unto God, the Almighty, the Best Beloved, to affirm that the Bayan and such as bear allegiance to it are but a present from me unto Thee and to express my un-doubting faith that there is no God but Thee, that the kingdoms of Creation and Revelation are Thine, that no one can attain anything save by Thy power and that He Whom Thou has raised up is but Thy servant and Thy Testimony, begging to address Thee by Thy leave in these words: "Shouldst Thou dismiss the entire company of the followers of the Bayan in the Day of the Latter Resurrection by a mere sign of Thy finger even while still a suckling babe, Thou wouldst indeed be praised in Thy indication. And though no doubt is there about it, do Thou grant a respite of nineteen years as a token of Thy favour so that those who have embraced this Cause may be graciously rewarded by Thee...' (Selections from the Writings of the Bab, 6-7)

Baha'u'llah

Husayn-Ali was born in Persia on November 12, 1817 and assumed the name Baha'u'llah—Arabic for the Glory of God. He died in 1892 near Acre in current day Israel, the final location in a series of banishments and imprisonments that began in 1853 in Tehran and lasted for forty years. Baha'u'llah announced His mission to the followers of the Bab in a garden in Baghdad prior to leaving the city to comply with an order for His further banishment to Constantinople. He is the promised one anticipated by all of the world's scriptures.

Verily I say, this is the Day in which mankind can behold the Face, and hear the Voice, of the Promised One. The Call of God hath been raised, and the light of His countenance hath been lifted up upon men. It behoveth every man to blot out the trace of every idle word from the tablet of his heart, and to gaze, with an open and unbiased mind, on the signs of His Revelation, the proofs of His Mission, and the tokens of His glory.

Great indeed is this Day! The allusions made to it in all the sacred Scriptures as the Day of God attest its greatness. The soul of every Prophet of God, of every Divine Messenger, hath thirsted for this wondrous Day. All the divers kindreds of the earth have, likewise, yearned to attain it. (Baha'u'llah. Gleanings, 10)

Baha'u'llah directed the birth and development of the Baha'i dispensation with the events of His life and with written documents that fill more than 100 volumes. His works articulate to humankind God's guidance for the development of a peaceful, prosperous, and ever-advancing global civilization.

The Center of the Covenant and the Guardian

A characteristic unique to the Baha'i dispensation is its clear articulation of the succession of leadership, which has protected the faith from division into sects. Baha'u'llah, through His written will and testament, instructs His followers to turn to His son to maintain the integrity and unity of the faith.

Whosoever turns to Him hath surely turned unto God, and whosoever turneth away from Him hath turned away from My beauty, denied My proof and is of those who transgress. Verily, He is the remembrance of God amongst you and His trust within you, and His manifestation unto you and His appearance among the servants who are nigh. Thus have I been commanded to convey to you the message of God, your Creator; and I have delivered to you that of which I was commanded. (Baha'u'llah, Baha'i World Faith, 205)

> When the ocean of My presence hath ebbed and the
> Book of My Revelation is ended, turn your faces towards
> Him Whom God hath purposed, Who hath branched from
> this Ancient Root. (Tablets of Baha'u'llah, 221)

Baha'u'llah referred in various writings to Abbas Effendi,
His eldest son, as He "Who hath branched from the Ancient
Root," the "Center of the Covenant," "the Master," the
"Perfect Exemplar" of His teachings. Abbas Effendi referred
to Himself as Abdul'Baha—the servant of the Glory of God.

Abdul'Baha was an intelligent, personable, charismatic leader
for the Baha'i community. He administered many of the
affairs of the faith during Baha'u'llah's lifetime. After
Baha'u'llah's passing in 1892, he had responsibility for its
administration until his own passing in 1921. In his own will
and testament, Abdul'Baha appointed his grandson, Shoghi
Effendi as the guardian of the faith and the interpreter of the
writings of the faith.

> O ye faithful loved ones of Abdul'Baha! It is incum-
> bent upon you to take the greatest care of Shoghi Effendi,
> the twig that hath branched from and the fruit given forth
> by the two hallowed and Divine Lote-Trees, that no dust
> of despondency and sorrow may stain his radiant nature,
> that day by day he may wax greater in happiness, in joy
> and spirituality, and may grow to become even as a fruitful
> tree. For he is, after Abdul'Baha, the guardian of the Cause
> of God. The Afnan, the Hands [pillars] of the Cause and
> the beloved of the Lord must obey him and turn unto
> him. He that obeyeth him not, hath not obeyed God; he
> that turneth away from him hath turned away from God
> and he that denieth him hath denied the True One. Be-
> ware lest anyone falsely interpret these words, and like unto
> them that have broken the Covenant after the Day of As-
> cension [Baha'u'llah] advance a pretext, raise the standard
> of revolt, wax stubborn and opened wide the door of false
> interpretation... (Abdul'Baha, Will and Testament of
> Abdul'Baha, 25-26)

Shoghi Effendi's contributions to the faith are most in evidence in his efforts to build the administrative infrastructure of the faith, to develop the Baha'i World Center, to interpret the writings through his own written work, to translate Baha'i scripture, and to direct the implementation of the teaching plans provided by Abdul'Baha.

Universal House of Justice

Foremost among the accomplishments of Shoghi Effendi was the implementation of the administrative order. In 1963, six years after Shoghi Effend's passing, enough of the Baha'i administrative order envisioned by Baha'u'llah was in place to elect the first members of the Universal House of Justice. The members of fifty-six national spiritual assemblies from around the world elected the pinnacle administrative institution for the continued expansion and consolidation of the Baha'i community. Its election realized an institution created by the pen of Baha'u'llah, elaborated by the efforts of Abdul'Baha, and constructed through the direction of Shoghi Effendi. The administrative order is derived from specific directives of Baha'u'llah.

> It is incumbent upon the members of the House of Justice to take counsel together regarding those things which have not outwardly been revealed in the Book, and to enforce that which is agreeable to them. God will verily inspire them with whatsoever He willeth, and He verily is the Provider, the Omniscient. (Baha'u'llah. Tablets of Baha'u'llah, 68)

The Universal House of Justice is the highest law of the land for Baha'is as is affirmed in the writings of Abdul'Baha.

> Unto the Most Holy Book [the Kitab-i-Aqdas] every one must turn, and all that is not expressly recorded therein must be referred to the Universal House of Justice. That which this body, whether unanimously or by a majority doth carry, that is verily the Truth and the Purpose of

God Himself. Whoso doth deviate there from is verily of them that love discord, hath shown forth malice, and turned away from the Lord of the Covenant. (Will and Testament of Abdul'Baha, 19-20)

Baha'i Administration

The Universal House of Justice has nine members and is elected every five years by the members of all of the National Spiritual Assemblies of the world. Each National Assembly has nine members who are elected annually by delegates who are correspondingly elected annually by the general Baha'i electorate. No nominating or campaigning processes are permitted. Any Baha'i in good standing over the age of twenty-one is eligible to vote and be elected.

Local Baha'i communities annually elect nine members from their respective communities to function as the Local Spiritual Assembly. The elections consist of private ballots. Each Baha'i selects nine community members. The votes are tallied. The nine members who received the most votes constitute the Local Spiritual Assembly for the year.

No individual has personal administrative authority outside of the collective decisions of the assembly. The primary mechanism for decision-making for the administration of the affairs of the Baha'i Faith is consultation. There are no clergy in the Baha'i Faith. The principles of the independent investigation of truth and the practices of consultation within the framework of the Baha'i administrative order provide the means for unity of action within the Baha'i community.

Some Teachings

The following is a sketch of some of the teachings which Baha'u'llah has provided for the development of harmonious and prosperous global community for humankind over the next millennium.

1. There is one God, one religion, and one people—one flock and one shepherd. There always has been. The underlying unity of those traditions is just beginning to be realized because of the ascendancy of science and technology and the convergence of the world community.

2. Global governance by law must replace war as the arbiter of disputes. We are in the final stages of nation building. It is now time to safeguard all of the world's borders with the creation of a binding set of rules for the peaceful interaction of the world's peoples. We are too big for war and must instead set policy and settle conflicts through political and legal processes.

3. Each individual is responsible for the development of his own relationship with and understanding of God. None can speak for God to another. All must seek the truth for themselves. Religious and civil law must reflect this essential human capacity and responsibility.

4. Science and faith are both knowledge, one proceeds from the mind through investigation and the other from the spirit. If we use reason without spiritual insight and integrity we are likely to create things that are unhealthy. Faith without reason is superstition and is likely to be as unhealthy as the former condition.

5. The people of the world need to evolve, by selection or creation, a secondary world language through which the practical and spiritual unity of the world's peoples will be expressed and its culture established.

6. Men and women must share equally in all aspects of the institutions of global community. The prophetic, or Adamic, cycle of the human race, its childhood and its hope for the future have been accompanied by the dominance of its social institutions by the male perspectives and proclivities. The institutions of global society must witness the ascendance to parity of feminine qualities.

7. The extremes of wealth and poverty must be eliminated if the world's peoples are to rid themselves of tumult and tyranny. This will not be accomplished solely through the development of political or economic systems. It will require spiritual maturity in the development of human economy.

8. The development of human capacity must be assisted through the global implementation of universal education.

In His writing and through His life's example during the middle to late nineteenth century, Baha'u'llah provided guidance for the health and well being of the peoples of the world. His teachings were not commonplace at the time neither in the heart of the Middle East nor in the more progressive environments of the Western world. Slavery still existed legally in the United States until the end of the Civil War. Women did not have the right to vote until the turn of the twentieth century. Compulsory education appeared in the later half of the nineteenth century. The oneness of God and the unity of religion has been slowly gaining acceptance. The trial of the State of Tennessee v. John T. Scopes took place in 1925 in reaction to the growing ascendance of science over religious superstition. The concept of global governance was first realized in the creation of the League of Nations after World War I. In the middle of the twentieth century, Martin Luther King, Jr. lifted the banner of unity in the ongoing struggle against racism. The cultural oneness of humanity is just now taking shape in economic interdependence, instantaneous global communication, and emerging concepts of world citizenship.

– 13 –

Unity of God, Religion, and Humankind

Give ear, O My servant, unto that which is being sent down unto thee from the Throne of the Lord, the Inaccessible, the Most Great. There is none other God but Him. He hath called into being His creatures, that they may know Him, Who is the Compassionate, the All-Merciful. Unto the cities of all nations He hath sent His Messengers, Whom He hath commissioned to announce unto men tidings of the Paradise of His good pleasure, and to draw them nigh unto the Haven of abiding security, the Seat of eternal holiness and transcendent glory. (Baha'u'llah, Gleanings, 144-45)

God's purpose in sending His Prophets unto men is two-fold. The first is to liberate the children of men from the darkness of ignorance, and guide them to the light of true understanding. The second is to ensure the peace and tranquility of mankind, and provide all the means by which they can be established. (Baha'u'llah. Gleanings, XXIV, 79-80)

The Great Being saith: O ye children of men! The fundamental purpose animating the Faith of God and His Religion is to safeguard the interests and promote the unity of the human race, and to foster the spirit of love and fellowship amongst men. Suffer it not to become a source of dissension and discord, of hate and enmity." (Baha'u'llah. Gleanings, CX, 215)

Religion forms the foundation of the world's cultures. The traditions, social customs, laws, literature, art, and music that unite a people derive the essence of their inspiration from the Messengers of God. It is critical to the peace and security of the modern world that its citizenry adopt not only a posture of pragmatic tolerance for each other's religions but wholeheartedly accept the legitimacy of their origin in one God and celebrate the diversity of God's dispensations of grace to humankind. The grace of God unites hearts regardless of the religious dispensation with which it is associated.

> Religion should unite all hearts and cause wars and disputes to vanish from the face of the earth, give birth to spirituality, and bring life and light to each heart. If religion becomes a cause of dislike, hatred and division, it were better to be without it, and to withdraw from such a religion would be a truly religious act. For it is clear that the purpose of a remedy is to cure, but if the remedy should only aggravate the complaint it had better be left alone. Any religion which is not a cause of love and unity is no religion. All the holy Prophets were doctors to the soul: they gave prescriptions for the healing of mankind; thus any remedy that causes disease does not come from the great and supreme Physician. (Paris Talks, p. 132)

An essential principle of Baha'u'llah's teaching is that religion must be the cause of unity and love amongst men; that it is the supreme effulgence of Divinity, the stimulus of life, the source of honor and productive of eternal existence. Religion is not intended to arouse enmity and hatred nor to become the source of tyranny and injustice. Should it prove to be the cause of hostility, discord and the alienation of mankind, assuredly the absence of religion would be preferable. Religious teachings are like a course of treatment having for its purpose the cure and healing of mankind. If the only outcome of a course of treatment should be mere diagnosis and fruitless discussion of symptoms, it would be better to abandon and abolish it. In this sense the absence of religion would be at least some progress toward unity. (Promulgation of Universal Peace, 394)

Religious absolutism is a more critical issue in the context of diversity. The world community is no longer a disparate collection of largely isolated cultural entities. It has converged into a neighborhood of cultural families. The realization of the underlying unity of religion is therefore central in the teachings of Baha'u'llah since His teachings are directed at the needs of global community. The Baha'i Faith specifically addresses current times. Central to its mission is the harmonization of the diverse cultural traditions in a unity that embraces and celebrates diversity. The spirit and teachings of the religions of God provide unity. The recognition that being without religious affiliation is better than subscribing to intolerance and fanaticism is not only a preferred value; it is a description of how things work.

When the Messenger appears with guidance to achieve the next level of human unity, the religious institutions that oppose the guidance lose credibility because of their opposition to beneficial outcomes for human society. To the degree that the primary purpose of religion, the unity of humankind at all levels of endeavor, is disregarded by the leaders of religion, fanaticism gains sway and serves to undermine the credibility of religion. The result is the abandonment of the religious practices that are contrary to the central purpose of religion.

We learn how reality works by choice and consequence. The Messengers of God provide us with guidance that we accept through choice over time. For example, the approach that Jesus submitted to the Sanhedrin to conquer the Romans with love was rejected. It was heard by some; but it was dismissed by most. The groups of religious zealots that were promoting armed resistance gained ascendancy over enough of the population that the Jewish leadership eventually had to choose war with Rome. In 70 AD the Jews rebelled against Rome to disastrous consequences. The Messengers tell us the truth about how things work and give us guidance sufficient to meet the particular demands for human cooperation and unity in the times that they address. We learn by the consequences of our choices.

Baha'u'llah brings guidance for the development of global community. His teachings address the questions and problems we are experiencing in the transition to global society. He wrote letters to the kings, queens, and religious leadership of the nineteenth-century world announcing His identity as the Messenger of God and calling them to put away war in favor of global cooperation. His guidance was dismissed. Since the rejection of His proposals for global unity, we have suffered two world wars that resulted in the deaths of more than seventy million men, women, and children and the suffering, through injury and loss, of nearly all of the inhabitants of the globe.

We are still struggling with acceptance of the advice to put away war in favor of governance structures for resolving conflict. Currently, religion has taken center stage as an underlying cause of conflict for global community. It is becoming more abundantly clear to greater numbers of people that absolutism and fanaticism are not healthy expressions of religion. They run counter to the central purpose of all of the Messengers of God. The Messengers of God are spiritual and practical teachers and they call everyone to the same profession.

> He Who is the Eternal Truth hath, from the Day Springs of Glory, directed His eyes towards the people of Baha, and is addressing them in these words, "Address yourselves to the promotion of the well being and tranquility of the children of men. Bend your minds and wills to the education of the peoples and kindreds of the earth, that haply the dissensions that divide it may, through the power of the Most Great Name, be blotted out from its face, and all mankind become the upholders of one Order, and the inhabitants of one City. Illumine and hallow our hearts; let them not be profaned by the thorns of hate or the thistles of malice. Ye dwell in one world, and have been created through the operation of one Will. Blessed is he who mingleth with all men in a spirit of utmost kindliness and love. (Baha'u'llah, Gleanings, 333-34)

The acceptance of the legitimacy of the Baha'i dispensation does not negate the legitimacy of any of the previous dispensations. Instead, it reaffirms and re-establishes their validity and reinvigorates them. The teachings of the new dispensation clarify the continuity of the guidance provided by the former Messengers. They fulfill the designs latent in the previous dispensations.

> Each of the divine religions embodies two kinds of ordinances. The first is those which concern spiritual susceptibilities, the development of moral principles and the quickening of the conscience of man. These are essential or fundamental, one and the same in all religions, changeless and eternal—reality not subject to transformation. Abraham heralded this reality, Moses promulgated it, and Jesus Christ established it in the world of mankind. All the divine Prophets and Messengers were the instruments and channels of this same eternal, essential truth.
>
> The second kind of ordinances in the divine religions is those which relate to the material affairs of human kind. These are the material or accidental laws which are subject to change in each day of manifestation, according to exigencies of the time, conditions and differing capacities of humanity. (Abdul-Baha, Promulgation of Universal Peace, 106)

Love for the former Messengers of God is infinitely enhanced by Baha'u'llah. For those previously confined to the love and trust of God through the religion they were raised in, the Baha'i Faith opens a depth and breadth of scriptural, cultural, and intellectual inspiration formerly unavailable, and it intimately connects individuals to others with richly diverse life experiences.

Trust, in each other and the institutions of society, is essential to human social order. The presence of God is its most potent source. Trust in God provides the spring of hope and creative energy essential to the well being of humankind. "The spirit that animateth the human heart is the knowledge of God" (Baha'u'llah. Gleanings, 291). The knowledge of God binds together the participants of society at both the spiritual and practical levels. At the spiritual level, communion with God provides the individual with the ability to love others selflessly.

At a practical level, members of a group with common beliefs are more likely to trust each other than strangers outside of the group. Global community is supported through recognition that all of the world's religions stem from the same source. We are all members of the same essential faith in God. We do not have to understand the particulars of all other faith traditions in order to realize that we each have access to a relationship with God. "Unto the cities of all nations He hath sent His Messengers, Whom He hath commissioned to announce unto men tidings of the Paradise of His good pleasure, and to draw them nigh unto the Haven of abiding security, the Seat of eternal holiness and transcendent glory" (Baha'u'llah, Gleanings, 145). At the level of personal experience, the Messengers show us that God takes care of everybody and that we do not have to personally understand or agree with someone's theology for this to be true. "Consort with the followers of all religions with a spirit of friendliness and fellowship" (Baha'u'llah. Gleanings, 95). Hindus, Jews, Zoroastrians, Moslems, Christians, Baha'is, and Buddhists all find their security and salvation in God, and they do this within the context of personal understandings of their respective faith traditions.

Baha'u'llah teaches explicitly that the various religions of the world were initiated by the Messengers of God. At the societal level, this is an essential realization for the maintenance of global social order. For institutions that hold to the absolute nature of religious truth and are therefore dedicated to the promotion of particular theologies, religious relativism is anathema. Globalization of civilization is seen as a threat to their survival unless they can enforce their version of religious hegemony. The path to harmonious and productive global civilization instead requires recognition of the unity underlying our diversity.

The Oneness of Humanity

The well-being of mankind, its peace and security, are unattainable unless and until its unity is firmly established. This unity can never be achieved so long as the counsels which the Pen of the Most High hath revealed are suffered to pass unheeded. (Baha'u'llah, Gleanings, 286)

The barriers to the unity of humankind in this age are the same as those that have plagued humanity throughout its social evolution—religious, racial, political and patriotic prejudices.

For a period of 6,000 years history informs us about the world of humanity. During these 6,000 years the world of humanity has not been free from war, strife, murder and bloodthirstiness. In every period war has been waged in one country or another and that war was due to either religious prejudice, racial prejudice, political prejudice or patriotic prejudice. It has therefore been ascertained and proved that all prejudices are destructive of the human edifice. As long as these prejudices persist, the struggle for existence must remain dominant, and bloodthirstiness and rapacity continue. Therefore, even as was the case in the past, the world of humanity cannot be saved from the darkness of nature and cannot attain illumination except through the abandonment of prejudices and the acquisition of the morals of the Kingdom. (Selections from the Writings of Abdul'Baha, 299)

The Messengers of God have always directed us to love one another. They have admonished us to transcend the prejudices of race, class, and culture. The consequences of heedlessness in the past, however, have not been as significant as today. There are no geographical barriers behind which we can hide from the potential now latent in our technical capacities for destruction. The world has become an interdependent neighborhood. Refusal to heed the directives of the Messengers of God to abandon our prejudices and join together to serve our common interests as creatures of the same God threatens destruction and human misery at levels unimaginable in the past.

> The earth is one native land, one home; and all mankind are the children of one Father. God has created them, and they are the recipients of His compassion. Therefore, if anyone offends another, he offends God. It is the wish of our heavenly Father that every heart should rejoice and be filled with happiness, that we should live together in felicity and joy. The obstacle to human happiness is racial or religious prejudice, the competitive struggle for existence and inhumanity toward each other. (Abdul-Baha, Promulgation of Universal Peace, 468)

> Therefore, it has been decreed by God in this day that these prejudices and differences shall be laid aside. All are commanded to seek the good pleasure of the Lord of unity, to follow His command and obey His will; in this way the world of humanity shall become illumined with the reality of love and reconciliation. (Abdul-Baha, Promulgation of Universal Peace, 316)

– 14 –

GLOBAL GOVERNANCE

This is the dawning of the age of peace. Baha'u'llah proclaims not only the desirability of peace, but its inevitability. It may not appear inevitable given the present state of armed conflict in the world; however, there are signs of its emergence that can be discerned in the experiences of the past century. After World War I, the League of Nations was formed in a first attempt at global governance. After World War II, the United Nations was formed as a second attempt. Neither of these institutions has been adequate to the task of insuring a cessation to war or of providing the foundations for peaceful and productive harmonization of the world's conflicted nations. But both are proof of a general acknowledgement of the desirability for global governance over war as a mechanism for resolution of conflict. It is also a demonstration that we are taking progressively surer steps forward.

Perhaps the most hopeful signs are in evidence in the emergence of the European Union. The institutions being developed by the countries of Europe can be viewed as the first comprehensive, detailed step toward global governance. The concept of nation-state in which some aspects of national sovereignty are willingly surrendered for the benefits associated with collective security and economic cooperation are being realized. These achievements are in harmony with the admonitions articulated by Baha'u'llah in the mid to latter part of the nineteenth century with respect to their advantages.

We see you adding every year unto your expenditures and laying the burden thereof on the people whom you rule; this verily is naught but grievous injustice. Fear the sighs and tears of this Wronged One, and burden not your peoples beyond that which they can endure....Be reconciled among yourselves, that ye may need armaments no more save in a measure to safeguard your territories and dominions. Be united, O concourse of the sovereigns of the world, for thereby will the tempest of discord be stilled amongst you and your peoples find rest. Should any one among you take up arms against another, rise ye all against him, for this is naught but manifest justice. (Shoghi Effendi, The World Order of Baha'u'llah, 40)

Shoghi Effendi, Guardian of the Baha'i Faith, comments on the passage in 1938.

What else could these weighty words signify if they did not point to the inevitable curtailment of unfettered national sovereignty as an indispensable preliminary to the formation of the future Commonwealth of all the nations of the world? Some form of a world Super-State must needs be evolved, in whose favor all the nations of the world will have willingly ceded every claim to make war, certain rights to impose taxation and all rights to maintain armaments, except for purposes of maintaining internal order within their respective dominions. Such a state will have to include within its orbit an International Executive adequate to enforce supreme and unchallengeable authority on every recalcitrant member of the commonwealth; a Word Parliament whose members shall be elected by the people in their respective countries and whose election shall be confirmed by their respective governments; and a Supreme Tribunal whose judgment will have a binding effect even in such cases where the parties concerned did not voluntarily agree to submit their case to its consideration. A world community in which all economic barriers will have been permanently demolished and the interdependence of Capital and Labor definitely recognized; in which the

clamor of religious fanaticism and strife will have been forever stilled; in which the flame of racial animosity will have
been finally extinguished; in which a single code of international law—the product of the considered judgment of
the world's federated representatives—shall have as its sanction the instant and coercive intervention of the combined
forces of the federated units; and finally a world community in which the fury of a capricious and militant nationalism will have been transmuted into an abiding consciousness of world citizenship—such indeed, appears, in its
broadest outline, the Order anticipated by Baha'u'llah, an
Order that shall come to be regarded as the fairest fruit of
a slowly maturing age. (Shoghi Effendi, The World Order
of Baha'u'llah, 40-41)

The broad outlines that Shoghi Effendi expressed in 1938
are taking tangible shape in the current world. The principles for a peaceful world order are being slowly established
in the fabric of today's world through choice and consequence. The European Union provides concrete hope for
the attenuation of the disastrous effects of "a capricious and
militant nationalism."

The European Union and NAFTA (North American Free
Trade Agreement) though flawed are evidence of the world's
movement toward open markets. And the increasing numbers of companies that provide their employees a share in
the profits are evidence of progress in the realization of the
interdependence of capital and labor.

The current ascendancy of fanaticism brings religion to
the forefront as the spirit of unity struggles to find religious
cooperation across theological and practical religious differences. The need for religious tolerance and open recognition
of the underlying unity of the world's religions is being
articulated by a broader percentage of the world's population as well as many of the leadership of the world's religions. The publication of *World Scripture: a Comparative
Anthology of Sacred Texts* by the International Religious Foundation is evidence of the growing accord among religionists.

World citizenship is emerging in the consciousness of larger percentages of the global population as individuals in increasing numbers interact in the global culture and economy.

"The Tabernacle of Unity," Baha'u'llah proclaims in His Message to all Mankind, "has been raised; regard ye not one another as strangers....Of one tree are all ye the fruit and of one bough the leaves....The world is but one country and mankind its citizens....Let not a man glory in that he loves his country; let him rather glory in this, that he loves his kind." (Shoghi Effendi, The World Order of Baha'u'llah, p. 41)

– 15 –

LANGUAGE

The day is approaching when all the peoples of the world will have adopted one universal language and one common script. When this is achieved, to whatsoever city a man may journey, it shall be as if he were entering his own home. These things are obligatory and absolutely essential. (Baha'u'llah, Gleanings, 249-50)

Language, technology, and culture are inseparably interwoven. The people of the world are evolving a global culture and will, over time, create or designate an official world language. The practical necessity of doing business, the need for ongoing communication required for political cooperation, the ever-increasing number of people crossing borders on a temporary or permanent basis, the shared technological advancements, and the rapidly evolving communication technologies that are increasing the rate of personal daily interaction for the people around the world are forces already at work in the creation of a global culture. The geographic boundaries that necessitated the development of separate languages and cultural groups are completely overwhelmed by today's political, economic, and technical changes. Isolation is no longer a practical option for any group of people. The twentieth century marks the full-scale reversal of the dispersion and cultural differentiation of humankind that has been proceeding for thousands of years as cultures evolved in geographic remoteness. The globe has been encompassed. The world's populations are now integrating at an ever-increasing rate.

The technological developments over the past 150 years have already created a shared global culture that is more significant than all the differences reflected in the myriad of cultures that developed over the previous 10,000 years. The differences between us attributable to cultural-historical origins are magnified by language differences, which, it could be argued, are the most significant differences among the peoples of the world in terms of erecting barriers. Religion, skin color, politics, and economics produce barriers as formidable as mountains for separating people. The ability to communicate provided by a common language is the primary material out of which roads over the mountains of our differences can be constructed.

In a broader context, our looks and language are a small, almost infinitesimal, fraction of characteristics compared with the overwhelming area of juncture we share as human beings. These differences, however, dominate the interactions of people crossing cultural borders. Human beings share millions or billions of years of common evolution depending on the starting point (i.e. some would start with the earliest primitive life forms). The visible differences—like hair and eye color—are a veneer. They are superficial but very noticeable and susceptible to overvaluation. Language barriers further exacerbate the difficulties they present.

Global human cultures afford differences in food, dress, aesthetics, body language, art, and literature—a myriad of subtle and not so subtle differences. The diversity potentially provides enjoyable accents to our shared humanity when we can communicate. The differences easily become the basis of fear and suspicion when we cannot. One of the most practical things the world community can do to promote its peace and prosperity is to teach a world language to all the inhabitants of the globe.

Travel to unfamiliar cultures feels significantly more comfortable with the ability to communicate. The psychological and social comfort of the traveler will not likely afford a strong enough motive for implementing a world language. However, survival in a nuclear age, profit from trade, global communication and entertainment systems, increased travel, scientific and educational cooperation, ever-increasing population migrations, along with increases in cultural and racial intermarriage rates may provide more persistent inducements.

Choose One or Create One

Arguments can be forwarded for the desirability of creating a world language rather than selecting an existing one. Some of the advantages are easily apparent. A language devised by linguists can be made to adhere to the dictates of reason instead of the rather subjective trends of cultural evolution. The learning of language can be considerably easier if its rules are logical and consistent. Vocabulary can initially be drawn from cognates of the world's existing language groups. Everyone will already know a percentage of the words. A created language will be closer to cultural and national neutrality.

Regardless of its practical benefits, efforts thus far to initiate the construction and acceptance of a secondary global language have failed. Esperanto enjoyed a modicum of support for a period of time but has been completely overshadowed by the prospect of English becoming a .global language. Esperanto, though it had the above mentioned benefits of a constructed language, had an Indo-European bias. Constructing an unbiased, reasonably culturally neutral language would be a monumental undertaking. It would, however, contribute beyond a selected language to cooperative processes essential to global community. The act of its creation would be a notable, proactive effort affirming the importance of global cooperation. Once created it would have staying power. A language that becomes dominant because of the dominance of a particular culture is subject to change as another culture becomes dominant. Whether a language is constructed or chosen, having a secondary language taught to all of the world's population is essential for harmonious global community.

– 16 –

INDEPENDENT
INVESTIGATION OF TRUTH

Suffer not yourselves to be wrapt in the dense veils of
your selfish desires, inasmuch as I have perfected in every
one of you My creation, so that the excellence of My handi-
work may be fully revealed unto men. It follows, therefore, that every man hath been, and will continue to be,
able of himself to appreciate the Beauty of God, the Glori-
fied. Had he not been endowed with such a capacity, how
could he be called to account for his failure? If, in the Day
when all the peoples of the earth will be gathered together,
any man should, whilst standing in the presence of God,
be asked: "Wherefore hast thou disbelieved in My Beauty
and turned away from My Self," and if such a man should
reply and say: "Inasmuch as all men have erred, and none
hath been found willing to turn his face to the Truth, I,
too, following their example, have grievously failed to recognize the Beauty of the Eternal," such a plea will, assuredly, be rejected. For the faith of no man can be conditioned by any one except himself. (Baha'u'llah, Gleanings,
143)

Individuals are responsible for their own spiritual development. Each has the faculty and responsibility to willingly
turn to God. This is an essential aspect of our nature and
applies to the members of all religions. However, it applies
to a further degree in the context of the current world.
Social evolution has reached a level that requires the indi-

vidual to consciously develop his own understanding of the scriptures. Baha'u'llah provides access for the individual to see what Moses saw on the mountain—the Glory of God. He has released this heightened spiritual capacity through the individual's independent investigation of truth and harnessed it to the processes of consultation. For the Baha'i dispensation, it is an integral aspect of the governance structures of the Faith.

Reason is given prominence in this dispensation. Submission to the will of God, sincerity and purity of motive are still essential in the approach to God. However, greater latitude is given to us in questioning God. The processes of search are an essential and integral aspect of this dispensation. Since there are no clergy in the Baha'i Faith and elected governing institutions have been established by Baha'u'llah for the administration of the affairs of the Baha'i Faith, the institutions function primarily using consensus formed through consultation. The independent investigation of truth with respect to the progressive development of a relationship with God, an understanding of the scripture, and making decisions is required for participating in the administration of the affairs of Baha'i community life.

> Know ye that God has created in man the power of reason, whereby man is enabled to investigate realty. God has not intended man to imitate blindly his fathers and ancestors. He has endowed him with mind, or the faculty of reasoning, by the exercise of which he is to investigate · and discover the truth, and that which he finds real and true he must accept. He must not be an imitator or blind follower of any soul. He must not rely implicitly upon the opinion of any man without investigation; nay, each soul must seek intelligently and independently, arriving at a real conclusion and bound only by that reality. The greatest cause of bereavement and disheartening in the world of humanity is ignorance based upon blind imitation. It is due to this that wars and battles prevail; from this cause hatred and animosity arise continually among mankind....

God has given man the eye of investigation by which he may see and recognize truth. He has endowed man with ears that he may hear the message of reality and conferred upon him the gift of reason by which he may discover things for himself. This is his endowment and equipment for the investigation of reality. Man is not intended to see through the eyes of another, hear through another's ears nor comprehend with another's brain. Each human creature has individual endowment, power, and responsibility in the creative plan of God. Therefore depend upon your own reason and judgment and adhere to the outcome of your own investigation; otherwise, you will be utterly submerged in the sea of ignorance and deprived of all the bounties of God. Turn to God, supplicate humbly at His threshold, seeking assistance and confirmation, that God may rend asunder the veils that obscure your vision. Then will your eyes be filled with illumination, face to face you will behold the reality of God and your heart become completely purified from the dross of ignorance, reflecting the glories and bounties of the Kingdom. (Promulgation of Universal Peace, 291-293)

The integration of the will of God into the fabric of the institutions of the Baha'i Faith proceeds through the instruments of both reason and faith. Justice is established in the context of Baha'i community through individuals submitting to the will of God in an active process of investigation, consultation, and decision making. The administrative structures that Baha'u'llah has provided harness both reason and faith for decisions and action. Consensus is the preferred mechanism for decisions but voting is used on the occasions it cannot be reached.

The best solutions often develop from the "clash of differing opinions" (Selections from the Writings of Abdul'Baha, 87). At the heart of Baha'i consultative processes is the willingness to find the truth in an opposing argument, particularly in the heat of discussion between individuals who hold painfully different views. The power that converts conflict into creative solutions is trust in God. A willingness to submit to the will of God, particularly under conflict, provides the flexibility for creative solutions. The Baha'i administrative order fulfills the Old Testament promise that "the government shall be upon His shoulders" (Isaiah 9.6) and the New Testament promise that "the meek shall inherit the earth" (Matthew 5:5). Individuals articulate the will of God into the fabric of community through their willingness in consultation to relinquish ownership of a position in favor of the love of God and service to the community.

– 17 –

SCIENCE AND RELIGION

The prominence of reason in the Baha'i dispensation has implications for the relationship of the institutions of science to those of religion. The past five hundred years has seen the development of a dialog stirred by the discoveries of science and the pronouncements of religion, albeit yielding at times more passionate argument than cooperative discussion. Baha'u'llah has explicitly compelled dialog between the two. He has set the parameters for the discussion. Science and reason must affirm the efficacy of religion in addressing our spiritual nature. Religious teachings must conform to the findings of science in matters concerning the physical world.

Furthermore, religion must conform to reason and be in accord with the conclusions of science. For religion, reason and science are realities; therefore, these three being realities, must conform and be reconciled. A question or principle which is religious in its nature must be sanctioned by science. Science must declare it to be valid, and reason must confirm it in order that it may inspire confidence. If religious teaching, however, be at variance with science and reason, it is unquestionably superstition. The Lord of mankind has bestowed upon us the faculty of reason whereby we may discern the realities of things. How then can man rightfully accept any proposition which is not in conformity with the processes of reason and the principles of science? Assuredly such a course cannot inspire man with confidence and real belief. (Promulgation of Universal Peace, 394)

Some Implications

Baha'u'llah noted that the universe is infinitely populated with life. Since His lifetime, we have discovered that the currently visible universe contains about 50 billion galaxies. Our galaxy contains about 100 billion suns. It takes light about 70,000 years to travel across our galaxy. Astronomers are just now beginning to observe the planetary systems of suns in our neighborhood. In a little more than one hundred years' time, we have advanced from travel by foot to space flight, extending our physical reach to our satellite world and throughout the solar system.

The unfolding of the adult capacities of humanity for the investigation of reality is just beginning. For example, science has just begun to unravel the genetic code that provides the blueprint to how everything works in our human biology as well as the other living organisms on this planet. There can be little doubt that we will use the information provided by our genetics for curing human disease. We will engage our knowledge to increase our average lifespan and the quality of our physical lives. Will we use it to make ourselves more intelligent? Will we use it to design our children?

Our science will become increasingly powerful and so will our ability to manipulate the phenomenal world. The increased capability requires mechanisms for the integration of values derived from spiritual insights into the processes that direct the use of our new understandings and technologies. With the potential for benevolent uses comes the capacity for destruction, i.e. nuclear fission. The guidance of Baha'u'llah's writings, including the amplified faculty to approach the presence of God, the admonition for the independent investigation of truth, and the use of consultative decision-making processes, provide tools to utilize the power of this stage of human evolution. The process of "beating our spears into plowshares," of harnessing our maturing strength for fruitful rather than destructive purposes, will unfold gracefully to the degree we utilize the gifts provided by Baha'u'llah.

– 18 –

EQUALITY OF WOMEN AND MEN

Male physical dominance has been used in most of the world's cultures to reinforce concepts of the superiority of men over women. Dominance has been reinforced through exclusion of women from education and participation in the institutions of society. Women have been powerless to fend for themselves in societies that afforded them little or no independent protection under the law, limited access to education, restricted rights to own property, and barriers to participation in the institutions of society. The dominance of men in all of the institutions of society along with greater physical strength ensured male dominance in personal relationships.

One of the developments of modern society is the ascendancy of women to full participation in the institutions of society. Baha'u'llah affirmed the equality of women and men within the culture and institutions of the nineteenth-century Islamic world. Abdul-Baha conditioned the degree of success and prosperity for global community on its achievement. The Baha'i writings use the analogy of the flight of a bird for the success of human society. It requires two equally strong wings for flight. Human society in this age requires the equality of women and men for its success.

And among the teachings of Baha'u'llah is the equality of women and men. The world of humanity has two wings—one is women and the other men. Not until both wings are equally developed can the bird fly. Should one wing remain weak, flight is impossible. Not until the world

of women becomes equal to the world of men in the acquisition of virtues and perfections, can success and prosperity be attained as they ought to be. (Selections from
the Writings of Abdul-Baha, 302)

At a meeting of the Women's Freedom League in Lon-
don, January 1913, Abdul'Baha spoke of the progress that
would result from the continued efforts of women to fulfill
their potential.

> Women must go on advancing; they must extend their
> knowledge of science, literature, history, for the perfec-
> tion of humanity. Erelong they will receive their rights.
> Men will see women in earnest, bearing themselves with
> dignity, improving the civil and political life, opposed to
> warfare, demanding suffrage and equal opportunities. I ex-
> pect to see you advance in all phases of life; then will your
> brows be crowned with the diadem of eternal glory.
> (Baha'u'llah and the New Era, 149)

Male and female qualities are different. The Baha'i writings insist that they must be equally respected and integrated into the institutions of society. With the development
of weapons of mass destruction that can potentially annihi-
late human life, the ordering of the affairs of humankind on
the planet will be well served by the articulation of the more
cooperative, supportive feminine qualities into the institutions of society and the de-accentuation of the more forceful
male characteristics.

> The world in the past has been ruled by force, and
> man has dominated over woman by reason of his more
> forceful and aggressive qualities both of body and mind.
> But the balance is already shifting; force is losing its domi-
> nance, and mental alertness, intuition, and the spiritual
> qualities of love and service, in which woman is strong, are
> gaining ascendancy. Hence the new age will be an age less
> masculine and more permeated with the feminine ideals,
> or, to speak more exactly, will be an age in which the mas-
> culine and feminine elements of civilization will be more
> evenly balanced. (Baha'u'llah and the New Era, 149)

– 19 –

ECONOMIC ISSUES

Elimination of the Extremes of Wealth and Poverty

Essential to the Baha'i concept of economic health and prosperity is the elimination of the extremes of wealth and poverty. The injustice apparent in the extreme polarization undermines human spiritual, social, and material well being. The economic extremes violate our spiritual capacities for compassion and our sensitivity to human life. The inherent injustice also destabilizes the political, social, and economic fabric of society. The Baha'i writings specify that we are to develop an organization in human economic affairs that mitigates the extremes of wealth and poverty. Abdul'Baha, however, warns against legislative mechanisms that attempt to homogenize the distribution of wealth. Equal justice cannot be established through treating everyone exactly the same.

Social and political order for humankind necessitates differences in rank and position. Different people are good at different tasks in the social order. Tasks are not equally valued by the individuals of society. There will always be differences in the values individuals hold concerning the phenomenal world. And individual initiative is an essential component of establishing justice in the context of economic well being.

> The arrangements of the circumstances of the people must be such that poverty shall disappear, that everyone, as far as possible, according to his rank and position, shall share in comfort and well-being. We see among us men

who are overburdened with riches on the one hand, and on the other those unfortunate ones who starve with nothing; those who possess several stately palaces, and those who have not where to lay their head....This condition of affairs is wrong, and must be remedied. Now the remedy must be carefully undertaken. It cannot be done by bringing to pass absolute equality between men. Equality is a chimera! It is entirely impracticable. Even if equality could be achieved it could not continue; and if its existence were possible, the whole order of the world would be destroyed. The Law of Order must always obtain in the world of humanity. Heaven has so decreed in the creation of man....

Certainly, some being enormously rich and others lamentably poor, an organization is necessary to control and improve this state of affairs. It is important to limit riches, as it is also of importance to limit poverty. Either extreme is not good....When we see poverty allowed to reach a condition of starvation, it is a sure sign that somewhere we shall find tyranny. Men must bestir themselves in this matter, and no longer delay in altering conditions which bring the misery of grinding poverty to a very large number of people.

The rich must give of their abundance; they must soften their hearts and cultivate a compassionate intelligence, taking thought for those sad ones who are suffering from lack of the very necessaries of life.

There must be special laws made, dealing with these extremes of riches and want....The government of the countries should conform to the Divine Law which gives equal justice to all....Not until this is done will the Law of God be obeyed. (Paris Talks, 156-59)

Sharing

The indication by Abdul'Baha that "the remedy [to economic injustice] be carefully undertaken" is a reflection of Baha'u'llah's teaching that "voluntary sharing is greater than (legally imposed) equality."

Among the teachings of Baha'u'llah is voluntary sharing of one's property with others among mankind. This
voluntary sharing is greater than (legally imposed) equality, and consists in this, that one should not prefer oneself
to others, but rather should sacrifice one's life and property for others. But this should not be introduced by coercion so that it becomes a law which man is compelled to
follow. Nay, rather, man should voluntarily and of his own
choice sacrifice his property and life for others, and spend
willingly for the poor, just as is done in Persia among the
Baha'is. (Abdul'Baha from a letter to the Central Organization for a Durable Peace written in 1919, Baha'u'llah
and the New Era, 142)

Capital and Labor

Abdul'Baha provided guidance in 1912 concerning the
relationship between capital and labor. The rich would "willingly divide" their wealth. They would, however, "come to
this gradually." The world community is still struggling with
these principles. Shoghi Effendi rearticulated this principle
in his comments concerning global governance. He described
"a world community in which all economic barriers will have
been permanently demolished and the interdependence of
Capital and Labor definitely recognized..." (Shoghi Effendi,
The World Order of Baha'u'llah, 40-41). The recognition of
the economic interdependence of capital and labor will come
about gradually through educative processes of choice and
consequence. As Abdul'Baha stated, it must be chosen. "The
rich must give of their abundance; they must soften their
hearts and cultivate a compassionate intelligence, taking
thought for those sad ones who are suffering from lack of the
very necessaries of life" (Abdul'Baha, Baha'u'llah and the
New Era, 141-42). It is a step beyond enlightened self-
interest—the phrase currently used to describe the attitude
of the rich person who is economically progressive, though
it addresses the same principle. All will benefit spiritually,
politically, and economically if we share rather than fight

over access to wealth. The particular mechanisms to safeguard against the development of the extremes of wealth
and poverty will be arrived at through agreement, not force.

> The solution of economic questions will not be brought
> about by array of capital against labor, and labor against
> capital, in strife and conflict, but by the voluntary attitude
> of goodwill on both sides. Then a real and lasting justness
> of conditions will be secured....
>
> Among the Baha'is there are no extortionate, merce-
> nary and unjust practices, no rebellious demands, no revo-
> lutionary uprisings against existing governments....
>
> It will not be possible in the future for men to amass
> great fortunes by the labors of others. The rich will will-
> ingly divide. They will come to this gradually, naturally, by
> their own volition. It will never be accomplished by war
> and bloodshed. (Abdul'Baha in a talk given in America in
> ⸱1912, Baha'u'llah and the New Era, 144-45)

Sharing the Profit

One of the mechanisms prescribed for the Baha'i dispensation is in evidence in the growing practice of profit sharing. Labor and capital merge perspectives through profit
sharing.

> Now I want to tell you about the law of God. Accord-
> ing to the divine law, employees should not be paid merely
> by wages. Nay, rather they should be partners in every
> work. The question of socialization is very difficult. It will
> not be solved by strikes for wages. All the governments of
> the world must be united, and organize an assembly, the
> members of which shall be elected from the parliaments
> and the noble ones of the nations. These must plan with
> wisdom and power, so that neither the capitalists suffer
> enormous losses, nor the laborers become needy. In the
> utmost moderation they should make the law, then an-
> nounce to the public that the rights of the working people
> are to be effectively preserved; also the rights of the capi-
> talists are to be protected. When such a general law is

adopted, by the will of both sides, should a strike occur, all the governments of the world should collectively resist it. Otherwise the work will lead to much destruction, especially in Europe. Terrible things will take place.

One of the several causes of a universal European war will be this question. The owners of properties, mines and factories, should share their incomes with their employees, and give a fairly certain percentage of their profits to their workingmen, in order that the employees should receive, besides their wages, some of the general income of the factory, so that the employee may strive with his soul in the work. (Abdul'Baha from a talk given at Dublin, New Hampshire in 1912, Baha'u'llah and the New Era, 145-46)

At the heart of this issue is the recognition of the value of talent—an individual's capacities and gifts, which are used to produce benefit to himself and others.

> The people of Baha should not deny any soul the reward due to him, should treat craftsmen with deference, and, unlike the people aforetime, should not defile their tongues with abuse. In this Day the sun of craftsmanship shineth above the horizon of the occident and the river of arts is flowing out of the sea of that region. One must speak with fairness and appreciate such bounty. By the life of God! The word 'Equity' shineth bright and resplendent even as the sun. We pray God to graciously shed its radiance upon everyone. He is in truth powerful over all things, He Who is wont to answer the prayers of all men. (Tablets of Baha'u'llah, 38-39)

Work

Work in the Baha'i dispensation is a form of worship. The use of talent to benefit ourselves and others is elevated in human consciousness to the level of awareness of God.

> It is enjoined on every one of you to engage in some occupation—some art, trade or the like. We have made this—your occupation—identical with the worship of God,

the True One. Reflect, O people, upon the Mercy of God and upon His Favors, then thank Him in mornings and evenings.

Waste not your time in idleness and indolence, and occupy yourselves with that which will profit yourselves and others beside yourselves. Thus hath the matter been decreed in this Tablet, from the Horizon of which the Sun of Wisdom and Divine Utterance is gleaming! The most despised of men before God is he who sits and begs. Cling unto the rope of means, relying upon God, the Causer of Causes. (Tablets of Baha'u'llah, 26)

— 20 —

UNIVERSAL
COMPULSORY EDUCATION

Baha'u'llah committed the Baha'i community to the principle of universal education before it was an established concept in any of the governments of the world. He made it mandatory for Baha'is to arrange for the education of their children. He instructed the governance structures of the Baha'i Faith to ensure the education of all children if some parents could not or would not provide it and explicitly directed the Baha'is concerning its funding and administration.

> Unto every father hath been enjoined the instruction of his son and daughter in the art of reading and writing and in all that hath been laid down in the Holy Tablet. He that putteth away that which is commanded unto him, the Trustees are then to take from him that which is required for their instruction, if he be wealthy, and if not the matter devolveth upon the House of Justice. Verily, have We made it a shelter for the poor and needy. He that bringeth up his son or the son of another, it is as though he hath brought up a son of Mine; upon him rest My Glory, My loving kindness, My Mercy, that have compassed the world. (Kitab-i-Aqdas, 37)

The emphasis on education is integral to Baha'i community. The reliance on science and reason, the lack of a clergy, the independent investigation of truth, elected administration, and consultation for problem solving necessitate an educated body of participants. Education is the means by which the latent capacities of human reality are revealed.

> Man is the supreme Talisman. Lack of a proper education hath, however, deprived him of that which he doth inherently possess. Through a word proceeding out of the mouth of God he was called into being; by one word more he was guided to recognize the Source of his education; by yet another word his station and destiny were safeguarded. The Great Being saith: Regard man as a mine rich in gems of inestimable value. Education can, alone, cause it to reveal its treasures, and enable mankind to benefit therefrom.... (Gleanings from the Writings of Bahá'u'lláh, 259–60)

Both the spiritual and material potential of human capacity should be developed.

> ...Schools must first train the children in the principles of religion, so that the Promise and the Threat recorded in the Books of God may prevent them from the things forbidden and adorn them with the mantle of the commandments; but this in such a measure that it may not injure the children by resulting in ignorant fanaticism and bigotry. (Tablets of Bahá'u'lláh, 68)

> Strain every nerve to acquire both inner and outer perfections, for the fruit of the human tree hath ever been and will ever be perfections both within and without. It is not desirable that a man be left without knowledge or skills, for he is then but a barren tree. Then, so much as capacity and capability allow, ye needs must deck the tree of being with fruits such as knowledge, wisdom, spiritual perception and eloquent speech. (Compilation on Bahá'í Education, 59)

Baha'u'llah provides additional guidance with respect to the content and usefulness of education. It should produce beneficial results for society by increasing the ability of individuals to serve humankind.

Knowledge is as wings to man's life, and a ladder for his ascent. Its acquisition is incumbent upon everyone. The knowledge of such sciences, however, should be acquired as can profit the peoples of the earth, and not those which begin with worlds and end with words. Great indeed is the claim of scientists and craftsmen on the peoples of the world. Unto this beareth witness the Mother Book on the day of His return. Happy are those possessed of a hearing ear. In truth, knowledge is a veritable treasure for man, and a source of glory of bounty, of joy, of exaltation, of cheer and gladness unto him. Thus hath the Tongue of Grandeur spoken in this Most Great Prison. (Tablets of Baha'u'llah, 51-52)

Conclusion

The cultures of the world that have evolved in relative isolation through the past five to ten thousand years are now converging into global community. The technological advances that have precipitated the process are accelerating as the collective capacities of the individuals who produce them are further advanced. The technologies, for example, that permit distance education bring ever more individuals into the arena of discovery and development. The advances in medicine that expand life expectancy increase the productiveness of individuals with mature knowledge and experience. National political, social, and economic environs are becoming increasingly interdependent as advanced information technologies afford broader and deeper interactions among the world's populations.

These changes are unprecedented for the participating cultures. Ways of thinking and living that have informed hundreds, even thousands, of years of human experience are being challenged, disrupted, and discredited. The faith and integrity associated with the institutions and belief systems of the world's cultures are being questioned along with the old ways of thinking and living. The institutions essential to the health and stability of human society are being dismantled by the frenetic nature and pace of change. To the degree that the presence and guidance of God are also lost, the global community is set adrift in a sea of capricious materialism, confusion, and hopelessness.

The transition to global culture can be characterized as a particular stage of development for humanity. The counterpart stage in an individual's development that shares its tumultuous nature is adolescence. Adolescence is a time for the faltering appearance of reason along with the emergence of heightened passions and increased physical power. The new motivational paradigm challenges the restraints on behavior formerly imposed through unquestioned submission to parental authority. The processes of development at this stage of maturation require the search for meaning and direction through an independent investigation of reality. Meaning, purpose, and integrity must emerge from the choices integral to a higher level of human capacity.

The Author of creation provided for humanity's earlier stages of development through Messengers, i.e. Zoroaster, Krishna, Buddha, Moses, Jesus, and Muhammad. They provided guidance relevant to the exigencies of their times. The guidance integral to the spiritual traditions they initiated has been reaffirmed and rearticulated into the fabric of human culture through the return of the Messenger of God, Baha'u'llah. His specific mission is the harmonization of human culture into a peaceful, productive, ever-advancing, global civilization. The Baha'i dispensation provides the spiritual, intellectual, and institutional tools requisite to the globalization of humankind and its emergence into adulthood.

Baha'u'llah extends the essential verities underlying past dispensations into the exigencies of the current stage of human development on this planet. God has been reflected through the Messengers of a progressive series of religions integral to the earlier developmental stages of human society. Central to Baha'u'llah's teachings for this age are the unity of God, religion, and humankind. Baha'u'llah provides for the harnessing of the diverse perspectives and increased capacities of this age through the fuller participation by the individual in the integration of spirituality into the fabric of human culture. He reinvigorates hope and trust in God through His presence and guidance and harnesses the use of reason in the independent investigation of truth to the ongoing spiritual and material advancement of global community.

Those who recognize Baha'u'llah as the fulfillment of the promise of the scriptures of the world's religions inherit the hope of God's purpose for humanity. The Baha'i dispensation provides an understanding of the course of human history as inevitably proceeding through the will of God toward the "Kingdom of God on earth." At this stage of social evolution on the planet, the vision is more substantially and specifically embodied in the scriptures of the Baha'i Faith than the earlier scriptures could provide because of the limits of earlier stages of development. The hope of a just and peaceful global civilization integral to a Baha'i view of human history transcends the frailty of utopian dreams on the one hand and the lethargy of cynicism and skepticism on the other. Substance is given to this hope through Baha'u'llah's provision of a "wondrous System" (Baha'u'llah, Gleanings, 136).

Baha'is expect the "wondrous System" to unfold in successive, interdependent developmental stages—disintegration of the institutions of the past, the establishment of a secular framework for the cessation of war (Baha'is refer to this as the Lesser Peace), and finally the realization of a just and spiritually enlightened global society (Baha'is refer to this as the Most Great Peace). The stages are essentially linked to each other and proceed through choice and consequence. Ineffectual methods and means for the establishment of global community become apparent as mankind learns through the successes and failures of responding to this stage of its development. The revelation of Baha'u'llah is integral to this process.

The world's equilibrium hath been upset through the vibrating influence of this most great, this new World Order. Mankind's ordered life hath been revolutionized through the agency of this unique, this wondrous System—the like of which mortal eyes have never witnessed (Baha'u'llah, Gleanings, 136).

The realization of a peaceful and bountiful world order will appear as the individuals articulate the admonitions of Baha'u'llah into the fabric of their lives through the independent expression of their love for God and each other.

Failure becomes apparent through human suffering. The Lesser Peace is the pragmatic realization of methods and systems that work in the establishment of global stability. The League of Nation, the United Nations, and the emerging European Union are examples of interrelated attempts to construct a framework for the resolution of conflict through governance rather than war.

The "wondrous System" that will afford a transformation toward the Most Great Peace is provided by the revelation of Baha'u'llah. The spiritual intensity of the revelation provides the basis for the unification of the peoples of the world in a just and peaceful global community. The following is a quote from Baha'u'llah translated by Shoghi Effendi.

This is the Day whereon naught can be seen except the splendors of the Light that shineth from the face of thy Lord, the Gracious, the Most Bountiful. Verily, We have caused every soul to expire by virtue of Our irresistible and all-subduing sovereignty. We have then called into being a new creation, as token of Our grace unto men. I am, verily, the All-Bountiful, the Ancient of Days. This is the Day whereon the unseen world crieth out: 'Great is thy blessedness, O earth, for thou hast been made the foot-stool of thy God, and been chosen as the seat of His mighty throne!' The realm of glory exclaimeth: 'Would that my life could be sacrificed for thee, for He Who is the Beloved of the All-Merciful hath established His sovereignty upon

thee, through the power of His name that hath been promised unto all things, whether of the past or of the future.'
(World Order of Baha'u'llah, 206)

This work closes with Shoghi Effendi's description of
the world community that is destined to evolve through
Baha'u'llah's renewed and heightened revelation of God for
this age.

The unity of the human race, as envisaged by
Baha'u'llah, implies the establishment of a world commonwealth in which all nations, races, creeds and classes are
closely and permanently united, and in which that au-
tonomy of its state members and their personal freedom
and initiative of the individuals that compose them are
definitely and completely safeguarded. This commonwealth
must, as far as we can visualize it, consist of a world legislature, whose members will, as the trustees of the whole of
mankind, ultimately control the entire resources of all the
component nations, and will enact such laws as shall be
required to regulate the life, satisfy the needs and adjust
the relationships of all races and peoples. A world executive, backed by an international Force, will carry out the
decisions arrived at, and apply the laws enacted by, this
world legislature, and will safeguard the organic unity of
the whole commonwealth. A world tribunal will adjudi-
cate and deliver its compulsory and final verdict in all and
any disputes that may arise between the various elements
constituting this universal system. A mechanism of world
inter-communication will be devised, embracing the whole
planet, freed from national hindrances and restrictions, and
functioning with marvelous swiftness and perfect regular-
ity. A world metropolis will act as the nerve center of a
world civilization, the focus towards which the unifying
forces of life will converge and from which its energizing
influences will radiate. A world language will either be in-
vented or chosen from among the existing languages and
will be taught in the schools of all the federated nations as
an auxiliary to their mother tongue. A world script, a world

literature, a uniform and universal system of currency, of weights and measure, will simplify and facilitate intercourse and understanding among the nations and races of mankind. In such a world society, science and religion, the two most potent forces in human life, will be reconciled, will cooperate, and will harmoniously develop. The press will, under such a system, while giving full scope to the expression of the diversified views and convictions of mankind, cease to be mischievously manipulated by vested interests, whether private or public, and will be liberated from the influence of contending governments and peoples. The economic resources of the world will be organized, its sources of raw materials will be tapped and fully utilized, its markets will be coordinated and developed, and the distribution of its products will be equitably regulated.

National rivalries, hatreds, and intrigues will cease, and racial animosity and prejudice will be replaced by racial amity, understanding and cooperation. The causes of religious strife will be permanently removed, economic barriers and restrictions will be completely abolished, and the inordinate distinction between classes will be obliterated. Destitution on the one hand, and gross accumulation of ownership on the other, will disappear. The enormous energy dissipated and wasted on war, whether economic or political, will be consecrated to such ends as will extend the range of human inventions and technical development, to the increase of the productivity of mankind, to the extermination of disease, to the extension of scientific research, to the raising of the standard of physical health, to the sharpening and refinement of the human brain, to the exploitation of the unused and unsuspected resources of the planet, to the prolongation of human life, and to the furtherance of any other agency that can stimulate the intellectual, the moral, and spiritual life of the entire human race.

A world federal system, ruling the whole earth and exercising unchallengeable authority over its unimaginably vast resources, blending and embodying the ideals of both the East and the West, liberated from the curse of war and its miseries, and bent on the exploitation of all the avail able sources of energy on the surface of the planet, a system in which Force is made the servant of Justice, whose life is sustained by its universal recognition of one God and by its allegiance to one common Revelation—such is the goal towards which humanity, impelled by the unifying forces of life, is moving (Shoghi Effendi. World Order of Baha'u'llah: Selected Letters, 203-4).

BIBLIOGRAPHY

I relied heavily on the compilation of scripture provided by *World Scripture: a Comparative Anthology of Sacred Texts,* a project of the International Religious Foundation, published at St. Paul, Minnesota: Paragon House in 1995. Throughout this bibliography, I used the citations provided in the bibliography of *World Scripture.* I included page numbers where the quoted material can be found in *World Scripture* [WS].

African Traditional Religions
Akan Prayer on Talking Drums, WS 105
> J. H. Nketia, *Drumming in Akan Communities of Ghana* (London: Thomas Nelson, 1963)

Yoruba Poem. Nigeria, WS 179
> Wande Abimbola, ed., *Yoruba Oral Tradition* (Ibadan, Nigeria: University Press Ltd., 1975)

Baha'i Faith
Baha'i Prayers, 13, 307-311
> *Baha'i Prayers* (Wilmette, IL: Baha'i Publishing Trust, 2002)

Baha'i World Faith, 205
> *Baha'i World Faith: Selectyed Writings of Baha'u'llah and Abdul-Baha* (Willmette, IL: Baha'i Publishing Trust)

Baha'u'llah and the New Era, 141-42, 144-45, 145-46, 147-48, 149, 152
> J. E. Esslemont, *Baha'u'llah and the New Era* (Willmette, IL: Baha'i Publishing Trust, 1980)

Divine Art of Living, 48
> Mabel Hyde Paine, ed., *The Divine Art of Living: Selections from Writings of Baha'u'llah and Abdul-Baha* (Willmette, IL: Baha'I Publishing Trust, 1979)

Divine Art of Living, 51-52
> Mabel Hyde Paine, ed., *The Divine Art of Living*

Compilation on Bahá'í Education, 59
> *Compilation on Bahá'í Education,* Compiled by the Research De-
> partment of the Universal House of Justice, Bahá'í World Cen-
> tre, August 1976
Gleanings, 5, 10, 46-47, 66-67, 68-69, 72, 74, 79-80, 95, 111, 132, 136, 143,
> 145, 195, 215, 249-50, 286, 291, 330-31, 333-34
> Shoghi Effendi, trans., *Gleanings from the Writings of
> Baha'u'llah* (Willmette, IL: Baha'i Publishing Trust, 1996)
Hidden Words: From the Persian, nos. 8, 24, 46, 70
Hidden Words: From the Arabic, nos. 7, 14
> Shoghi Effendi, trans., *The Hidden Words: Baha'u'llah*
> (Willmette, IL: Baha'i Publishing Trust, 1994)
King of Glory, 78
> H. M. Balyuzi, *Baha'u'llah: The King of Glory* (Kidlington, Ox-
> ford, Great Britain: George Ronald, Publisher, 1991)
Kitab-i-Aqdas, 37
> Baha'u'llah, *The Kitab-i-aqdas* (Ann Arbor, MI: Edwards Broth-
> ers, 1992)
Lights of Guidance, 474
> Helen Hornby, ed., *Lights of Guidance: A Baha'i Reference File* (
> New Delhi, India: Baha'i Publishing Trust, 1988)
Paris Talks, 29
> Paris Talks*: Addresses Given by Abdul'Baha in 1911* (UK Bahá'í
> Publishing Trust, 1972 eleventh edition reprint)
Paris Talks, 132, 156-159
> *Paris Talks: Addresses Given by Abdul'Baha in 1911,* (Nepean,
> ON, Canada: Nine Pines Publishig, Baha'i Publishing Trust,
> 1999)
Promise of World Peace, 17
> The Universal House of Justice, *Promise of World Peace: To the
> Peoples of the World* (Canberra, Australia: Bahai' Publications of
> Australia, 1986)
Promulgation of Universal Peace, 106, 291-293, 296, 316, 378-79, 394, 468
> Howard MacNutt, ed., *The promulgation of Universal Peace:
> Talks Delivered by Abdul-Baha during His Visit to the United
> States and Canada in 1912* (Willmette, IL: Baha'i Publishing
> Trust, 1982)
Selections from the Writings of Abdul'Baha 53-54, 87, 299, 302
> A Committee at the Baha'i World Center and Marzieh Gail,
> trans., *Selections from the Writings of Abdul-Baha,* (Chatham,
> Great Britain: W & J MacKay Limited, 1978)
Selections from the Writings of the Bab, 6-7, 9, 12, 48, 91
> Habib Taherzadeh, trans., *Selections from the Writings of the Bab*
> (Chatham, Great Britain: W & J MacKay Limited, 1976)

Seven Valleys and the Four Valleys 59
    Baha'u'llah, *Seven Valleys and the Four Valleys* (Wilmette, IL: US
    Baha'i Publishing Trust, 1991 Pocketbook edition)
Some Answered Questions, 100-102, 151, 283, 286
    Laura Clifford Barney, trans., *Some Answered Questions: Abdul-Baha* (Wilmette, IL: Baha'i Publishing Trust, 1981)
Tablets of Baha'u'llah, 26, 38-39, 51-52, 64, 68, 90, 221
    Habib Taherzadeh, trans., *Tablets of Baha'u'llah* (Willmette, IL:
    Baha'i Publishing Trust, 1988)
Talk Given to Women's Freedom League
    Abdul'Baha, *Talk Given to Women's Freedom League*, London,
    January, 1913
Will and Testament of Abdul'Baha, 19-20, 25-26
    Abdul-Baha, *The Will and Testament of Abdul-Baha* (Wilmette,
    IL: US Baha'i Publishing Trust, 1990 reprint) Online at http://
    reference.bahai.org/en/t/ab/WT/
World Order of Baha'u'llah, 40 41, 203-4, 206
    Shoghi Effendi, *The World Order of Baha'u'llah* (Wilmette, IL:
    US Baha'i Publishing Trust, 1986)

Buddhism

Anguttara Nikaya iv.91, Sujata Sutta, WS 182
    F. L. Woodward and E. M. Hare, trans., *Gradual Sayings*, 5 vol.
    (London: Pali Text Society, 1951-65)
Dhammapada 46, WS 231; 54, WS 221, 730; 69, WS 123; 127, WS 124
    Narada Maha Thera, trans., *The Dhammapada* (Columbo, Sri
    Lanka: Vajirarama, 1972)
Dhammapada 136, WS 123
    David J. Kalupahana, trans., A Path of Righteousness:
    Dhammapada (Lanham: University Press of America, 1986)
Dhammapada 151, WS 78; 194, WS 185, 195; 219-20, WS 238; 223 WS
655; 239, WS 510; 393, 396, WS 191
    Narada Maha Thera, trans., *The Dhammapada* (Columbo, Sri
    Lanka: Vajirarama, 1972)
Diamond Sutra 26, WS 287
    A. F. Price, trans., The Diamond Sutra (Boston: Shambhala,
    1969)
Digha Nikaya iii.74, Cakkavatti-Sihanada Suttanta, WS 792-93
    T. W. Rhys Davids and C. A. F. Rhys Davids, trans., *Dialogues of
    the Buddha (Digha Nikaya)*, Parts 1-3, Sacred Books of the
    Buddhists, vols. 2-4 (London: Pali Text Society, 1956-59)
Digha Nikaya iii.74-75, Cakkavatti-Sihanada Suttanta, WS 792-93
    T. W. Rhys Davids and C. A. F. Rhys Davids

Digha Nikaya iii.92-93, Agganna Suttanta, WS 748
>   Wm. Theodore de Bary, ed., *Sources of Indian Tradition* (New York: Columbia University Press, 1958)
Digha Nikaya: Brahmajala Sutta, WS 231
>   T. W. Rhys Davids and C. A. F. Rhys Davids, trans., *Dialogues of the Buddha (Digha Nikaya)*, Parts 1-3, Sacred Books of the Buddhists, vols. 2-4 (London: Pali Text Society, 1956-59)
Itivuttaka 11, WS 188
>   F. L. Woodward, trans., *Minor Anthologies of the Pali Canon: Part 2 Udana: Verses of Uplift and Itivuttaka: As it Was Said* (London: Pali Text Society, 1948)
Khuddaka Patha, WS 29
>   F. L. Woodward, *Some Sayings of the Buddha* (London: Oxford University Press, 1973)
Lion's Roar of Queen Srimala 5, WS 466
>   Diani Y. Paul, *The Buddhist Feminine Ideal* (Missoula, Mont.: Scholars Press, 1980)
Lotus Sutra 2, WS 247; 3, WS 253-54; 3, WS 406; 5, WS 361; 13, WS 775
>   W. E. Soothill, trans., *The Lotus of the Wonderful Law* (Oxford: Oxford University Press, 1930)
Meditation on Buddha Amitayus 27, WS 171
>   *Shinshu Seiten: Jodo Shin Buddhist Teaching* (San Fransisco: Buddhist Churches of America, 1978)
Nagarjuna, Mulamadhyamaka Karika 25, pp. 59-60
>   Kenneth K. Inada, trans., *Nagarjuna: Mulamadhyamakakarika* (Tokyo: Hokuseido Press, 1970)
Nagarjuna, Precious Garland 8-9, WS 112; 283, WS 614; 327, WS 749
>   J. Hopkins and L. Rimpoche, trans., *Nagarjuna, The Precious Garland and the Song of the Four Mindfulnesses* (London: George Allen & Unwin, 1975)
Perfection of Wisdom in Eight Thousand Lines
>   3.51-54 WS 105; 31.1 WS 52
>   Edward Conze, ed. and trans., *The Perfection of Wisdom in Eight Thousand Lines and Its Verse Summary* (San Fransisco: Four Seasons Foundation, 1983)
Samyutta Nikaya v.455, WS 239
>   F. L. Woodward, *Some Sayings of the Buddha* (London: Oxford University Press, 1973)
Samyutta Nikaya xlvii.37, WS 657
>   Nyanaponika Thera, *The Heart of Buddhist Meditation: A Handbook of Mental Training Based on the Buddha's Way of Mindfulness (Satipatthana)* (York Beach, Maine: Samuel Weiser, 1965)
Smaller Skhavativyuha Sutra 10, WS 592
>   Cowell, Muller, and Takakusu, *Buddhist Mahayana Texts.*

Sutra of Hui Neng 2, WS 58
> Wong Mou-lam, trans., *The Sutra of Hue Neng* (Boston: Shambhala, 1969)

Sutta Nipata 672-76, WS 254; 705, WS 114
> H. Saddhatissa, trans., *The Sutta-Nipata* (London: Curzon Press, 1985)

Sutta Nipata, 249, WS 614
> David Maurice, ed., *The Lion's Roar: An Anthology of the Buddha's Teachings Selected from the Pali Canon* (London: Rider & Co., 1962)

Sutta Nipata 798 WS 39
> K. R. Norman, trans., *The Group of Discourses* (London: Pali Text Society, 1984)

Udana 6, WS 614
> F. L. Woodward, trans., *Minor Anthologies of the Pali Canon: Part 2 Udana: Verses of Uplift and Itivuttaka: As it Was Said* (London: Pali Text Society, 1948)

Christianity

The Holy Bible, Revised Standard Version (New York: National Council of Churches of Christ in the USA, 1946, 1971) *Holy Bible*: Old and New Testaments, King James Version (Nashville, TN: Broadman Press, 1973) [All passages are from the Revised Standard Version unless marked KJV]

1 Corinthians 12:4-7, WS 53
1 Corinthians 13:9-12, WS 576
1 Corinthians 15:40-44, WS 226
1 Corinthians 7:1   KJV
1 Thessalonians 5:17, WS 593
2 Timothy 3:1-5, WS 775
Acts 10:34-35, WS 37
Colossians 3:5, WS 288
Ephesians 5:21-23, WS 180
Ephesians 5:27-33, WS 181
Galatians 3:28, WS 191
Galatians 6:7, WS 122
Hebrews 12:22-24, WS 249
James 1:25, WS 105
John 1:12   KJV
John 1:12-13, WS 406
John 1:1-4, 14, WS 466
John 1:9   KJV
John 10:25-30   KJV
John 10:16, WS 36
John 11.25, WS 410

Confucianism

Analects 2.4, WS 510; 3.3, WS 614; 3.13, WS 593; 11.11,
> WS 237; 21.2.1, WS 232
>> Arthur Waley, trans., *The Analects of Confucius* (London: George
>> Allen & Unwin; New Yourk: Random House, 1938)

Book of Ritual
>> James Legge, trans., *The Sacred Books of China, Part 4, The Li
>> Ki, a Collection of Treatises on the Rules of Propriety or Ceremo-
>> nial Usages*, Sacred Books of the East, vol. 27 (Oxford:
>> Clarendon Press, 1885)

Classic on Filial Piety 1
>> James Legge, trans., *The Sacred Books of China, Part 4, The Li
>> Ki, a Collection of Treatises on the Rules of Propriety or Ceremo-
>> nial Usages*, Sacred Books of the East, vol. 27 (Oxford:
>> Clarendon Press, 1885)

Doctrine of the Mean 12, WS 101, 175
>> Lin Yutang, ed. and trans., *The Wisdom of Confucius* (New York:
>> Random House, 1938)

I Ching 37: The Family, WS 180
>> John Blofeld, trans., *I Ching: The Book of Change* (London:
>> George Allen & Unwin, 1965)

Mencius IV.A.17, WS 616; VII.A.4, WS 114
>> D. C. Lau, trans., *Mencius* (London: Penguin Books, 1979)

Hinduism

Atharva Veda 14.2.71, WS 174
>> Raimundo Panikkar, ed., Mantramanjari: *The Vedic Experience*
>> (Berkeley: University of California Press, 1977)

Atharva Veda 7.52.1-2. WS 187
>> Abinash Chandra Bose, ed., *Hymns from the Vedas* (Bombay:
>> Asia Publishing House, 1966)

Basavanna, Vacana 239, WS 249
>> H. Deveerappa, ed., *Vacanas of Basavanna*, trans. L. M. A. Menezes
>> and S. M. Angadi (Sirigere, India: Annana Balaga, 1967)

Basavanna, Vacana 642, WS 614
>> Shivamurthy Shivacharya Mahaswamiji, his own transla-
>> tions submitted to *World Scripture*

Bhagavad Gita 2.19-25, WS 233
>> Eknath Easwaran, ed., *The Bhagavad Gita* (Petaluma, Calif.:
>> Nilgiri Press, 1985)

Bhagavad Gita 3.20-21
>> Kees W. Bolle, ed., The Bhagavadgita: A New Translation (Ber-
>> keley: University of California Press, 1979)

Bhagavad Gita 4.7-8; 4.11, WS 34
>> Eknath Easwaran, ed., *The Bhagavad Gita* (Petaluma, Calif.:
>> Nilgiri Press, 1985)

Bhagavad Gita 9.11-12
> Kees W. Bolle, ed., The Bhagavadgita: A New Translation (Berkeley: University of California Press, 1979)

Bhagavad Gita 9.29, WS 190; 9.32-33, WS 192
> Eknath Easwaran, ed., The Bhagavad Gita (Petaluma, Calif.: Nilgiri Press, 1985)

Laws of Manu 2.146, WS 407; 4.172, WS 123; 4.238-39, WS 238; 5.153-65, WS 181; 6.92, WS 112
> Georg Buhler, trans., The Laws of Manu, Sacred Books of the East, vol. 25 (Oxford: Clarendon Press, 1886)

Mahabharata, Anusasana Parva 113.8, WS 114
> V. Raghavan, trans., The Indian Heritage (Bangalore: Indian Institute of World Culture, 1963)

Ramayana, Aranya Kanda 29, WS 123
> Hari Prasad Shastri, trans., The Ramayana of Valmiki, 3 vols. (London: Shanti Sada, 1962)

Rig Veda 10.191.2-4, WS 187
> Abinash Chandra Bose, ed., Hymns from the Vedas (Bombay: Asia Publishing House, 1966)

Srimad Bhagavatam 1.1, WS 467; 11.12, WS 450; 11.15, WS 242; 11.3, WS 179; 11.5, WS 594
> Swami Prabhavananda, ed., Srimad Bhagavatam: The Wisdom of God (Hollywood: Vedanta Press, 1943)

Upanishad Brihadaranyaka 1.3.28, WS 31
> R. C. Zaehner, ed. and trans., Hindu Scriptures, Everyman's Library 944 (London: J. M. Dent & Sons, 1966)

Upanishad Brihadaranyaka 4.3.35, WS 235
> Swami Prabhavananda, ed., The Spiritual Heritage of India (Hollywood, Calif.: Vedanta Press, 1963)

Upanishad Isha 17, WS 231
> Abinash Chandra Bose, ed., Hymns from the Vedas (Bombay: Asia Publishing House, 1966)

Upanishad Kena 2.1-3, WS 56

Upanishad Mundaka 1.2.7-11
> Swami Pradhavananda and Fredeerick Manchester, trans., The Upanishads: Breath of the Eternal (Hollywood, Calif.: Vedanta Press, 1948)

Upanishad Mundaka 3.1.6, WS 102
> Eknath Easwaran, trans., The Upanishads (Petaluma, Calif.: Nilgiri Press, 1985)

Upanishad Svetasvatara 6.11
> F. Max Muller, trans., The Upanishads, 2 vols., Sacred Books of the East, Vols. 1, 15 (Oxford: Clarendon Press, 1879)

Vishnu Purana 3.12, WS 730
> Horace H. Wilson, trans., The Vishnu Purana (London: John Murray, 1840); London: Trubner, 1864)

Islam

Forty Hadith of an-Nawawi 13 WS 114; 36 WS 186
> Eric F. F. Bishop, "The Forty Traditions of An-Nawawi," in The Moslem World 29, no.2 (April 1939) 163-77 (Hartford, Conn.:Gartford Seminary Foundation)

Hadith (RGC p. 108) WS 137
> Etham Ruhi Figlali (Paper presented at the 6th Conference on God in April 1988 sponsored by the International Religious Foundation)

Hadith of Baihaqi (RGC p. 112) WS 748
> Ghazi Ahmad, trans., Sayings of Muhammad (Lahore, Pakistan: Sh. Muhammad Ashraf, 1968)

Hadith of Bukhari (RGC p. 112, 125) WS 748
> James Robson, trans., Mishkat Al-Masabih (Lahore, Pakistan: Sh. Muhammad Ashraf, 1981)

Hadith of Bukhari (RGC p. 133 All of you) WS 180
> Muhammad Muhsin Khan, trans., The Translation of the Meanings of Sahih Al-Bukhari, 9 vols. (Chicago:Kazi Publications, 1976-1979)

Hadith of Bukhari (RGC p. 133, Your wife) WS 178
> Emile Dermenghem, Muhammad and the Islamic Tradition, trans. from French by J. M. Watt (Westport, Conn.:Greenwood Press, 1974)

Qur'an 2.177 WS 615
> Arthur J. Arberry, trans., The Koran Interpreted (New York: Macmillan, 1955)

Qur'an 2.223 WS 178
> A. Yusuf Ali, trans., The Meaning of the Glorious Qur'an (Cairo, Egypt: Dar Al-Kitab Al-Masri, 1938)

Qur'an 2.256 WS 39
> Arthur J. Arberry, trans., The Koran Interpreted (New York: Macmillan, 1955)

Qur'an 3.178 WS 123-24; 4.129 WS 179
> Muhammad Marmaduke Pickthall, trans., The Meaning of the Glorious Qur'an (Mecca and New York: Muslim World League, 1977)

Qur'an 6.103 WS 55; 10.99-100 WS 39
> A. Yusuf Ali, trans., The Meaning of the Glorious Qur'an (Cairo, Egypt: Dar Al-Kitab Al-Masri, 1938)

Qur'an 14.15-16 WS 253; 16.36 WS 286
> Muhammad Marmaduke Pickthall, trans., The Meaning of the Glorious Qur'an (Mecca and New York: Muslim World League, 1977)

Qur'an 16.74 WS 55; 17.23 WS 171
> A. Yusuf Ali, trans., The Meaning of the Glorious Qur'an (Cairo, Egypt: Dar Al-Kitab Al-Masri, 1938)

Qur'an 18.46 WS 237
> Muhammad Marmaduke Pickthall, trans., *The Meaning of the Glorious Qur'an* (Mecca and New York: Muslim World League, 1977)

Qur'an 21.104-5 WS 789
> Arthur J. Arberry, trans., *The Koran Interpreted* (New York: Macmillan, 1955)

Qur'an 22.67 WS 36
> Muhammad Marmaduke Pickthall, trans., *The Meaning of the Glorious Qur'an* (Mecca and New York: Muslim World League, 1977)

Qur'an 24.54 WS 453
> Arthur J. Arberry, trans., *The Koran Interpreted* (New York: Macmillan, 1955)

Qur'an 29.45 WS 592
> A. Yusuf Ali, trans., *The Meaning of the Glorious Qur'an* (Cairo, Egypt: Dar Al-Kitab Al-Masri, 1938)

Qur'an 30.21 WS 176
> Thomas Ballantine Irving, trans., *The Qur'an: First American Version* (Brattleboro, Vermont: Amana Books, 1985

Qur'an 32.8-9 WS 230
> Arthur J. Arberry, trans., *The Koran Interpreted* (New York: Macmillan, 1955)

Qur'an 33.40 WS 450; 40.78 WS 36
> Muhammad Marmaduke Pickthall, trans., *The Meaning of the Glorious Qur'an* (Mecca and New York: Muslim World League, 1977)

Qur'an 42.13 WS 188
> Thomas Ballantine Irving, trans., *The Qur'an: First American Version* (Brattleboro, Vermont: Amana Books, 1985

Qur'an 42.30 WS 122
> Arthur J. Arberry, trans., *The Koran Interpreted* (New York: Macmillan, 1955)

Qur'an 45.23 WS 288 293
> Muhammad Marmaduke Pickthall, trans., *The Meaning of the Glorious Qur'an* (Mecca and New York: Muslim World League, 1977)

Qur'an 57.20 WS 231
> Arthur J. Arberry, trans., *The Koran Interpreted* (New York: Macmillan, 1955)

Qur'an 69.13-37 WS 781
> Muhammad Marmaduke Pickthall, trans., *The Meaning of the Glorious Qur'an* (Mecca and New York: Muslim World League, 1977)

Qur'an 78.21-30 WS 253
> Thomas Ballantine Irving, trans., *The Qur'an: First American Version* (Brattleboro, Vermont: Amana Books, 1985

Qur'an 84.6, 19 WS 510; 98.7-8 WS 411
> A. Yusuf Ali, trans., *The Meaning of the Glorious Qur'an* (Cairo, Egypt: Dar Al-Kitab Al-Masri, 1938)

Qur'an 112 WS 51
> Muhammad Marmaduke Pickthall, trans., *The Meaning of the Glorious Qur'an* (Mecca and New York: Muslim World League, 1977)

Jainism

Acarangasutra 5.135-40, WS 58
> Muni Mahendra Kumar, trans., *Acararigasutra* (Delhi, Motilal Banarsidass, 1981)

Jinasena, Adipurana, WS 188

Kundakaunda, Niyamasara 176-77, WS 153

Somadeva, Nitivakyamrita 1.1, WS 191

Sutrakritanga 1.1.50 WS 39
> Bhagchandra Jain Bhaskar, his own translation submitted to *World Scripture*

Sutrakritanga 1.11.33, WS 114
> Hermann Jacobi, trans., *Jaina Sutras*, 2 vols., Sacred Book of the East, vols. 22, 45(Oxford: Clarendon Press, 1884, 1895; reprint, New York: Dover, 1968)

Tatthvarthasutra 9.6, WS 112
> A. Jain trans., *Reality* (Calcutta: Vira Shasan Sangha, 1960)

Uttaradhyayana Sutra 4.2, WS 123
> K. C. Sogani, *Ethical Doctrines in Jainism* (Solapur: Jain Sam. Samraksaka Sangh, 1967)

Judaism

The Holy Bible, Revised Standard Version (New York: National Council of Churches of Christ in the USA, 1946, 1971) *The Holy Bible*, Authorized King James Version (New York: Oxford University Press, 1945) [Marked KJV]; James Moffatt, ed., A New Translation of the Bible Containing the Old and New Testaments (New York: Harper & Row, 1922) [Marked M]; All passages are from the Revised Standard Version unless marked otherwise.

Amos 5.23-24, WS 197

Deuteronomy 6:4, WS 51

Deuteronomy 18.15, WS 473

Ecclesiastes 12.7, WS 230

Exodus 20.1-2, WS 110

Exodus 20.1-17, WS 110

Genesis 2.7, WS 230

Genesis 2.18, WS 175

Genesis 18.17-19, WS 451   M

Hosea 8.7, WS 123

Isaiah 2.2-4, WS 790

Isaiah 9.6, WS 783
Isaiah 24.18-23, WS 781
Isaiah 24.23, WS 781
Isaiah 45.15, WS 55
Isaiah 45.5, WS 51
Isaiah 55.8-9, WS 55
Isaiah 56.7, WS 188
Leviticus 19.18, WS 114
Leviticus 25.10, WS 197
Malachi 1:11, WS 36
Malachi 2.10, WS 190
Psalm 50.23, WS 104
Psalm 81.10,   KJV
Psalm 133, WS 187

Midrash. Mekilta Exodus 12:6, WS 287
        Joseph L. Baron, ed., *A Treasury of Jewish Quotations*
        (Northvale, New Jersy: Jason Aronson, 1985)
Midrash Psalms 18, WS 407
        Louis I. Newman and Samuel Spitz, eds., *The Talmudic Anthol-
        ogy* (New York: Behrman House, 1945)
Mishnah, Abot 1.2, WS 197
        R. Travers Herford, ed., *The Ethics of the Talmud: Sayings of the
        Fathers* (New York: Schocken Books, 1925, 1962)
Mishnah, Abot 2.4, WS 188
        Joseph L. Baron, ed., *A Treasury of Jewish Quotations*
        (Northvale, New Jersey: Jason Aronson, 1985)
Mishnah, Abot 3.2, WS 747; 4.22, WS 237
        R. Travers Herford, ed., *The Ethics of the Talmud: Sayings of the
        Fathers* (New York: Schocken Books, 1925, 1962)
Seder Eliyyahu Rabbah 10, WS 191
        Jacob J. Petuchowski, *Our Masters Taught: Rabbinic Stories and
        Sayings* (New York: Crossroad, 1982)
Shabbat 105b, WS 288
        George Foote Moore, *Judaism in the First Centuries of the
        Christian Era*, vol. 1 (Cambridge: Harvard University Press,
        1927)
Talmud Baba Batra 10b, WS 37
        A. Cohen, ed., *Everyman's Talmud* (New York: E. P. Dutton,
        1949)
Talmud, Berakot 30b, WS 594
        C. G. Montefiroe and H. Loewe, eds., *A Rabbinic Anthology*
        (New York: Schocken Books, 1974)
Talmud, Erubin 100b, WS 178
        I. Epstein, trans., *The Babylonian Talmud* (New York Soncino
        Press, 1948)

Talmud, Hullin 92a, WS 730
>   C. G. Montefiroe and H. Loewe, eds., *A Rabbinic Anthology*
>   (New York: Schocken Books, 1974)

Talmud, Pesahim 50a, WS 249
>   A. Cohen, ed., *The Minor Tractates of the Talmud*, 2 vols., 2d
>   ed. (New York: Soncino Press, 1971)

Talmud, Sanhedrin 108a, WS 230
>   I. Epstein, trans., *The Babylonian Talmud* (New York Soncino
>   Press, 1948)

Talmud, Yebamot 62, WS 178
>   Louis I. Newman and Samuel Spitz, eds., *The Talmudic Anthology* (New York: Behrman House, 1945)

Native American Religions

A Winnebago Father's Precepts, WS 178
>   Paul Radin, *The Autobiography of a Winnebago Indian* (New
>   York: Dover, 1920)

Hiawatha, Onondaga Tradition, WS 188
>   Erdos and Oriz, *American Indian Myths and Legends*, 197

Sikhism

Adi Granth, Asa Chhant, M. 4, 442, WS 465
>   Gurbachan Singh Talib, trans., *Sri Guru Granth Sahib*, 4 vols.
>   (Patiala: Publication Bureau of Punjabi University, Patiala, 1984-)

Adi Granth, Gauri, M.5, 188, WS 233
>   Gurbachan Singh Talib, trans., *Sri Guru Granth Sahib*, 4 vols.
>   (Patiala: Publication Bureau of Punjabi University, Patiala, 1984-)

Adi Granth, Gauri Var, M.4, 308, WS 122-23
>   Gurbachan Singh Talib, trans., *Sri Guru Granth Sahib*, 4 vols.
>   (Patiala: Publication Bureau of Punjabi University, Patiala, 1984-)

Adi Granth, Japuji 1, WS 31; 2, M.1, 1, WS 101; 28, M.1 6,
>   WS 188; 37 M.1, 8, WS 248
>   Harbans Singh, *The Message of Sikhism* (Delhi: Delhi Sikhi
>   Gurdwara Manangement Committee, 1978)

Adi Granth, Kanara, M.5, 1299, WS 195
>   Surindar Singh Kohli, *A Critical Study of Adi Granth* (Delhi:
>   Motilal Banarsidass, 1961)

Adi Granth, Maru Solahe, M.1, 1026, WS 253
>   Surindar Singh Kohli, *A Critical Study of Adi Granth* (Delhi:
>   Motilal Banarsidass, 1961)

Adi Granth, Ramkali, M.5, 885, WS 36
>   Trilochan Singh et al., trans., *Selections from the Sacred Writings
>   of the Sikhs* (London: George Allen & Unwin, 1960)

Adi Granth, Sri Raga, M.1, 22, WS 237
>   Gurbachan Singh Talib, trans., *Sri Guru Granth Sahib*, 4 vols.
>   (Patiala: Publication Bureau of Punjabi University, Patiala, 1984-)

Adi Granth, Sri Raga, M.3, 68, WS 451
>Surindar Singh Kohli, *A Critical Study of Adi Granth* (Delhi: Motilal Banarsidass, 1961)

Adi Granth, Sri Raga Ashtpadi, M.1, 62, WS 104
>Gurbachan Singh Talib, trans., *Sri Guru Granth Sahib*, 4 vols. (Patiala: Publication Bureau of Punjabi University, Patiala, 1984-)

Adi Granth, Var Suhi, M.3, 788, WS 174
>Gurbachan Singh Talib, trans., *Sri Guru Granth Sahib*, 4 vols. (Patiala: Publication Bureau of Punjabi University, Patiala, 1984-)

Taoism

Chuang Tzu 19, WS 136
>Burton Watson, trans., *Chuang Tzu: Basic Writings* (New York: Columbia University Press, 1964)

Chuang Tzu 23, WS 234
>Herbert A. Giles, trans., *Chuang Tzu: Mystic, Moralist, and Social Reformer*, 2d ed. (Shanghai: Kelly & Walsh, 1926; reprint, New York: AMS Press, 1974)

Tao Te Ching 1, WS 57
>D. C. Lao, ed. and trans., *Lao Tzu: Tao Te Ching* (London: Penguin Books, 1963)

Tao Te Ching 16, WS 383
>Wing-tsit Chan, trans., *The Way of Lao Tzu: Tao Te Ching* (New York: Bobbs-Merrill Co., 1963)

Tao Te Ching 22, WS 51; 54, WS 106
>Arthur Waley, *The Way and Its Power: A Study of the Tao Te Ching and Its Place in Chinese Thought* (New York: Grove Press, 1958)

Tao Te Ching 73, WS 124
>D. C. Lao, ed. and trans., *Lao Tzu: Tao Te Ching* (London: Penguin Books, 1963)

Treatise on Response and Retribution, Appended Tales, WS 255
>D. T. Suzuki and Paul Carus, trans. *Lao Tze, Treatise on Response and Retribution* [First published as *T'ai-Shang Kan-Ying P'ien: Treatise of the Exalted One on Response and Retribution*] (Peru, Illinois: Open Court Publishing Co., 1906; paperback, 1973)

Zoroastrianism

Avesta, Yasna 30.8-10, WS 780-81; 45.5, WS 105
>H. K. Mirza, his own translations submitted to *World Scripture*

Avesta, Yasna 44.7, WS 171
>S. Insler, *The Gathas of Zarathustra*, Acta Inranica 8, vol. 1 (Leiden: E.J. Brill, 1975)

Avesta, Zamayad Yasht 19.11-12, WS 794
>H. K. Mirza, his own translations submitted to *World Scripture*